Annotated Teacher Edition

JAMESTOWN ✦ EDUCATION

Literature

An Adapted Reader

Course 3

McGraw Hill Glencoe

New York, New York   Columbus, Ohio   Chicago, Illinois   Peoria, Illinois   Woodland Hills, California

JAMESTOWN EDUCATION

ACKNOWLEDGMENTS
Grateful acknowledgment is given authors, publishers, photographers,
museums, and agents for permission to reprint the following copyrighted
material. Every effort has been made to determine copyright owners. In
case of any omissions, the Publisher will be pleased to make suitable
acknowledgments in future editions.
Acknowledgments continued on p. 284.

Send all inquiries to:
Glencoe/McGraw-Hill
8787 Orion Place
Columbus, OH 43240-4027

ISBN-13: 978-0-07-874315-3 (Student Edition)
ISBN-10: 0-07-874315-X (Student Edition)

ISBN-13: 978-0-07-874328-3 (Annotated Teacher Edition)
ISBN-10: 0-07-874328-1 (Annotated Teacher Edition)

Printed in the United States of America
4 5 6 7 8 9 10 079 11 10 09 08

Contents

To the Teacher

Program Overview

The *Jamestown Literature* program gives students who are reading below grade level the opportunity to read and comprehend the same selections that are taught in grade-level literature classrooms. The program consists of five consumable books, Grades 6–10, each containing a wide range of fiction and nonfiction reading selections from a grade-specific literary canon. Most of the selections in *Jamestown Literature* will appear in basal literature programs, including Glencoe's *Reading with Purpose* and *The Reader's Choice*.

Up to 75 percent of the selections in *Jamestown Literature* have been adapted from their original form—the vocabulary may have been adjusted, the sentence structure simplified, the selection abridged, or all three. The lines of text per page are controlled in all selections, and all selections offer guided reading support. The reading levels of the selections in each book are at least two grades below grade level. *Jamestown Literature* supports students' efforts before, during, and after reading by introducing literary elements and reading skills, preteaching vocabulary, guiding comprehension, and reinforcing skills and strategies.

Before Reading

The unit opener introduces the genre, literary elements, and reading skills for that unit. The clear and concise explanation of the genre, familiar examples, and interactive prompts give the students a better understanding of the genre's characteristics before they begin reading. The Literary Elements and Reading Skills charts on pages xiv–xvii provide students with additional help in understanding literary elements and reading skills.

The opener for each selection prepares students to read by asking questions that activate their prior knowledge and by helping them set a purpose for reading. These features can be used as a springboard for classroom discussions. The opener also includes information about the author and provides further background information to help students understand the selection in its proper context. Finally, the introduction preteaches the vocabulary words that are glossed within the selection. By reading aloud the definitions and example sentences, students gain a better understanding of the pronunciation and proper use of each word.

During Reading

As students read, interactive side margin notes help them perform crucial reading tasks such as monitoring their reading comprehension and making connections with the text. Literary Element and Reading Skill notes reinforce what students learned in the unit opener and show them how to apply their knowledge and skills as they read. Did You Know? features are embedded in selections to provide relevant contextual

After Reading

A variety of after-reading activities assess students' reading comprehension and their understanding of new skills and concepts. Students use critical thinking skills and recall specific information from the selection to answer comprehension questions. Additional exercises give students the opportunity to solidify their understanding of new vocabulary, demonstrate their comprehension of the selection's literary element and reading skills, and complete a creative writing activity based on the selection. An end-of-selection assessment in multiple-choice format provides practice for standardized reading tests. Finally, the Compare and Contrast graphic organizer at the end of each unit helps students apply what they learned about one of the literary elements to the selections they have read.

English Language Learners

The features in *Jamestown Literature* support the reading efforts of English language learners. The adapted nature of the selections, including simplified vocabulary and sentence structure, allow ELLs access to the same literature canon as their English-speaking peers. The pretaught vocabulary and accompanying activities facilitate language acquisition, including academic English words that would not generally be included in the typical ELL lexicon without direct instruction. Additionally, the side margin notes provide the type of guided reading instruction that ELLs need in order to comprehend text. English Coach notes call out and define unfamiliar words. Did You Know? and Background Info notes provide additional definitions as well as cultural references that help English language learners connect to the text. In addition to these features, the accessible instruction and format of the *Jamestown Literature* program benefit ELLs by increasing their ability to derive meaning from text, thereby allowing them to transfer acquired skills to other academic disciplines.

information or to help students develop vocabulary and comprehend important terms through words and pictures. Other notes provide additional background information or language support for English language learners. Each side margin note is color-coded to the text with which it corresponds. The text is either highlighted or boxed in color for easy tracking.

In addition to margin note support, the selection vocabulary is glossed at point of use, helping students connect their prereading vocabulary instruction to the contextualized use of each word.

The unique Break Time feature in longer selections allows students to take a strategy break during reading. A graphic organizer offers students the opportunity to organize information or ideas from what they have read so far.

Why Use This Book?

Read a Variety of Texts

The notes and features of *Jamestown Literature* guide you through the process of reading and understanding each literature selection. As you use these notes and features, you practice the skills and strategies that good readers use whenever they read.

UNIT 1

Short Story

What's a Short Story?

What keeps your eyes glued to the pages of a story? Is it interesting characters, an unusual problem that a character must solve, or a plot that has many unexpected twists and turns?

A **short story** is a brief piece of fiction—writing that is about imaginary people, places, and events. In a limited amount of space, a short story can get your heart pounding, make you cry, or make you laugh.

Check the boxes next to the kinds of short stories you like to read:

☐ adventure
☐ science fiction
☐ horror
☐ romance
☐ reality
☐ fantasy
☐ other _____

Why Read Short Stories?

Reading a short story, even if you are reading it for a class, is almost always entertaining. Reading a short story takes very little time, but it can spark all kinds of ideas. A good story may whisk you away to another time or place. It can help you find out something interesting about yourself and others. It can give wings to your imagination.

How Do I Read Short Stories?

Focus on key **literary elements** and **reading skills** to get the most out of reading the four short stories in this unit. Here are two key literary elements and two key reading skills that you will practice in this unit.

Key Literary Elements

• Climax
The **climax** is the turning point of a story. It is an exciting moment that all the earlier events lead up to. After the climax, you can almost figure out how the story will end. Some very suspenseful stories have more than one climax.

• Point of View
Point of view is the relationship of the narrator to the story. The person who is telling the events is the narrator. In first-person point of view, the narrator is a character in the story. The story is told by a character who uses the pronoun I. In third-person point of view, the narrator is outside the story. A third-person point of view can describe the thoughts and feelings of one or all the characters in a story.

Key Reading Skills

• Predict
Readers often use clues in a story to guess what will happen next. This is called **predicting**. Predicting is thinking ahead to guess how things might turn out. For example, in a mystery you might guess who committed the crime. When you read how events actually turn out, you are checking your prediction. Predictions don't have to be right! What's important is that you get involved in your reading from the start of the story.

• Cause and Effect
A **cause** is something that happens that sets something else in motion. An **effect** is the result or outcome. For example, a character may refuse to study for a test, causing him to fail. To find a cause-and-effect relationship, ask yourself: Did this happen because of something else? Sometimes clue words, such as *because, as a result, therefore, since,* and *so,* let you know of a cause-and-effect relationship.

What Is It? Why Read?

The genre, or type of writing, is defined for you at the beginning of the unit. Learn why a particular genre offers important and entertaining reading.

Literary Elements and Reading Skills

New literary elements and reading skills are introduced in each unit opener. Use these elements and skills to get the most out of your reading.

UNIT 2 — Short Story

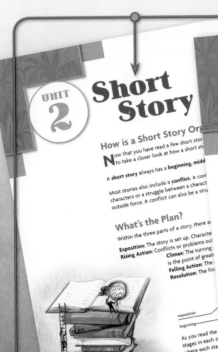

How is a Short Story Org...
Now that you have read a few short stor... to take a closer look at how a short sto...

A **short story** always has a **beginning, midd**...

Most stories also include a **conflict**. A con... characters or a struggle between a charact... outside force. A conflict can also be a stru...

What's the Plan?
Within the three parts of a story, there a...

Exposition: The story is set up. Characte...
Rising Action: Conflicts or problems occ...
Climax: The turning ... is the point of great...
Falling Action: The ...
Resolution: The fina...

exposition

beginning:

As you read the n... stages in each sto... where each stage...

Understanding t... become a better...

60

UNIT 3 — Drama

What's Drama?
Have you ever acted out a scene from... imitated a conversation to make so... creating a drama.

A **drama**, also called a play, is a story... on a stage or before a movie camera.... story or novel.

Understanding the elements of dra...

- **Stage directions** tell the actors... they should move on the stage.... the stage. Stage directions are...
- **Acts** divide long plays into sh... even shorter sections.
- **Dialogue** is the conversation... and the personalities of the...

Dramas take many forms, fro... stage plays. What types of d... next to the types of dram...

130

UNIT 4 — Folktale and Myth

What's a Folktale? What's a Myth?
Long before superheroes and animated troublemakers began entertaining people in comic books and movies, people amused themselves by telling stories. Stories were passed from generation to generation, helping to keep ideas and customs alive. Many of these stories are in the form of folktales and myths.

A **folktale** is a traditional story that entertains, amazes, or explains something. Many folktales are about larger-than-life characters, or animals that act like humans.

A **myth** is a story handed down from an ancient culture. Myths explain events in nature or the beliefs and customs of a people. Mythical characters include gods and goddesses, magical creatures, and heroes.

> **You probably have read a folktale or myth that included one of the following things. Circle one that you know about. Write the title of a folktale or myth it describes.** For example, you might circle "talking animals" and write "The Three Little Pigs."

talking animals   people tricking others or getting tricked

a test of love   the wise against the unwise

three wishes

Why Read Folktales and Myths?
You can read a folktale or myth to enjoy a good story. But folktales and myths provide more than entertainment. They often include a lesson or an explanation of something in the world. Through these stories, readers learn about the values and concerns of different cult...

UNIT 5 — Nonfiction

What's Nonfiction?
Pick up a newspaper or magazine, or check out many Web sites, and you will find writing that is nonfiction.

Nonfiction is the name for writing that is about real people and real events. Many types of nonfiction are meant to inform or to relate experiences. Nonfiction can go beyond just telling facts to include the use of vivid descriptions. Sometimes nonfiction writing also tries to influence the reader's opinion. There are many kinds of nonfiction. Essays, biographies, and autobiographies are popular types of this kind of writing.

- An **essay** is a short piece of nonfiction about a single topic.
- A **biography** is the story of a person's life written by someone other than that person.
- An **autobiography** is the story of a person's life written by that person.

Nonfiction can deal with many topics—the life of a famous person, historical events, or observations about a place.

> **On the line below, write a nonfiction subject that you would like to read about.**

Why Read Nonfiction?
Read nonfiction to learn about new places, new people, and new ideas. By reading nonfiction and learning new things, you can better understand the world around you. Nonfiction can even help you better understand yourself.

Explore Literature
Your book features several of the most popular types of writing. Find out what makes each genre unique. Discover new and exciting types of writing.

Get Set!

The first page of each lesson helps you get ready to read. It sets the stage for your reading. The more you know about the reading up front, the more meaning it will have for you.

Get Ready to Read!

Chanclas

Meet Sandra Cisneros

Sandra Cisneros (sis nä´ rōs´) was born in Chicago in 1954. She is the only daughter in a family of seven children. Her family moved between Chicago and Mexico City, where her father's parents lived. Cisneros often writes about the life experiences of Hispanic girls. Cisneros says, "They're all stories I lived, or witnessed, or heard." "Chanclas," which is part of the novel *The House on Mango Street*, was first published in 1983.

What You Know

Think about a time in the past when you felt awkward or embarrassed. With a partner, discuss things that you can do, or that friends can help you do, to feel more comfortable in an embarrassing situation.

Reason to Read

Read "Chanclas" to find out how a girl overcomes what she thinks will be an embarrassing event.

Background Info

Hispanics are the fastest-growing minority group in the United States. More than one in eight people in the United States are of Hispanic origin. Over 60 percent of Hispanics have roots in Mexico. Other places of origin include countries in South and Central America, Puerto Rico, and Cuba. Hispanics make up a large part of the population of many large cities in the West and the South and work in almost every sector of the U.S. economy.

What You Know

Think about your own experience and share your knowledge and opinions. Then, build on what you know as you read the lesson.

Reason to Read

Set a purpose for reading. Having a reason to read helps you get involved in what you read.

Background Info

Get a deeper insight into the reading. Knowing some background information helps you gain a greater appreciation and understanding of what you read.

Meet the Author

Meet the authors to get to know where they come from, what or who inspires them, and why they write.

Build Vocabulary

Each lesson introduces you to words that help build your vocabulary. You'll find these words in the reading. Understanding these words before you read makes reading easier.

Word Power

In an after-reading activity, you practice the vocabulary words you learned in the lesson.

Word Power

arrogant (ar´ə gant) *adj.* full o...
Amanda is *arrogant* because sh...

banished (ban´ishd) *v.* forced t...
After the man was caught settin...

commotion (ka mō´shan) *n.* no...
Because of the car accident, ther...

conquer (kong´kar) *v.* to take ov...
Napoleon said he was going to co...

commended (ka men´did) *v.* gav...
My teacher *commended* me for w...

Answer the following questions t...
Write your answers in the spaces ...

1. Did Alexander the Great *conquer*...

2. If you are *commended*, did you do...

3. Would a *commotion* be silent and...

4. What kind of a student would be *ba*...
well-behaved or one who causes tro...

5. Would someone *arrogant* brag or be...

Adapted from

The Wise Old Woma...

Yoshiko U...

Background Info

Japan used to have a government run by an emperor. Each village also had its own ruler, called a *lord*, who owned the land and made the laws. The people who lived in the village worked for the lord.

Many long years ago, there lived an **arrogant** and cr...
lord who ruled over a small village in Japan. "I have n...
people in my village," he said. "They are neither usefu...
work for a living. Therefore anyone over seventy-on...
banished from the village and left in the mountain...

"What a cruel and unreasonable lord we have," ...
of the village murmured. But the lord punished a...
disobeyed him, and so villagers who turned sev...
tearfully carried into the mountains, never to r...

Gradually there were fewer and fewer old p...
village and soon they disappeared altogether...
was pleased.

"What a fine village of young, healthy an...
have," he bragged. "Soon it will be the fine...

Now there lived in this village a kind y...
mother. They were poor, but the farmer...
and the two of them lived happily toge...
went by, the mother grew older, and b...
terrible age of seventy-one.

Word Power

arrogant (ar´ə gant) *adj.* full of unde...
banished (ban´ishd) *v.* forced to lea...

162

Respond to Literature

C Word Power

Complete each sentence below, using one of the words in the box.

arrogant	banished
commotion	conquer	commended

1. Lisa was _____ for getting good grades on her report card.

2. After the big _____ in the hallway, the teachers told the students to go back to their classes.

3. The queen was so _____ she thought she was the fairest in the kingdom.

4. The leader's plan was to _____ all his neighbors so he would rule the entire land.

5. Some fans were _____ from the game after they threw tomatoes.

Circle the word that best completes each sentence.

6. The president was too **(commended, arrogant)** to be a good leader.

7. Fireworks during the parade always cause a huge **(commotion, conquer)**.

8. The general **(banished, commended)** his troops for their bravery.

9. The large country wanted to **(conquer, arrogant)** the small island.

10. A long time ago, villages **(commotion, banished)** thieves to the forest.

170

Word Power

Before you read, you learn key vocabulary words and their definitions. The definitions and sample sentences help you complete the questions that follow.

Word Power Footnotes

Look for pronunciations and definitions of vocabulary words at the bottom of pages throughout the reading. Vocabulary words appear in dark type in the text.

My Personal Dictionary

My Personal Dictionary

As you read, jot down words in your personal dictionary that you want to learn more about. Later, ask a classmate or your teacher what they mean, or look them up in a dictionary.

Read, Respond, Interact

Notes in "My Workspace" support and guide you through the reading process. Interact with and respond to the text by answering the questions or following the directions in the workspace notes.

Background Info notes give information about a particular event, time, person, or place mentioned in the reading. Whenever you read text that is boxed in orange, look for a Background Info note in your workspace.

Literary Element notes help you understand important features of literature. Whenever you read text that is highlighted in blue, look for a Literary Element note in your workspace.

English Coach notes explain difficult or unusual words and cultural references. Whenever you read text that is highlighted in red, look for an English Coach note in your workspace.

Connect to the Text notes help you connect what you're reading to something in your own life. Whenever you read text that is boxed in purple, look for a Connect to the Text note in your workspace.

Adapted from

Icarus and Daedalus
Josephine Preston Peabody

Background Info

Crete is a Greek island in the Mediterranean Sea. The Minoan culture, named after King Minos, may have begun on Crete as early as 3000 B.C. This culture was the first major civilization in ancient Greece. It flourished between 1700 and 1400 B.C. Minoans were known for their cleverness.

Literary Element

Symbol Reread the highlighted text. When Daedalus looks at the sea gulls, he sees more than the birds. What do they symbolize to Daedalus?

Among all those humans who became so wise that they learned the secrets of the gods, none was more **cunning** than Daedalus.

He once built, for King Minos of Crete, a wonderful Labyrinth of winding ways. It was so cunningly tangled up and twisted around that, once inside, you could never find your way out again without a magic clue. But the king's friendship changed with the wind, and one day he had his master architect imprisoned in a tower. Daedalus managed to escape, but it seemed impossible to leave the island. Every ship that came or went was well guarded by order of the king.

After watching the sea gulls in the air—the only creatures that were sure of liberty—Daedalus thought of a plan for himself and his young son Icarus, who was **captive** with him.

Did You Know?
The Labyrinth (lab´ ə rinth´) was a huge maze. Its complicated and twisted path enclosed by high walls made it impossible for people to find their way out once they had entered it.

Word Power
cunning (kun´ing) *adj.* skillful and clever; sly
captive (kap´ tiv) *adj.* imprisoned; kept within bounds

194

My Workspace

English Coach

When the author writes, "that language had never lived in our mouths," she means that she and her brother do not speak Arabic. The language did not actually inhabit their mouths. Check the phrases below that don't actually mean what they say.

☐ He was on her mind.
☐ My lips are sealed.
☐ Her eyes hurt from the strain.

Connect to the Text

Reread the boxed sentences. *Shookrun* is Arabic for "thank you." Do you know how to say "thank you" in more than one language? Why is "thank you" an important phrase to learn?

We had never met our Palestinian grandmother, Sitti Khadra, or seen Jerusalem, where our father had grown up. Our mother hadn't either. We did not speak Arabic, though the sound of the language was familiar to us—our father's musical blessings before meals. But that language had never lived in our mouths.

And that's where we were going, to Jerusalem.

The first plane flight of my whole life was the night flight out of New York City across the ocean. I was fourteen years old.

We stopped in Portugal for a few weeks. We were making a slow change. We stopped in Spain and Italy and Egypt, where the pyramids shocked me by sitting right on the edge of the giant city of Cairo. While we waited for our baggage to clear customs, I stared at six tall African men in a discussion with an Egyptian customs agent and realized I did not even know how to say "thank you" in Arabic. How was this possible? The most elemental and important of human phrases in my father's own tongue had been unknown to me till now. "Daddy," I said, "Daddy, I have to know. Daddy, tell me. Daddy, why didn't we ever *learn?*" Always thereafter, the word *shookrun*, so simple, would remind me of the vast African baggage.

We stayed one or two nights at the old Shepheard's Hotel downtown but couldn't sleep due to the heat and honking traffic beneath our windows. So our father moved us to the famous Mena House Hotel next to the pyramids.

That night, my brother and I both awakened burning with fever. We lay in bed for a week. An aged doctor tripped over my suitcase every time he entered to take our temperatures. We smothered our laughter. "*Shookrun*," I would say. But as soon as he left, to my brother, "I feel bad. How do you feel?"

222

x

Comprehension Check

notes help you understand what you're reading. Whenever you read text that is boxed in green, look for a Comprehension Check note in your workspace.

My Workspace

Literary Element
Symbol Reread the sentences highlighted in blue. What does flying symbolize to the enslaved men and women?

_____
_____
_____

Reading Skill
Visualize Reread the sentences highlighted in green. In the frame below, draw a picture of what you think the flying people look like. If you have room, you can add the fields, fences, streams, or the Overseer.

Your Sketch

The young woman lifted one foot on the air. Then the other. She flew clumsily at first, with the child now held tightly in her arms. Then she felt the magic, the African mystery. Say she rose just as free as a bird. As light as a feather.

The Overseer rode after her, hollerin. Sarah flew over the fences. She flew over the woods. Tall trees could not snag her. Nor could the Overseer. She flew like an eagle now, until she was gone from sight. No one dared speak about it. Couldn't believe it. But it was, because they say that was there saw that it was.

Say the next day was dead hot in the fields. A young man slave fell from the heat. The Driver come and whipped him. Toby come over and spoke words to the fallen one. The words of ancient Africa once heard are never remembered completely. The young man forgot them as soon as he heard them. They went way inside him. He got up and rolled over on the air. He rode it awhile. And he flew away.

Another and another fell from the heat. Toby was there. He cried out to the fallen and reached his arms out to them. "*Kum kunka yali, kum ... tambe!*" Whispers and sighs. And they too rose on the air. They rode the hot breezes. The ones flyin were black and shinin sticks, wheelin above the head of the Overseer. They crossed the rows, the fields, the fences, the streams, and were away.

"**Seize** the old man!" cried the Overseer. "I heard him say the magic *words*. Seize him!"

Power

(ēz) v. to grab and take hold of someone or something, possibly

207

My Workspace

Comprehension Check

Reread the boxed text. What does Terry assume happened to his father when he does not meet him? Underline the answer in the passage.

Reading Skill
Cause and Effect Reread the highlighted paragraph. What causes Terry to think that his father may be in trouble at the hardware store? Check the correct response.

☐ Terry's father's car is not in the parking lot.

☐ Terry's father asks Terry not to come to the store with him.

☐ Terry sees people moving toward the hardware store.

When they got to the mall they split up. His father went to the hardware store, Terry to a record store to look at albums.

Terry browsed so long that he was late meeting his father at the mall's front door. But his father wasn't there, and Terry looked out to the car to make sure it was still in the parking lot. It was, and he supposed his father had just gotten busy, so he waited.

Still his father didn't come, and he was about to go the hardware store to find him when he noticed the commotion.

Later, he thought of it and couldn't remember when the feeling first came to him that there was something wrong. The people were moving toward the hardware store and that might have been what made Terry suspicious.

There was a crowd blocking the entry to the store, and he couldn't see what they were looking at.

Terry squeezed through the crowd until he got near the front. There were still some people in front of him, so he pushed a crack between them. Then he saw it: His father was squirming along the floor on his stomach. He was crying, looking terrified, his breath coming in short, hot pants like some kind of hurt animal.

It burned into Terry's mind, the picture of his father down on the floor. It burned in and in, and he wanted to walk away, but something made his feet move forward. He knelt next to his father and helped the owner of the store get him up on his feet. His father didn't speak at all but continued to make little whimpering sounds, and they led him back into the owner's office and put him in a chair. Then Terry called his mother and she came in a taxi to take them home. Waiting, Terry sat in a chair next to his father, looking at the floor, wanting only for the earth to open and let him drop in a deep hole. He wanted to disappear.

Did You Know?
Before music was recorded on CDs, it was recorded on record albums. A record is a thin black disc with grooves on it.

20

The margin notes let you interact with what you're reading in several ways. Some notes ask you to write out your response. Other notes may ask you to draw a picture, underline answers in the text, or interact in some other way.

Reading Skill notes let you practice active reading strategies that help good readers think as they read. Whenever you read text that is highlighted in green, look for a Reading Skill note in your workspace.

Use the **Did You Know?** feature to get a clear picture of something interesting in the text.

Wrap It Up!

The Break Time, Respond to Literature, and Compare and Contrast pages help you focus your understanding of the text. You apply the skills and strategies you've practiced during reading.

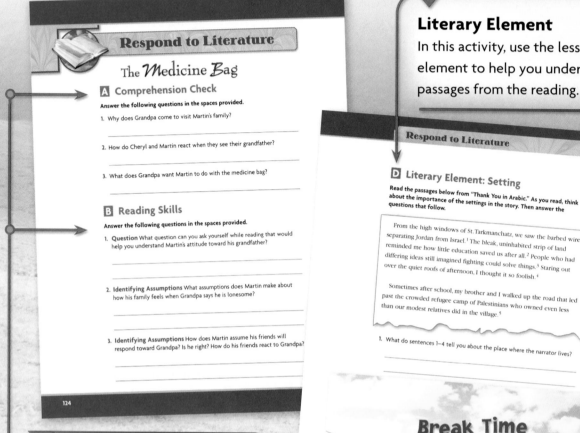

Respond to Literature

The Medicine Bag

A Comprehension Check

Answer the following questions in the spaces provided.

1. Why does Grandpa come to visit Martin's family?

2. How do Cheryl and Martin react when they see their grandfather?

3. What does Grandpa want Martin to do with the medicine bag?

B Reading Skills

Answer the following questions in the spaces provided.

1. **Question** What question can you ask yourself while reading that would help you understand Martin's attitude toward his grandfather?

2. **Identifying Assumptions** What assumptions does Martin make about how his family feels when Grandpa says he is lonesome?

3. **Identifying Assumptions** How does Martin assume his friends will respond toward Grandpa? Is he right? How do his friends react to Grandpa?

124

Respond to Literature

D Literary Element: Setting

Read the passages below from "Thank You in Arabic." As you read, think about the importance of the settings in the story. Then answer the questions that follow.

From the high windows of St. Tarkmanchatz, we saw the barbed wire separating Jordan from Israel.[1] The bleak, uninhabited strip of land reminded me how little education saved us after all.[2] People who had differing ideas still imagined fighting could solve things.[3] Staring out over the quiet roofs of afternoon, I thought it so foolish.[4]

Sometimes after school, my brother and I walked up the road that led past the crowded refugee camp of Palestinians who owned even less than our modest relatives did in the village.[5]

1. What do sentences 1–4 tell you about the place where the narrator lives?

Literary Element

In this activity, use the lesson's literary element to help you understand passages from the reading.

Break Time

As you read *The Diary of Anne Frank*, look for details describing each character. Details make the characters come to life. Complete the chart below to help you imagine and understand the characters in this drama and their behavior. Characters are listed in the left column. In the right column, list details that describe each character. Use information from the story to help you. An example has been provided.

Character	Description
Miep	A young Dutch woman; she is kind; she helps hide the families in the attic.
Mr. Frank	
Mr. Van Daan	
Mrs. Van Daan	
Peter Van Daan	
Mrs. Frank	
Margot	
Anne	
Mr. Kraler	

GO Continue reading on the next page.

142

Comprehension Check and Reading Skills

In the Comprehension Check activity, you recall events and facts from the text. In the Reading Skills activity, you apply the reading skills you practiced while reading.

Break Time

The Break Time page helps you organize your thoughts about the text.

E Journal Entry

Imagine that you are Martin. You keep a journal in which you write about things that have happened and how you feel. Write journal entries describing the day Grandpa gave you the medicine bag and the day you put the sacred sage in the medicine bag.

Tuesday:

Grandpa asked me to see him today. He wanted to give me the medicine bag. I ran home from school. When I entered Grandpa's room, _____

_____

I felt _____

_____

Saturday:

It has been two
Today, we trave
got there, _____

_____

I felt _____

Writing Activity

Develop your writing skills by completing various types of activities. Here's your chance to be creative!

Assessment

Fill in the circle next to each correct answer.

1. What is being dedicated at Gettysburg?
   - ○ A. a cemetery
   - ○ B. a monument
   - ○ C. a park
   - ○ D. a new nation

2. Why does Lincoln deliver the speech "The Gettysburg Address"?
   - ○ A. He wants to congratulate the soldiers on winning the war.
   - ○ B. He is honoring the dead at a battleground.
   - ○ C. He is trying to get votes to become president.
   - ○ D. He is surrendering to the Southern army.

3. Lincoln is dedicating a cemetery at Gettysburg because
   - ○ A. it was the location of the final battle of the Civil War.
   - ○ B. it was where the Southern troops surrendered.
   - ○ C. it was a battlefield where many brave soldiers fought.
   - ○ D. it was the meeting place of the country's founding fathers.

4. Choose one of the following statements that **best** paraphrases one of the main ideas of "The Gettysburg Address."
   - ○ A. Everyone should always support the military.
   - ○ B. We should learn from our mistakes and not repeat errors.
   - ○ C. We should continue to fight for freedom and democracy.
   - ○ D. To survive, the country needs to constantly change.

   ns "an idea or a suggestion"?

245

Assessment

The lesson assessment helps you evaluate what you learned in the lesson.

UNIT 4 Wrap-up

Compare and Contrast

Both "Icarus and Daedalus" and "The People Could Fly" include **symbols**. This is an important literary element in both stories. Although the setting and the characters of the stories are very different, a symbol in both stories—the ability to fly—stands for similar ideas. Think about the symbols in these stories. Think about what the symbols stand for. Finally, think about how the symbols reflect the meanings of the stories.

In the Venn diagram below, describe how the symbols of flying in "Icarus and Daedalus" and "The People Could Fly" are alike and how they are different. Write about how the symbols are different in the outer parts of the circles. Write about how the symbols are alike in the overlapping part of the circles. Examples have been provided.

"Icarus and Daedalus"
- Flying ends in tragedy.

Alike
- Flying means freedom.

"The People Could Fly"
- Enslaved people successfully fly to their freedom.

215

Compare and Contrast

The Compare and Contrast activity helps you see how two texts are alike and different.

The What, Why, and How of Reading

LITERARY ELEMENTS

Each lesson focuses on one literary element. Before you begin a lesson, read carefully the explanations of the literary elements found at the beginning of the unit. You can refer to this chart for an overview. The more familiar you become with these important features, the more you will understand and appreciate each reading.

Unit 1	What Is It?	Example
	Climax The climax is the turning point of a story. It is an exciting or intense moment that all the earlier events lead up to.	In "The Tell-Tale Heart," there are two climaxes. Both are turning points in the story and moments of great excitement.
	Point of View The point of view is the relationship of the narrator to the story. In *first-person* point of view, the narrator is a character in the story. In *third-person* point of view, the narrator is outside the story and can describe the feelings of one or all the characters in the story.	In "Everybody Knows Tobie," the point of view is first person. We get to know how Joey feels and how he interacts with people in his town from the character's own point of view.
Unit 2	**Conflict** Conflict is the struggle between two opposing forces. An external conflict is a struggle between a character and an outside force. An internal conflict is a struggle within a character's mind.	In "Raymond's Run," the character of Squeaky has an external conflict with her rival Gretchen because they both think that they can win the race.
	Theme A theme of a story is its central message. Sometimes a theme is stated directly. However, sometimes the reader must figure out the theme by looking carefully at the characters and the plot.	The theme of "The Medicine Bag," that people should respect and preserve their cultures, is represented by an old man's handing down of a cherished possession to his great-grandson.

Unit 3	What Is It?	Example
	Characterization Characterization is the way an author reveals information about characters. An author may directly describe a character. A character's personality can also be revealed through his or her words and actions or through what others think and say about him or her.	In *The Diary of Anne Frank*, we get to know Anne through the descriptions of her in the stage directions, her diary entries, and conversations she has with the other characters.
Unit 4	**Tone** Tone is the writer's attitude toward the subject. The reader can identify the tone of a story by looking at the writer's word choices. Tone can vary from serious to funny or from tense to happy.	In "Racing the Great Bear," the author expresses a respectful and serious tone toward the Great Peace that has been established among the Native American groups.
	Symbol A symbol is an object, person, place, or experience that also stands for something else. Symbols can add an extra layer of meaning to a story.	Wings and flying are symbols of freedom in both "Icarus and Daedalus" and "The People Could Fly."
Unit 5	**Setting** Setting is the time and place in which the events in the text take place. Setting can also include the culture, values, and beliefs of a time and place.	"Thank You in Arabic" is set in many different locations, including Jerusalem. The text provides details about what life in Jerusalem is like.
	Author's Purpose The author's purpose is his or her reason for writing. The purpose can be to inform, to persuade, or to entertain—or a combination of several different purposes.	In "This We Know," the purpose of Chief Seattle's speech is to persuade the U.S. government to take care of the land they want to buy.

READING SKILLS

You will use reading skills to respond to questions in the lessons. Before you begin a lesson, read carefully the explanations of the reading skills found at the beginning of the unit. You can refer to this chart for an overview. The more you practice the skills in the chart, the more these active reading strategies will become a natural part of the way you read.

Unit 1	What Is It?	Why It's Important	How To Do It
	Predict Predicting is making a guess about how things might turn out.	Predicting gives you a reason to read. It helps you get involved in your reading from the start.	Combine what you already know with clues in the text to guess what will happen next.
	Cause and Effect A cause is something that happens that sets something else in motion. An effect is the result or the outcome.	Identifying cause and effect helps you to understand why things happen. It also lets you examine the results of events or actions.	Ask yourself: Did this happen because of something else? Look for clue words or phrases, such as *because* and *as a result*, to help you find cause-and-effect relationships.
Unit 2	**Question** Questioning is asking yourself what information about what you are reading helps you get the most from the text.	As you answer your questions, you're making sure you understand the most important aspects of a story.	Ask yourself *who, what, where, when,* and *why* questions. Also ask yourself: How can I understand this better?
	Identifying Assumptions Assumptions are beliefs that are based on experiences or opinions.	Identifying assumptions that characters make can help you better understand why the characters act the way they do.	Carefully observe how characters behave and think. Identify whether their behaviors are affected by their beliefs.

Unit 3	What Is It?	Why It's Important	How To Do It
	Respond Responding is considering your thoughts and feelings about something you've read.	When you react in a personal way to what you read, you enjoy it more and understand it better.	Consider how you feel about what you read. Also ask yourself, "How would I act in this situation?"
	Sequence Sequence is the order in which events occur—first, next, and last.	Following the sequence of events helps you see how a text is organized. It also helps you understand how events relate to each other.	As you read, look for clue words like *first*, *then*, and *finally*. These words can help you figure out the order in which things happen.
Unit 4	**Visualize** Visualizing is picturing in your mind what you are reading.	Visualizing is one of the best ways to understand and remember ideas, characters, and other details in a story.	Use details in the text to help you create mental pictures. Also use your own experiences to help you imagine the scene.
	Infer Inferring is making an educated guess about information that is not directly stated.	Inferring helps you look more deeply at characters and understand the theme or message of the story.	Connect your own knowledge with details in the story to figure out what the writer is hinting at.
Unit 5	**Evaluate** Evaluating is making judgments about what you are reading and how it is presented.	When you make judgments about what you are reading, you can better understand its purpose and how effective it is.	Think about the writer's words. Evaluate by asking yourself questions: Does this make sense? Is the speech convincing?
	Paraphrase Paraphrasing is restating all or part of a text in your own words.	Paraphrasing helps you understand what you've read and what the author means.	To put text into your own words, replace large words with smaller words and leave out unnecessary details.

UNIT 1

Short Story

What's a Short Story?

What keeps your eyes glued to the pages of a story? Is it interesting characters, an unusual problem that a character must solve, or a plot that has many unexpected twists and turns?

A **short story** is a brief piece of fiction—writing that is about imaginary people, places, and events. In a limited amount of space, a short story can get your heart pounding, make you cry, or make you laugh.

Check the boxes next to the kinds of short stories you like to read:

✔ ☐ adventure
☐ science fiction
☐ horror
☐ romance
☐ reality
✓ ☐ fantasy
✓ ☑ other _____Sample response: mystery_____

Why Read Short Stories?

Reading a short story, even if you are reading it for a class, is almost always entertaining. Reading a short story takes very little time, but it can spark all kinds of ideas. A good story may whisk you away to another time or place. It can help you find out something interesting about yourself and others. It can give wings to your imagination.

How Do I Read Short Stories?

Focus on key **literary elements** and **reading skills** to get the most out of reading the four short stories in this unit. Here are two key literary elements and two key reading skills that you will practice in this unit.

Key Literary Elements

• Climax

The **climax** is the turning point of a story. It is an exciting moment that all the earlier events lead up to. After the climax, you can almost figure out how the story will end. Some very suspenseful stories have more than one climax.

• Point of View

Point of view is the relationship of the narrator to the story. The person who is telling the events is the narrator. In first-person point of view, the narrator is a character in the story. The story is told by a character who uses the pronoun I. In third-person point of view, the narrator is outside the story. A third-person point of view can describe the thoughts and feelings of one or all the characters in a story.

Key Reading Skills

• Predict

Readers often use clues in a story to guess what will happen next. This is called **predicting.** Predicting is thinking ahead to guess how things might turn out. For example, in a mystery you might guess who committed the crime. When you read how events actually turn out, you are checking your prediction. Predictions don't have to be right! What's important is that you get involved in your reading from the start of the story.

• Cause and Effect

A **cause** is something that happens that sets something else in motion. An **effect** is the result or outcome. For example, a character may refuse to study for a test, causing him to fail. To find a cause-and-effect relationship, ask yourself: Did this happen because of something else? Sometimes clue words, such as *because, as a result, therefore, since,* and *so,* let you know of a cause-and-effect relationship.

Get Ready to Read!

The Tell-Tale Heart

Meet Edgar Allan Poe

Edgar Allan Poe was born in 1809. "The Tell-Tale Heart" was first published in *Pioneer* magazine in 1843. Poe became known for writing stories and poems about mysterious forces, wicked crimes, and death. Sadly, his life was like those of his characters. He was two when his mother died and his foster parents eventually wanted nothing to do with him. Poe's wife died of tuberculosis when she was only twenty-four. Poe died in 1849.

What You Know

How do you see yourself? How do you think others see you? Do you think the way others see you is the same way you do? Why or why not? Compare your responses with the responses of other students in your class.

Reason to Read

Read this short story to find out what a man thinks about himself and his actions. Also think about how you feel about him.

Background Info

An important part of many stories is where they take place. A dark old house makes the perfect setting for this horror story. The narrator of the "The Tell-Tale Heart" lives in this house and takes care of a rich, old man. In addition to the house itself, the author's description of features within the house adds to the eerie feeling. For example, because the house does not have electricity, the narrator uses a lantern to see at night. Like the house in this story, many old houses have floors made out of wooden boards that can be pulled up. Under these floorboards are spaces to hide things.

Word Power

stalking (stô´king) *v.* following someone in a secretive manner; p. 6
The spy was *stalking* the mysterious man.

[handwritten: stalk + ing → stalking]

rouses (rou´zez) *v.* stirs up emotion or excites; p. 7
The dogs bark excitedly when the mail carrier *rouses* them.

[handwritten: rouse + s → rouses]

conceal (kən sēl´) *v.* to hide something; p. 8
With chocolate all over my face, it was difficult to *conceal* that I had eaten the cake.

[handwritten: con + ceal → conceal]

suspicion (sə spish´ən) *n.* a feeling that something is wrong; p. 8
The police arrested the thief after their *suspicion* turned out to be true.

[handwritten: su + spic + ion → suspicion]

mock (mok) *v.* to tease or make fun of someone; p. 10
My friends will *mock* me if I wear a suit to the party.

hideous (hid´ē əs) *adj.* horrible, ugly, or nasty; p. 10
I cannot believe you wore such a *hideous* mask to the costume party!

[handwritten: ? hide + ous → hideous   ? hideous]

Answer the following questions, using one of the new words above.
Write your answers in the spaces provided.

1. Which word goes with "awful to look at"? _____hideous_____

2. Which word goes with "to hide so no one else can see something"?____conceal____

3. Which word goes with "thinking someone is guilty"? _____suspicion_____

4. Which word goes with "to make fun of someone for something they did"?

_____mock_____

5. Which word goes with "watching other people without their knowledge"?

_____stalking_____

6. Which word goes with "makes excited"? _____rouses_____

The Tell-Tale Heart

Edgar Allan Poe

Reading Skill

Predict Reread the title and the highlighted sentences. What do you think the story will be about?

Possible response: It will be

about a heart that makes

the narrator go mad.

English Coach

Film is a word with more than one meaning. In this story, it means a thin cover over the eye. What other word means film? Check the correct response.

- ☐ theater
- ☑ movie
- ☐ glasses
- ☐ vision

True!—nervous—very, very nervous I had been and am! But why will you say that I am mad? My disease had sharpened my senses not destroyed them. My sense of hearing was the strongest. I heard all things in heaven and earth. I heard many things in hell. How then am I mad? Listen how calmly I can tell you the whole story.

I don't know how the idea first entered my brain, but once it did it haunted me day and night. There was no reason for it. I was not angry. I loved the old man. He had never wronged me. He had never insulted *me*. And I did not desire his gold.

I think it was his eye! Yes, it was this! One of his eyes was like that of a vulture. It was a pale, blue eye with a film over it. Whenever I saw it my blood ran cold.

Slowly, very slowly, I made up my mind to take the old man's life. And thus I would rid myself of the eye forever.

Now this is the point. You think I'm mad. Madmen know nothing. But you should have seen *me*. You should have seen how wisely I prepared. How careful I was! How clever I was about my work!

I was never kinder to the old man than during the week before I killed him. And every night, about midnight, I turned the latch of his door and opened it—oh so gently! And then, when I had made an opening just large enough for my head, I put in a dark lantern, all closed so that no light shone out.

Oh, you would have laughed to see how cleverly I did it! I did it slowly, very slowly so that I wouldn't disturb the old man's sleep. It took me an hour to place my head within the opening just far enough to see him in bed. Ha! would a madman have been as wise as this?

Then, when my head was inside the room, I undid the lantern. I was so careful—for the hinges squeaked, you see. I undid it just so much that one ray of light fell upon the vulture eye.

I did this for seven long nights, every night just at midnight. But I always found the eye closed. So it was impossible to do the work. You must understand—it was not the old man I hated. It was his Evil Eye.

And every morning I went bravely into his room and spoke to him. I called him by name, as usual. And I asked how had he passed the night. So, you see, he did not suspect that each night, just at twelve, I looked in at him while he slept.

Comprehension Check

Reread the boxed sentences. Why can't the narrator bring himself to kill the old man?

He can't kill the old man

because the old man's eye is

not open.

Connect to the Text

Reread the text boxed in purple. Think about a time you heard a sound and didn't know what it was. How did you feel? What did you do?

Possible response: I was

scared and screamed.

Background Info

Death watches are beetles that live between walls. They make a ticking sound, which some people believe is a sign of death. A death watch also refers to keeping watch over a dying person.

On the eighth night I was more careful than usual in opening the door. The hand of a watch moves faster than mine did. Never had I felt more wise—more powerful! To think that he did not even dream of my secret deeds and thoughts. I chuckled at the idea. And perhaps he heard me. He moved suddenly on the bed as if startled.

Now you may think that I drew back—but no, I kept pushing the door—steadily, steadily. I had my head in and was about to open the lantern, when my thumb slipped. It made a noise and the old man sprang up in bed.

"Who's there?" he cried.

I kept very still and said nothing. For a whole hour I did not move a muscle. And during that time I did not hear him lie down. He was still sitting up in bed listening. He was doing what I had done night after night. He was listening to the death watches in the wall.

In a while I heard a slight groan. I knew it was a groan of deadly terror. It was not a groan of pain. Oh, no! It was a groan that rises from the bottom of a soul that is filled with fear. I knew what the old man felt. And I pitied him.

Still, I chuckled at heart. I knew the old man had been lying awake ever since I made the noise. His fears were increasing. And he would try to tell himself there was nothing to fear.

"It is nothing but the wind. Perhaps it is only a mouse. Ah, it was a cricket that chirped."

Yes, he had been trying to comfort himself. But he had found it all useless. He had felt Death **stalking** him. The black shadow had fallen over the victim. He *felt* the presence of my head within the room.

Word Power

stalking (stô′ king) *v.* following someone in a secretive manner

When I had waited a long time without hearing him lie down, I decided to open a tiny crack in the lantern. So I opened it. You cannot imagine how carefully I opened it.

At last, a single ray, like the thread of a spider, shot from the crack and fell upon the vulture eye. It was open, wide open! And I grew furious as I looked at it. I saw it clearly—all dull blue with a horrible veil over it. It chilled me to the bone.

I could see nothing else of the old man's face, for I had aimed the light exactly on the one damned spot.

Suddenly, there came to my ears a low, dull, quick sound, such as a watch makes when wrapped in cotton. It was the beating of the old man's heart. It made me even more angry, just as the beating of a drum **rouses** the soldier into courage. But I remained quiet. I hardly breathed. I held the lantern steady and aimed the ray on the eye.

Meanwhile the hellish beat of the heart grew quicker and quicker, and louder and louder every minute. The old man's terror must have been extreme! At the dead hour of night, in the dreadful silence of the old house, so strange a noise as this excited me to uncontrollable terror. Yet, for some minutes longer I remained still. But the beating grew louder, louder—I thought the heart must burst.

And now a new fear seized me—the sound would be heard by a neighbor. The old man's hour had come. With a loud yell I threw open the lantern and leaped into the room. He screamed once—only once. In an instant I dragged him to the floor, and pulled the heavy bed over him. For many minutes the heart beat on with a muffled sound. Finally, it stopped. I removed the bed and placed my hand on the old man's heart. There was no pulse; he was stone dead. His eye would trouble me no more.

Reading Skill

Cause and Effect Reread the sentences highlighted in green. The narrator describes the beating of the heart. What effect does the beating have on him?

Possible response: It makes
him angry.

Literary Element

Climax Reread the paragraph highlighted in blue. Poe builds suspense as the story gets closer to its first climax by repeating words. Underline two pairs of repeated words in this passage.

quicker, louder

Word Power

rouses (rou´zez) v. stirs up emotion or excites

7

Comprehension Check

Reread the boxed sentences. Where does the narrator hide the old man's body?

He hides the body beneath

the floorboards.

_____

English Coach

Foul play is a term used to describe a violent act, such as a murder. Can you think of another situation in which the word *foul* is used?

Possible response: Foul is

used in basketball when

someone breaks a rule.

Foul smell ; foul ball

The night faded, so I worked quickly and silently to **conceal** the body. First of all I cut the corpse into pieces. I cut off the head, then the arms, and finally the legs.

I then took up three boards from the flooring of the room and put the pieces of the body between the floor studs. I then replaced the boards so cleverly that no human eye could have detected anything wrong. There were no blood stains to wash out either for I had caught it all in a tub—ha! ha!

When I had finished this, it was four o'clock—still dark as midnight. As the clock chimed the hour, there was a knock at the front door. I went down to answer it with a light heart—for what had I *now* to fear?

There entered three men who introduced themselves as officers of the police. A scream had been heard by a neighbor during the night. **Suspicion** of foul play had been aroused, and they were assigned to search the house.

I smiled and welcomed the officers, for what had I to fear? The scream, I said, was my own in a dream. The old man, I mentioned, was visiting in the country. I took the police all over the house and invited them to search—search well.

I led them, finally, to *his* room and showed them his treasures safe and untouched. With eager confidence, I brought chairs into the room, and asked them *here* to rest from their labors. Then I boldly placed my own seat on the very spot under which lay the body of the victim.

Word Power

conceal (kən sēl´) *v.* to hide something

suspicion (sə spish´ ən) *n.* a feeling that something is wrong

The officers were satisfied. My *manner* had convinced them, for I was very relaxed. They sat, and while I answered cheerily, they chatted about many things. But, after awhile, I felt myself getting pale, and wished they would leave. My head ached, and I thought I heard a ringing in my ears. But still they sat and chatted. The ringing became clearer, and I talked more freely to get rid of the feeling. But it continued and became more clear—until finally, I found that the noise was not within my ears.

No doubt I now grew very pale;—but I talked faster, and with a high-pitched voice. Yet the sound increased—and what could I do? It was a low, dull, quick sound—much like the sound a watch makes when wrapped in cotton. I gasped for breath—and still the officers did not hear it.

I arose and argued about unimportant things in a high-pitched voice and with violent gestures, but the noise steadily increased. Why would they not leave?

Hidden Room of 1,000 Horrors (The Tell-Tale Heart), 1963. Movie still.

What seems to be tormenting the man in the picture? How does the picture reflect this story?

Reading Skill

Cause and Effect Reread the highlighted paragraph. What causes the narrator to speak faster and louder?

Possible response: He thinks he hears the sound grow louder and louder.

Literary Element

Climax Reread the highlighted passage. The story has a second climax. What event marks the second climax in the story?

The narrator confesses.

_____

_____

_____

_____

I paced the floor to and fro with heavy steps, but the noise got louder. Oh God! What could I do? I foamed—I raved—I swore! I swung the chair I had been sitting on and scraped it across the boards, but the noise rose over it. It grew louder—louder—louder!

And still the men chatted pleasantly and smiled. Was it possible they did not hear it? Almighty God! No, no! They heard!—they suspected!—they *knew*—they were laughing at my horror. But anything was better than this agony! I could bear their false smiles no longer. I felt that I must scream or die!—and now—again!—louder—louder—louder—louder!

"Villains!" I shrieked, "**Mock** me no more! I admit the deed!—tear up the boards!—here, here!—it is the beating of his **hideous** heart!"

Word Power

mock (mok) *v.* to tease or make fun of someone
hideous (hid′ē əs) *adj.* horrible, ugly, or nasty

Respond to Literature

The Tell-Tale Heart

A Comprehension Check

Answer the following questions in the spaces provided.

1. What reason does the narrator give for wanting to kill the old man?

   He says that he has to get rid of the old man's eye—it makes his blood run

   cold. He thinks it's an evil eye.

2. What does the narrator do with the old man's body?

   He cuts up the body and hides the parts under the floorboards.

B Reading Skills

Answer the following questions in the spaces provided.

1. **Cause and Effect** What effect does the visit from the police have on the narrator?

   Possible response: He acts normally when they first arrive, but then he

   becomes nervous and eventually confesses to the murder.

2. **Cause and Effect** Why does the narrator confess to the crime?

   Possible response: He thinks he hears the old man's heart beating.

3. **Predict** Read the prediction you made at the start of the story. Was the story about what you thought it would be? How was it similar or different?

   Answers will vary.

C Word Power

Complete each sentence below, using one of the words in the box.

stalking	rouses	conceal
suspicion	mock	hideous

1. Do not _____mock_____ my laugh even though it sounds funny.

2. The police arrested the woman on the _____suspicion_____ that she stole a car.

3. The lizard changed colors to _____conceal_____ itself from a passing hiker.

4. A wolf was _____stalking_____ the chickens, hoping to get an easy meal.

5. The rotten apples looked _____hideous_____ so I threw them out.

6. When the band plays our school song, it always _____rouses_____ the football team.

D Literary Element: Climax

Read the passage below from "The Tell-Tale Heart." As you read, think about how the author creates suspense that leads to the climax. Also think about the details the narrator describes that lead to his actions. Then answer the questions that follow.

At the dead hour of night, in the dreadful silence of the old house, so strange a noise as this excited me to uncontrollable terror.[1] Yet, for some minutes longer I remained still.[2] But the beating grew louder, louder—I thought the heart must burst.[3]

And now a new fear seized me—the sound would be heard by a neighbor.[4] The old man's hour had come.[5] With a loud yell I threw open the lantern and leaped into the room.[6] He screamed once—only once.[7] In an instant I dragged him to the floor, and pulled the heavy bed over him.[8]

1. What does the narrator describe in sentences 1–3 that creates suspense?

   Possible response: The narrator describes terror and the heartbeat growing

   louder and louder.

2. Reread sentences 4–8. How do you know that this is the turning point in the story?

   Possible response: The narrator has been waiting to kill the old man. Finally,

   he makes his move, leaps into the room, and attacks the old man.

E A Police Report

Imagine that you are one of the police officers in the story. You remove the floorboards and are shocked at what you see. Now you have to write a police report.

Police Report

Reported by Officer _____

What was the complaint and who made it? Possible response: A neighbor

heard a scream and suspected foul play.

How did the suspect react when you arrived? Possible response: He was calm

and acted innocently.

What did you find on your first search of the house?

Possible response: I did not find any sign of foul play.

How did the suspect act after you searched the house?

Possible response: He was calm at first, but then became more and

more nervous.

What did he say that led you to remove the floorboards?
Possible response: He said the old man's heart was under the floorboards.

What did you find? Possible response: The body of the old man cut into pieces.

Assessment

Fill in the circle next to each correct answer.

1. Which sentence from the story **best** helps you predict that the narrator is going to do something awful?
   - ○ A. I loved the old man.
   - ● B. And thus I would rid myself of the eye forever.
   - ○ C. My sense of hearing was the strongest.
   - ○ D. I was not angry.

2. What is the turning point in the story when you know the old man is about to die?
   - ○ A. when the narrator greets the old man in the morning
   - ○ B. when the narrator sees that the old man's eye is closed
   - ● C. when the narrator leaps into the old man's room
   - ○ D. when the police come to the door

3. How does the narrator kill the old man?
   - ○ A. He leaves him in the country.
   - ○ B. He traps him under the floorboards.
   - ○ C. He cuts off his head.
   - ● D. He pulls a heavy bed over him.

4. Which sentence from the story **best** describes the effect sound has on the narrator?
   - ○ A. But I remained quiet. I hardly breathed.
   - ○ B. The scream, I said, was my own in a dream.
   - ● C. I gasped for breath — and still the officers did not hear it.
   - ○ D. It was open, wide open! And I grew furious as I looked at it.

5. Which of the following words means "to hide something"?
   - ● A. conceal
   - ○ B. rouses
   - ○ C. stalking
   - ○ D. mock

Get Ready to Read!

STOP THE SUN

Meet Gary Paulsen

Gary Paulsen was born in 1939. This award-winning author says his hero is a librarian. Paulsen explains, "There's nothing that has happened to me that would have happened if she hadn't got me to read." Paulsen writes and reads from 5:30 A.M. until he goes to bed at midnight. He says, "You really have to be able to read to learn things. You try to learn to grow to be more." "Stop the Sun" was first published in 1986.

What You Know

When might someone your age have trouble talking with a family member? With a partner, make a list of problems that can cause poor communication among family members. Next to each problem, list a way you think the problem can be solved.

Reason to Read

Read to find out what happens when a teenage boy digs into his father's battle-scarred past.

Background Info

From 1965 to 1973, U.S. troops fought alongside the South Vietnamese in their struggle against Communist North Vietnam in what has become known as the Vietnam War. Some of the soldiers who returned home after the fighting suffered from mental problems. Doctors call these problems *post-traumatic stress disorder* or *Vietnam syndrome*. This condition can cause anger, nervousness, and nightmares. Special doctors worked with the soldiers to help them handle these problems.

Word Power

veterans (vet´ ər ənz) *n.* people who served in the armed forces, such as the navy, air force, marines, or army; p. 18
Our Fourth of July parade honors the *veterans* who have fought in past wars.

persisted (pər sist´ id) *v.* refused to give up; continued in a stubborn way; p. 19
All the way home, my little brother *persisted* in asking me to buy him some ice cream.

involvement (in volv´ mənt) *n.* the act of being a part of or taking part in something; p. 19
Her *involvement* in the practical joke was revealed when she started to laugh.

afterthought (af´ tər thôt´) *n.* an idea that occurs or comes to mind later; p. 21
Because the apology came as an *afterthought*, I didn't think he really meant it.

psychiatrists (sī kī´ ə trists) *n.* doctors who specialize in helping people with mental problems; p. 23
Several *psychiatrists* agreed that the man should stay in the hospital for a few weeks.

Answer the following questions, using one of the new words above.
Write your answers in the spaces provided.

1. Which word goes with "continued without changing"? ___persisted___

2. Which word goes with "a late idea"? ___afterthought___

3. Which word goes with "the act of being part of something"? ___involvement___

4. Which word goes with "mental health doctors"? ___psychiatrists___

5. Which word goes with "former soldiers"? ___veterans___

Adapted from

STOP THE SUN

Gary Paulsen

English Coach

Reread the highlighted words. The phrase *eyes went away* does not actually mean that his eyes left. It means that Terry's father is thinking about another event or another time in his life. Check the phrases below that have meanings that are different from their word-for-word meanings.

☑ His mind wandered.
☑ I smell trouble.
☐ I opened my eyes.

Terry Erickson was a tall boy, 13, starting to fill out with muscle but still a little awkward. He was on the edge of being a good athlete, which meant a lot to him. He felt it coming too slowly, though, and that bothered him.

But what bothered him even more was when his father's eyes went away.

Sometimes during a meal his father's fork would stop halfway to his mouth, just stop, and there would be a long pause while the eyes went away, far away.

After several minutes his mother would reach over and take the fork and put it gently down on his plate, and they would go back to eating—or try to go back to eating—normally.

They knew what caused it. When it first started, Terry had asked his mother in private what it was, what was causing the strange behavior.

"It's from the war," his mother had said. "The doctors at the **veterans'** hospital call it the Vietnam syndrome."

Word Power

veterans (vet´ ər ənz) *n.* people who served in the armed forces, such as the navy, air force, marines, or army

"Will it go away?"

"They don't know. Sometimes it goes away. Sometimes it doesn't."

"But what happened? What actually caused it?"

"I told you. Vietnam."

"But there had to be something," Terry **persisted.** "Something made him like that. Not just Vietnam. Billy's father was there, and he doesn't act that way."

"That's enough questions," his mother said sternly. "He doesn't talk about it, and I don't ask. Neither will you. Do you understand?"

"But, Mom."

"That's enough."

And he stopped pushing it. But it bothered him whenever it happened. When something bothered him, he liked to stay with it until he understood it, and he understood no part of this.

Words. His father had trouble, and they gave him words like Vietnam syndrome. He knew almost nothing of the war, and when he tried to find out about it, he kept hitting walls. Once he went to the school library and asked for anything they might have that could help him understand the war and how it affected his father. They gave him a dry history that described French **involvement,** Communist involvement, American involvement. It was all numbers, cold numbers, and nothing of what had happened.

And it may have gone on and on like that, with Terry never really knowing any more about it except that his father's eyes started going away more and more often. It might have just gone the rest of his life that way except for the shopping mall.

It started as a normal shopping trip. His father had to go to the hardware store, and he asked Terry to go along.

Word Power

persisted (pər sist´ id) *v.* refused to give up; continued in a stubborn way
involvement (in volv´ mənt) *n.* the act of being a part of or taking part in something

Reading Skill

Predict Reread the paragraph highlighted in green. Terry is determined to find out why his father acts strangely. Predict what Terry will find out and how he will find it out.

Possible responses: Terry will ask his father about his life. His father will tell him about something bad that happened that causes him to behave this way.

English Coach

Dry often means that something is not wet. In this sentence, *dry* means that the history book is "not interesting" or "boring." Write a sentence using *dry* as it is used in the story.

Possible response: The movie was so dry that I fell asleep before it ended.

19

Comprehension Check

Reread the boxed text. What does Terry assume happened to his father when he does not meet him? Underline the answer in the passage.

Reading Skill

Cause and Effect Reread the highlighted paragraph. What causes Terry to think that his father may be in trouble at the hardware store? Check the correct response.

☐ Terry's father's car is not in the parking lot.

☐ Terry's father asks Terry not to come to the store with him.

☑ Terry sees people moving toward the hardware store.

When they got to the mall they split up. His father went to the hardware store, Terry to a record store to look at albums.

Terry browsed so long that he was late meeting his father at the mall's front door. But his father wasn't there, and Terry looked out to the car to make sure it was still in the parking lot. It was, and <u>he supposed his father had just gotten busy</u>, so he waited.

Still his father didn't come, and he was about to go the hardware store to find him when he noticed the commotion.

Later, he thought of it and couldn't remember when the feeling first came to him that there was something wrong. The people were moving toward the hardware store and that might have been what made Terry suspicious.

There was a crowd blocking the entry to the store, and he couldn't see what they were looking at.

Terry squeezed through the crowd until he got near the front. There were still some people in front of him, so he pushed a crack between them. Then he saw it: His father was squirming along the floor on his stomach. He was crying, looking terrified, his breath coming in short, hot pants like some kind of hurt animal.

It burned into Terry's mind, the picture of his father down on the floor. It burned in and in, and he wanted to walk away, but something made his feet move forward. He knelt next to his father and helped the owner of the store get him up on his feet. His father didn't speak at all but continued to make little whimpering sounds, and they led him back into the owner's office and put him in a chair. Then Terry called his mother and she came in a taxi to take them home. Waiting, Terry sat in a chair next to his father, looking at the floor, wanting only for the earth to open and let him drop in a deep hole. He wanted to disappear.

Did You Know?

Before music was recorded on CDs, it was recorded on record albums. A record is a thin black disc with grooves on it.

Words. They gave him words like Vietnam syndrome, and his father was crawling through a hardware store on his stomach.

When the embarrassment became so bad that he would cross the street when he saw his father coming, when it ate into him as he went to sleep, Terry realized he had to do something. He had to know this thing, had to understand what was wrong with his father.

When it came, it was simple enough at the start. It had taken some courage, more than Terry thought he could find. His father was sitting in the kitchen at the table and his mother had gone shopping. Terry wanted it that way; he wanted his father alone. His mother seemed to try to protect him, as if his father could break.

Terry got a soda out of the refrigerator and popped it open. As an **afterthought,** he handed it to his father and got another for himself. Then he sat at the table.

His father smiled. "You look serious."

"Well . . ."

It went nowhere for a moment, and Terry was just about to drop it altogether. It may be the wrong time, he thought, but there might never be a better one.

"I was wondering if we could talk about something, Dad," Terry said.

His father shrugged. "We already did the bit about girls. Some time ago, as I remember it."

"No. Not that." It was a standing joke between them. When his father finally got around to explaining things to him, they'd already covered it in school. "It's something else."

"Something pretty heavy, judging by your face."

"Yes."

Word Power
afterthought (af´ tər thôt´) *n.* an idea that occurs or comes to mind later

Reading Skill
Cause and Effect Reread the highlighted paragraph. What makes Terry decide to do something about understanding his father's behavior?

Possible responses: Terry

avoids his father because

he's embarrassed. It bothers

Terry as he tries to sleep.

Connect to the Text
Reread the boxed text. Think of a time you tried to talk about something difficult with a parent or someone close to you. Was it hard to bring up the subject? How did you feel during the conversation?

Answers will vary.

Literary Element

Climax Reread the sentences highlighted in blue. Terry does something that begins to lead up to the climax, or the turning point in the story. What does Terry do that he has been waiting to do since the beginning of the story? Underline the sentence where he does this.

Reading Skill

Cause and Effect Reread the paragraph highlighted in green. What effect does bringing up Vietnam have on Terry's father?

His father's eyes go away

again.

_____

_____

"Well?"

I still can't do it, Terry thought. I can still drop this thing.

"Vietnam," Terry blurted out.

"No!" his father said sharply. It was as if he had been struck a blow.

"But, Dad."

"No. That's another part of my life. A bad part. A rotten part. It was before I met your mother, long before you. It has nothing to do with this family, nothing. No."

So, Terry thought, so I tried. But it wasn't over yet. It wasn't started yet.

"It just seems to bother you so much," Terry said, "and I thought if I could help or maybe understand it better . . ." He looked at the table, then out the window. It was all wrong to bring it up, he thought. "I'm sorry."

But now his father didn't hear him. Now his father's eyes were gone again, and something horrible went through Terry's heart as he thought he had done this thing to this father, caused his eyes to go away.

War & Peace, 1990. Tsing-Fang Chen. Acrylic on canvas, 66 x 95 in. Lucia Gallery, New York.

How does the artist reflect opposite ideas—war and peace—in this painting?

"You can't know," his father said after a time.

"This thing that you want to know—there is so much of it that you cannot know it all, and to know only a part is . . . is too awful. I can't tell anybody what it was really like."

It was more than he'd ever said about Vietnam, and his voice was breaking. Terry hated himself and felt he would hate himself until he was an old man. In one second he had caused such ruin. Now he had done this, and he wanted to hide, to leave. But he sat, waiting, knowing that it wasn't done.

His father looked to him, through him, somewhere into and out of Terry. He wasn't in the kitchen anymore. He was back in the green places, back in the hot places, the wet-hot places.

"You think that because I act strange, that we can talk and it will be all right," his father said. "That's what you think, isn't it?

"That's what the shrinks say," his father continued. "The **psychiatrists** tell me that if I talk about it, the whole thing will go away. But they don't know. They weren't there. Nobody was there but me and some other dead people, and they can't talk because they couldn't stop the morning."

Terry pushed his soda can back and forth, looking down, frightened at what was happening.

"I don't understand, Dad."

"No. You don't." His voice hardened, then softened again, and broke at the edges. "But see, see how it was . . ." He trailed off, and Terry thought he was done.

Background Info

Many soldiers who returned from Vietnam did not want to talk about their experiences. It was not a popular war, and Americans were deeply divided about the war. Some soldiers felt their sacrifices were not appreciated, and many had trouble adjusting back to their daily lives.

English Coach

The word *shrinks* is a slang term for psychiatrists. These doctors specialize in treating people with mental problems and illnesses. What other meaning does the word *shrink* have?

to make smaller

Word Power

psychiatrists (sī kī′ ə trists) *n.* doctors who specialize in helping people with mental problems

Background Info

A *rice paddy* is a field in which rice is grown. Because rice requires much water to grow, the fields are often ankle deep with water.

Reading Skill

Predict Terry's father tells his story to Terry. Reread the prediction you made on page 19. Does it match what happened in the story? (Don't worry if it doesn't match! You can change your predictions as you get new information from the story!) Now predict how the retelling of the father's experience will affect Terry and his father.

Possible responses: It will

help Terry understand what

his father went through. His

father might feel better if

he tells the story aloud.

_____

_____

_____

_____

"We were crossing a rice paddy in the dark," he said, and suddenly his voice flowed like a river breaking loose. "We were crossing the paddy, and it was dark, so black you couldn't see the end of your nose. There was a light rain, and I was thinking that during the next break I would whisper and tell Petey Kressler how nice the rain felt. But of course I didn't know there wouldn't be a Petey Kressler."

He took a deep breath. At that moment Terry felt his brain swirl, and he felt the darkness and the light rain because it was in his father's eyes, in his voice.

"So we were crossing the paddy, and then we caught it. We began taking fire from three sides, automatic weapons, and everybody went down. We tried to get low, but we couldn't. We could never get low enough, and you could hear the rounds hitting people. It was just a short time before they brought in the mortars. We should have moved, should have run, but nobody got up, and after a time nobody *could* get up. The fire just kept coming and coming, and then incoming mortars. I heard screams as they hit, but there was nothing to do. Nothing to do."

"Dad?" Terry said. He thought, maybe I can stop him. Maybe I can stop him before . . . before it gets to be too much. Before he breaks.

"Mortars," his father went on, "I hated mortars. You just heard them *wump* as they fired, and you didn't know where they would hit, and you always felt like they would hit your back. They swept back and forth with the mortars, and the automatic weapons kept coming in. There was no radio, no way to call for artillery. Just the dark to hide in. So I crawled to the side and found Jackson, only he wasn't there, just part of his body, the top part, and I hid under it and waited, and waited, and waited.

"Finally the firing quit. But see, see how it was in the dark with nobody alive but me? I yelled once, but that brought fire again, so I shut up and there was nothing, not even the screams."

His father cried, and Terry tried to understand, and he thought he could feel part of it. But it was so much, so much and so strange to him.

"You cannot know this," his father repeated. "You cannot know the fear. It was almost dark, and I was the only one left alive out of 54 men, all dead but me, and I knew that the Vietcong were just waiting for light. When the dawn came, 'Charley' would come out and finish everybody off, the way they always did. And I thought if I could stop the dawn, just stop the sun from coming up, I could make it."

Terry felt the fear, and he also felt the tears coming down his cheeks. His hand went out across the table, and he took his father's hand and held it. It was shaking.

"I mean I actually thought that if I could stop the sun from coming up, I could live. I made my brain work on that because it was all I had. Through the rest of the night in the rain in the paddy, I thought I could do it. I could stop the dawn." He took a deep breath. "But you can't, you know. You can't stop it from coming, and when I saw the gray light, I knew I was dead. It would just be minutes, and the light would be full, and I just settled under Jackson's body, and hid."

He stopped, and his face came down into his hands. Terry stood and went around the table to stand in back of him, his hands on his shoulders, rubbing gently.

"They didn't shoot me. They came, one of them poked Jackson's body and went on and they left me. But I was dead. I'm still dead, don't you see? I died because I couldn't stop the sun. Inside where I am—I died."

Terry was still in back of him, and he nodded, but he didn't see. He understood only that he didn't understand, and that he would probably never understand what had truly happened. And maybe his father would never be truly normal.

But Terry also knew that it didn't matter. He would try to understand, and the trying would have to be enough. He would try hard from now on, and he would not be embarrassed when his father's eyes went away. He would not be embarrassed no matter what his father did. Terry had knowledge now. Maybe not enough and maybe not all that he would need.

But it was a start.

Reading Skill

Predict Does your prediction from page 24 match what happened in the story, or were you surprised by the outcome? How do you think Terry will act toward his father in the future?

Possible responses:

Terry will keep trying to

understand him. He will

keep trying to help his

father and to deal with his

father's behavior.

Rice Paddies—Vietnam, 1966. Augustine Acuna. Watercolor, 18 x 28 in. United States Army Center of Military History, Washington, D.C.

How is the scene in this painting similar to what Terry's father describes?

Respond to Literature

STOP THE SUN

A Comprehension Check

Answer the following questions in the spaces provided.

1. What do the doctors say Terry's father is suffering from?

   The doctors say he is suffering from Vietnam syndrome.

2. What does Terry's father say happened to him because he could not stop the sun from coming up? Terry's father says he died inside.

B Reading Skills

Answer the following questions in the spaces provided.

1. **Cause and Effect** What causes Terry to want to disappear at the hardware store? His father is found crawling and whimpering on the floor of the store.

2. **Cause and Effect** When Terry hears about Vietnam from his father, what effect does it have on him? Possible responses: Terry realizes that he will never really understand his father's experiences, but he begins to understand how much his father suffers. He won't be embarrassed by his father again.

3. **Predict** Predict whether or not Terry will be able to help his father overcome his problems. Why do you think so? Possible responses: Yes, Terry will help his father by listening to his experiences and being supportive. No, no one can help Terry's father get over such a horrible experience.

C Word Power

Complete each sentence below, using one of the words in the box.

veterans	persisted	involvement
afterthought	psychiatrists	

1. The _____psychiatrists_____ at the hospital are trained to work with people who have suffered through terrible tragedies.

2. We showed our _____involvement_____ in the community by attending the town hall meetings.

3. The dedication of the World War II memorial was attended by families of the _____veterans_____.

4. Although it was not supposed to rain, my mother _____persisted_____ in telling us to take our umbrellas.

5. As an _____afterthought_____, I told the audience that I had written the play.

Circle the word that best completes each sentence.

6. My (**involvement**, **afterthought**) in running the new club was temporary.

7. The memorial honors the (**veterans**, **persisted**) who served in Vietnam.

8. As an (**afterthought**, **involvement**) to our discussion about San Francisco, Ashley added that she had seen the Golden Gate Bridge.

9. For several days, Maria (**psychiatrists**, **persisted**) in asking the entire class to join the chess club.

10. After the disaster, (**psychiatrists**, **veterans**) were available to talk with the survivors.

D Literary Element: Climax

Read the passage below from "Stop the Sun." As you read, think about what the sentences reveal about the climax of the story. Then answer the questions that follow.

"Well?"[1]

I still can't do it, Terry thought.[2] I can still drop this thing.[3]

"Vietnam," Terry blurted out.[4]

"No!" his father said sharply.[5] It was as if he had been struck a blow.[6]

"I'm still dead, don't you see?[7] I died because I couldn't stop the sun.[8] Inside where I am—I died."[9]

1. How are sentences 1–6 building up to the climax of the story?

   Possible responses: Terry finally gets the courage to bring up Vietnam. The

   tension has been building up to this moment. This conversation leads to

   the turning point in the story.

   _____

   _____

2. Read sentences 7–9. How is this moment a turning point for both Terry and

   his father? Possible responses: Terry's father finally tells the story that he

   has kept inside for so long. Terry finally hears the reason why his father

   behaves the way he does.

   _____

   _____

E A Letter

Imagine that you are Terry. Write a letter to your father, telling him how much you care about him. Explain that you understand a little of what he experienced and hope that he will start to heal inside.

Dear Dad,

On the day we went to the mall, I was really worried about you. I saw you crawling on the floor of the hardware store.

I got really scared and wanted to understand Possible response: what was causing you to behave this way.

Then you told me about Vietnam and that you were

Possible response: trapped in the rice paddy. You and the other men

were being attacked. Soon you were the only one left alive.

You knew that when the sun came up, you would die. But you didn't die. I know that you said you feel like you are dead inside.

But I see you as being very much alive, and I hope that you will Possible response: start to feel alive again.

I don't understand everything, but I love you.

Your son,

Terry

Assessment

Fill in the circle next to each correct answer.

1. Why does Terry go to the library to research Vietnam?
   - ○ A. He wants to know how many people fought in the war.
   - ○ B. He thinks his mother is hiding important information.
   - ○ C. He wants to know more about the people of Vietnam.
   - ● D. He wants to understand how the war affected his father.

2. Which sentence from the story **best** helps you predict that Terry will try to learn what his father is thinking?
   - ○ A. It was all wrong to bring it up, he thought.
   - ○ B. "Billy's father was there, and he doesn't act that way."
   - ● C. Terry realized he had to do something.
   - ○ D. Now he had done this, and he wanted to hide, to leave.

3. Why does Terry want his father to stop in the middle of telling his story?
   - ○ A. Terry feels disappointed by what his father is telling him.
   - ● B. Terry is afraid that his father will break.
   - ○ C. Terry feels good because he understands everything.
   - ○ D. Terry is proud of himself for getting his father to share.

4. At what point in the story does Terry realize that his father's pain is much deeper than he ever imagined?
   - ● A. when he talks about death and fearing the dawn
   - ○ B. when he is unable to finish eating a meal
   - ○ C. when he asks Terry to go to the store with him
   - ○ D. when he tells Terry what the psychiatrists say

5. Which of the following words means "continued on"?
   - ● A. persisted
   - ○ B. involvement
   - ○ C. afterthought
   - ○ D. psychiatrists

Chanclas

Meet
Sandra Cisneros

Sandra Cisneros (sis nā′ rōs′) was born in Chicago in 1954. She is the only daughter in a family of seven children. Her family moved between Chicago and Mexico City, where her father's parents lived. Cisneros often writes about the life experiences of Hispanic girls. Cisneros says, "They're all stories I lived, or witnessed, or heard." "Chanclas," which is part of the novel *The House on Mango Street*, was first published in 1983.

What You Know

Think about a time in the past when you felt awkward or embarrassed. With a partner, discuss things that you can do, or that friends can help you do, to feel more comfortable in an embarrassing situation.

Reason to Read

Read "Chanclas" to find out how a girl overcomes what she thinks will be an embarrassing event.

Background Info

Hispanics are the fastest-growing minority group in the United States. More than one in eight people in the United States are of Hispanic origin. Over 60 percent of Hispanics have roots in Mexico. Other places of origin include countries in South and Central America, Puerto Rico, and Cuba. Hispanics make up a large part of the population of many large cities in the West and the South and work in almost every sector of the U.S. economy.

Word Power

baptism (bap´ tiz´ əm) *n.* a ceremony in which a person becomes a member of the Christian religion; p. 34
After her *baptism*, Sara went to church every Sunday.

precious (presh´ əs) *adj.* valuable; highly cherished; p. 34
When my father wrote letters to my mother, he addressed them to his *precious* friend.

scuffed (skufd) *adj.* scraped or scratched through use; p. 35
My shoes were *scuffed* and dirty after my long walk on the dusty road.

plungers (plun´ jərz) *n.* large rubber cups attached to long handles that are used to unclog drains; p. 35
My dad bought two *plungers* at the store for our bathrooms.

linoleum (li nō´ lē əm) *n.* a type of material used for covering floors; p. 35
We couldn't decide whether to cover the floor with *linoleum* or carpeting.

**Answer the following questions that contain the new words above.
Write your answers in the spaces provided.**

1. Would *plungers* be used in a sink or in an oven? _____ in a sink _____

2. If a tabletop is *scuffed,* is it smooth or rough? _____ rough _____

3. Would a *baptism* take place in a church or in a store? _____ in a church _____

4. If a painting is *precious,* is it treasured or considered worthless? _____ treasured _____

5. Would *linoleum* be used inside a house or in a garden? _____ inside a house _____

Chanclas

Sandra Cisneros

English Coach

It's is a contraction for "it is." A contraction is the shortening of a word or group of words. In *it's,* the apostrophe takes the place of the letter *i.* Underline another contraction in the same paragraph. What is it short for?

she is, she has, *or* I am

Reading Skill

Predict Reread the sentence highlighted in green. Predict how the narrator will feel after her mother forgets to buy her shoes.

Possible response: She will

be disappointed and mad.

It's me—Mama, Mama said. I open up and she's there with bags and big boxes, the new clothes and, yes, she's got the socks and a new slip with a little rose on it and a pink and white striped dress. What about the shoes? I forgot. Too late now. I'm tired. Whew!

Six-thirty already and my little cousin's **baptism** is over. All day waiting, the door locked, don't open up for nobody, and I don't till Mama gets back and buys everything except the shoes.

Now Uncle Nacho is coming in his car, and we have to hurry and get to **Precious** Blood Church quick because that's where the baptism party is in the basement rented for today for dancing and tamales and everyone's kids running all over the place.

Did You Know?

Tamales are made from cornmeal stuffed with beans, peppers, meat, vegetables, or cheese. They are wrapped in corn husks and cooked by steaming or roasting.

Word Power

baptism (bap´ tiz´ əm) *n.* a ceremony in which a person becomes a member of the Christian religion

precious (presh´ əs) *adj.* valuable; highly cherished

Mama dances, laughs, dances. All of a sudden, Mama is sick. I fan her hot face with a paper plate. Too many tamales, but Uncle Nacho says too many this and tilts his thumb to his lips.

Everybody laughing except me, because I'm wearing the new dress, pink and white with stripes, and new underclothes and new socks and the old saddle shoes I wear to school, brown and white, the kind I get every September because they last long and they do. My feet **scuffed** and round, and the heels all crooked that look dumb with this dress, so I just sit.

Meanwhile that boy who is my cousin by first communion or something, asks me to dance and I can't. Just stuff my feet under the metal folding chair stamped Precious Blood and pick on a wad of brown gum that's stuck beneath the seat. I shake my head no. My feet growing bigger and bigger.

Then Uncle Nacho is pulling and pulling my arm and it doesn't matter how new the dress Mama bought is because my feet are ugly until my uncle who is a liar says, You are the prettiest girl here, will you dance, but I believe him, and yes, we are dancing, my Uncle Nacho and me, only I don't want to at first. My feet swell big and heavy like **plungers,** but I drag them across the **linoleum** floor straight center where Uncle wants to show off the new dance we learned. And Uncle spins me, and my skinny arms bend the way he taught me, and my mother watches, and my little cousins watch, and the boy who is my cousin by first communion watches, and everyone says, wow, who are those two who dance like in the movies, until I forget that I am wearing only ordinary shoes, brown and white, the kind my mother buys each year for school.

Word Power

scuffed (skufd) *adj.* scraped or scratched through use

plungers (plun´ jərz) *n.* large rubber cups attached to long handles that are used to unclog drains

linoleum (li nō´ lē əm) *n.* a type of material used for covering floors

Reading Skill

Predict Reread the prediction you made at the beginning of the story. Does it match what actually happens? (Don't worry if it doesn't match! You can change your predictions as you get more information from the story.) Do you predict the narrator will dance at the party? Why or why not?

Possible responses: Yes, she will get over her embarrassment. No, she will be too ashamed to dance.

Literary Element

Point of View Reread the highlighted sentence. This story is written from the first-person point of view. The main character is the narrator and talks about the people in the story as they relate to her. Underline the phrases that show how other people at the party are related to the narrator. What pronoun in these phrases shows that the passage is told from the first-person point of view?

my

Reading Skill

Cause and Effect Reread the highlighted sentences. What effect does dancing with Uncle Nacho have on the narrator?

Possible responses: She feels good about herself. She stops feeling embarrassed about her shoes because she knows that people care about her dancing, not what she is wearing.

And all I hear is the clapping when the music stops. My uncle and me bow and he walks me back in my thick shoes to my mother who is proud to be my mother. All night the boy who is a man watches me dance. He watched me dance.

Do you think the clothes you wear reflect who you are? Why or why not?

Respond to Literature

Chanclas

A Comprehension Check

Answer the following questions in the spaces provided.

1. Why is the narrator excited at the beginning of the story? What changes her mood? She is excited about getting a new outfit. She feels disappointed when she realizes that her mother forgot to buy new shoes for her.

2. How does Uncle Nacho help the narrator have a good time at the party? He insists that she dance with him and tells her she is pretty. They dance so well together that the narrator forgets all about her ugly shoes.

B Reading Skills

Complete the following activities in the spaces provided.

1. **Predict** Predict how the narrator will feel about herself and her shoes after the end of the story. Possible responses: She will feel happy and confident. She will not mind wearing the old shoes.

2. **Cause and Effect** What causes the narrator's attitude to change at the end of the story? When the narrator dances with her uncle, everyone is impressed by how well they dance. This response makes her feel confident.

C Word Power

Complete each sentence below, using one of the words in the box.

baptism	precious	scuffed	plungers	linoleum

1. After the workers put the _____linoleum_____ on the kitchen floor, it looked much better.

2. We bought several _____plungers_____ because our drains are always getting clogged.

3. After the dog had lived with us for three months, all the furniture in the house was _____scuffed_____ and damaged.

4. A _____baptism_____ ceremony is often followed by a party.

5. The poem my grandmother wrote about her homeland is a _____precious_____ gift for our entire family.

Circle the word that best completes each sentence.

6. The father bought a beautiful white outfit for his baby's (**baptism**, **scuffed**).

7. The most (**precious**, **plungers**) gift Jill ever received was a quilt her mother had made.

8. The ballroom's (**baptism**, **linoleum**) dance floor was easy to clean.

9. Before Antonio called a plumber, we tried to use (**plungers**, **precious**) to drain the water.

10. The rubber tires on the old car were dirty and (**linoleum**, **scuffed**).

D Literary Element: Point of View

Read the passage below from "Chanclas." As you read, think about the point of view in the story. Then answer the questions that follow.

> Everybody laughing except me, because I'm wearing the new dress, pink and white with stripes, and new underclothes and new socks and the old saddle shoes I wear to school, brown and white, the kind I get every September because they last long and they do. My feet scuffed and round, and the heels all crooked that look dumb with this dress, so I just sit.

1. Is the passage told in the first- or third-person point of view? How do you know?

   The passage is written in the first-person point of view. The sentences use the pronouns *me, I,* and *my.*

2. How does the point of view of the passage help you understand how the narrator feels?

   Since it is told in first person, we get to directly hear her thoughts about how she feels.

E A Letter

Imagine that you are the narrator. You want to write a letter to Uncle Nacho thanking him for making you feel better at the party. Remember to include a funny statement that reflects how you feel about your shoes!

Dear Uncle Nacho,

What a lifesaver you are. There I was at the baptism party, sitting in my chair, feeling Possible response: miserable

and embarrassed because I had to wear my old shoes.

My shoes Possible responses: were so lame it hurt my eyes just to look

at them; looked like clown shoes.

You probably thought I looked pretty sad, but you still insisted that I dance with you. How did you know that dancing Possible response: with you would make me feel so much

better?

We sure make great dance partners. Even with my worn-out shoes, I was able to spin around like a pro. Later at the party, Possible response: I met a nice boy who had

watched me dance all night.

Thanks again, Uncle Nacho. You're the best!

Your loving niece.

Assessment

Fill in the circle next to each correct answer.

1. What causes the narrator to feel embarrassed at the dance?
   ○ A. Her uncle is a show-off.
   ○ B. Her family is late to the party.
   ● C. Her shoes are old and worn out.
   ○ D. Her mother eats too many tamales.

2. Who helps the narrator overcome being embarrassed?
   ● A. the narrator's uncle
   ○ B. the narrator's mother
   ○ C. the narrator's little cousins
   ○ D. no one

3. Which sentence from the story **best** helps you predict that the narrator and "the boy who is a man" might become better friends?
   ○ A. I shake my head no.
   ● B. He watched me dance.
   ○ C. Uncle wants to show off the new dance we learned.
   ○ D. And all I hear is the clapping when the music stops.

4. Which of the following phrases from the story shows that it is written in the first-person point of view?
   ○ A. she's got the socks and a new slip
   ○ B. that's where the baptism party is
   ○ C. You are the prettiest girl here, will you dance
   ● D. my skinny arms bend the way he taught me

5. Which of the following words means "highly valued"?
   ● A. precious
   ○ B. baptism
   ○ C. scuffed
   ○ D. plungers

Get Ready to Read!

Everybody Knows
Tobie

Meet
Daniel Garza

Daniel Garza (gär ′ zä) was born in Texas in 1938. His family was originally from Mexico. They moved to Texas in the early 1900s. Garza was born and raised in a small town close to Hillsboro, Texas. Garza studied for a few years at a university and later joined the U.S. Army. He has received awards for his writing, which is often about the lives of seasonal workers in Texas. "Everybody Knows Tobie" was first published in 1963.

What You Know

Have you ever felt that you did not quite belong to any group? How did it make you feel? Do you think it is important to belong? Discuss your ideas with the class.

Reason to Read

Read to find out about how a boy deals with not fitting in.

Background Info

For over sixty years, many Mexican workers have moved to the United States to improve their lives. Some settled in the country and have become U.S. citizens. Many Mexicans and Mexican Americans became farmworkers known as migrant workers. A migrant farmworker is a person who moves regularly, from crop to crop or from labor camp to labor camp, in order to find work. In many places, the workers were treated poorly and denied basic needs, such as food and shelter. Today, migrants continue to work throughout the United States.

Word Power

prejudiced (prej´ə disd) *adj.* having a bad opinion without enough knowledge or good reasons; p. 45
The girls were *prejudiced* against fishing, even though they had never tried to catch fish.

rejected (ri jekt´ id) *adj.* unwanted; unaccepted; p. 49
The dog looked lonely and *rejected* as it waited for someone to take it home.

incident (in´sə dənt) *n.* an event that happens; an experience; p. 51
There was a strange *incident* at school in which all the chairs were overturned.

astonishment (əs ton´ ish mənt) *n.* surprise; amazement; p. 52
The student's face had a look of *astonishment* when the teacher told him that he was now at the top of his class.

meaningless (mē´ ning lis) *adj.* pointless; without importance; p. 53
The foreign words were *meaningless* to me.

**Answer the following questions, using one of the new words above.
Write your answers in the spaces provided.**

1. Which word goes with "reaction to something unexpected"? _____astonishment_____

2. Which word goes with "something that occurs"? _____incident_____

3. Which word goes with "having no point"? _____meaningless_____

4. Which word goes with "not liking something for no good reason"? _____prejudiced_____

5. Which word goes with "turned away"? _____rejected_____

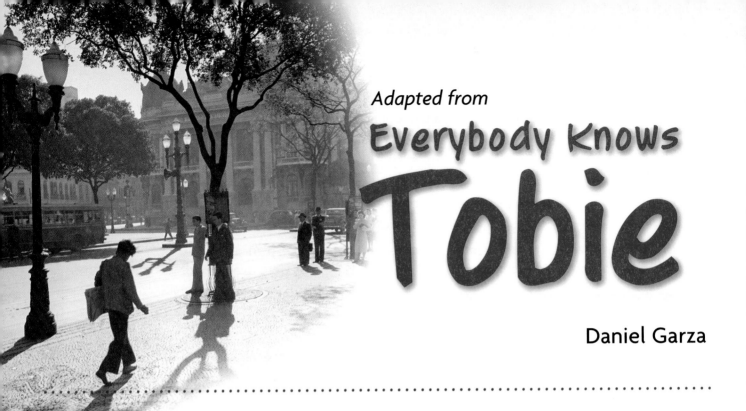

Adapted from

Everybody Knows Tobie

Daniel Garza

Reading Skill

Predict Reread the title of the story and the highlighted sentence. Predict how the people of the town will treat Tobie's brother.

Possible responses: They

will be nice to him. They

will accept him.

Background Info

Gringo (gring´gō) is a word used to refer to foreigners who speak English. In this story, it describes the Anglos in the town. The word *Chicano* (chi kä´ nō) describes people of Mexican descent who were born in the United States.

When I was thirteen years old my older brother, Tobie, had the town newspaper route. Everyone in the town knew him well because he had been delivering their papers for a year and a half. Tobie used to tell me that he had the best route of all because his customers would pay on time each month. Sometimes, he used to brag that the nice people of the town would tip him a quarter or maybe fifty cents at the end of the month because he would walk up many stairs to deliver the paper personally.

Yes, Tobie had it good.

Because of his paper route, Tobie knew the Gringos of the town so well that he could go into a Gringo barbershop and get a haircut. The barber wouldn't tell him to go to the Mexican barber in our town or embarrass him in front of all the Gringo customers in the shop as they often did when Chicano cotton pickers came into their places during the fall months.

The Gringo barbers of my town were careful whom they allowed in their shops during the cotton harvest season in the fall. September and October and cotton brought Chicanos from the south to the north of Texas where I lived. Chicanos is what we say in our language. It means the Mexicans of Texas. These Chicano cotton pickers came from the Rio Grande Valley in South Texas. Sometimes, even people from Mexico made the trip to the north of Texas.

When the Chicanos came to my town on Saturdays after working in the cotton fields all week, they would go to the town market for food or to the local movie house. And then maybe those who had never been to the north of Texas before would go to the Gringos' barbershops for haircuts, not knowing that they would be refused. The Gringo barbers would be very careful not to let them come too close to their shops because the regular Gringo customers would get mad. Sometimes they would curse the Chicanos.

"Hell, it's them damn pepper bellies again. Can't seem to get rid of 'em in the fall," the **prejudiced** Gringos of my town would say. Some of the nicer people would only become uneasy at seeing so many Chicanos with long, black, greasy hair wanting haircuts.

Did You Know?

The *Rio Grande* (rē´ ō grand´) is a river that forms the border between Texas and Mexico. The Rio Grande Valley is located near the mouth of the river.

Comprehension Check

Reread the boxed sentences. When do the Chicanos from the south come to Joey's town? Why do they come?

In September and October

they come to pick cotton.

_____

_____

_____

Reading Skill
Cause and Effect

Reread the highlighted sentences. If the Gringo barbers let the Chicanos come close to their shops, what effect would it have? Check the correct response.

☐ More Gringos would come to town.

☐ The Chicanos would lose ther jobs.

☑ The Gringo customers would get mad.

Word Power

prejudiced (prej´ ə disd) *adj.* having a bad opinion without enough knowledge or good reasons

Background Info

A *flat-top* is a type of haircut. The hair on top is so short that it stands up to form a flat surface.

The barbers of the town liked Tobie, and they invited him to their shops for haircuts. Tobie said that the barbers told him that they would cut his hair because he did not belong to that group of people who came from the south of Texas. Tobie understood. And he did not argue with the barbers because he knew how Chicanos from South Texas were, and how maybe Gringo scissors would get all greasy from cutting their hair.

During that fall Tobie encouraged me to go to the Gringo's place for a haircut. "Joey, when are you going to get rid of that mop of hair?" he asked.

"I guess I'll get rid of it when Mr. López learns how to cut flat-tops."

"Mr. López is a good ole guy and all that, but if he doesn't know how to give flat-tops then you should go to some other barber for flat-tops. Really, kid-brother, that hair looks awful."

"Yeah, but I'm afraid."

"Afraid of what?" Tobie asked.

"I'm afraid the barber will mistake me for one of those guys from South Texas and kick me out of his shop."

"Mr. Brewer . . . you know, the barber who cuts my hair . . . is a nice man, and he'll cut your hair. Just tell him you're my kid-brother."

I thought about this new adventure for several days. Then on a Saturday, when there was no school, I decided to get a haircut at Mr. Brewer's. I hurriedly rode my bike to town and parked it in the alley close to the barbershop. As I walked into the shop, I noticed that all of a sudden the Gringos inside stopped their conversation and looked at me. The shop was silent for a moment. I thought then that maybe this was not too good and that I should leave. I remembered what Tobie had told me about being his brother, and about Mr. Brewer being a nice man. I was convinced that I belonged in the Gringo barbershop.

Literary Element

Point of View Reread the highlighted passage. A story told from the first-person point of view often takes place in the mind of the narrator. Underline the phrases that show that this passage is taking place inside Joey's head.

I found an empty chair and sat down to wait my turn for a haircut. One Gringo customer sitting next to me rose and explained to the barber that he had to go to the courthouse for something. Another customer left without saying anything. And then one, who was dressed in dirty coveralls, got up from Mr. Brewer's chair and said to him, "Say, Tom, looks like you got yourself a little tamale to clip.'"

Mr. Brewer smiled only.

My turn was next, and I was afraid. But I remembered again that this was all right because I was Tobie's brother, and everybody liked Tobie. I went to Mr. Brewer's chair. As I started to sit down, he looked at me and smiled a nice smile.

He said, "I'm sorry, sonny, but I can't cut your hair. You go to Mr. López's. He'll cut your hair."

Mr. Brewer took me to the door and pointed the way to López's barbershop. He pointed with his finger and said, "See, over there behind that service station. That's his place. You go there. He'll clip your hair."

Tears were welling in my eyes. I felt a lump in my throat. I was too choked up to tell him I was Tobie's brother, and that it was all right to cut my hair. I only looked at him as he finished giving directions. He smiled again and patted me on the back. As I left, Mr. Brewer said, "Say hello to Mr. López for me, will you, sonny?"

I did not turn back to look at Mr. Brewer. I kept my head bowed as I walked to Mr. López's because tears filled my eyes. These were tears of hurt to the pride and confidence which I had slowly gained in my Gringo town.

I thought of many things as I walked slowly. Maybe this was a foolish thing which I had done. There were too many Gringos in the town, and too few of us who lived there all the year long. This was a bad thing because the Gringos had the right to say yes or no, and we could only follow what they said. It was useless to go against them. It was foolish.

Reading Skill

Predict Reread the prediction you made at the beginning of the story. Does it match what happens? (Don't worry if it doesn't match! You can change your predictions as you get new information from the story!) Why do the Gringos treat Tobie and Joey differently?

Possible response:
Everybody knows Tobie, but the Gringos assume Joey is with the cotton pickers.

Reading Skill

Cause and Effect Reread the highlighted sentence. What happens to Joey at the Gringo barbershop? Complete the Cause and Effect chart below by adding the cause.

Cause

The barber refuses to cut Joey's hair.

Effect
Joey feels badly.

47

Connect to the Text

Reread the boxed sentences. Have you ever been in a situation in which you felt you had no choices? How did it make you feel?

Answers will vary.

_____

_____

_____

_____

_____

But I was different from the Chicanos who came from the south, not much different. I did live in the town the ten months of the year when the other Chicanos were in the south or in Mexico. Then I remembered what the barber had told my brother about the South Texas people, and why the Gringo customers had left while I was in Mr. Brewer's shop. I began to understand. But it was very hard for me to realize that even though I had lived among Gringos all of my life I still had to go to my own people for such things as haircuts. Why wouldn't Gringos cut my hair? I was clean. My hair was not long and greasy.

I walked into Mr. López's shop. There were many Chicanos waiting their turn for a haircut. Mr. López paused from his work as he saw me enter and said, "Sorry, Joey, full up. Come back in a couple of hours."

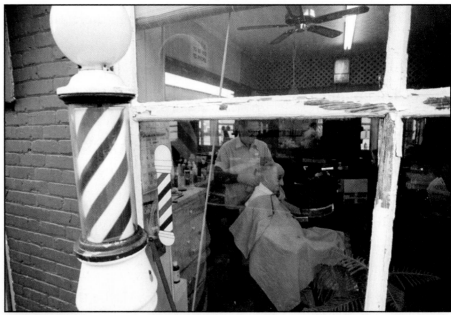

Have you ever been to a barbershop? How was it like or unlike the shops in this story?

_____

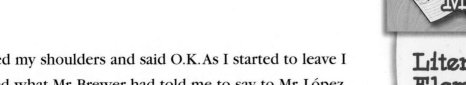

I shrugged my shoulders and said O.K. As I started to leave I remembered what Mr. Brewer had told me to say to Mr. López. "Mr. López," I said, and all the Chicanos, the ones who were waiting, turned and looked at me with curious eyes. "Mr. Brewer told me to tell you hello."

Mr. López shook his head approvingly, not taking in the content of my statement. The Chicanos looked at me again and began to whisper among themselves. I did not hear, but I understood.

I went away feeling **rejected** both by the Gringos and even my people, the entire world I knew.

Back in the alley where my bike was parked I sat on the curb for a long while thinking how maybe I did not fit into this town. Maybe my place was in the south of Texas where there were many of my kind of people, and where there were more Chicano barbershops and less Gringo barbers. Yes, I thought, I needed a land where I could belong to one race. I was so concerned with myself that I did not notice a Chicano, a middle-aged man dressed in a new shirt and faded pants, studying me.

"Maybe the cotton has not been good for you this year," he said.

"No, *señor*. I live here in the town."

And then the Chicano said, "Chico, I mistook you for one of us."

Suddenly the Chicano became less interested in me and walked away unconcerned.

I could not have told him that I had tried for a haircut at the Gringo's because he would have laughed at me and called me a *pocho*; a Chicano who prefers Gringo ways. These experienced Chicanos knew the ways of the Gringos in the north of Texas.

Literary Element

Point of View Reread the sentence highlighted in blue. Underline the pronouns that tell you that this story is being told by Joey from a first-person point of view. How would this sentence read if it were told from a third-person point of view?

Joey went away feeling rejected both by the Gringos and even his own people, the entire world he knew.

English Coach

Joey and the man speak Spanish to each other. *Señor* (sā nyor´) means "sir" or "mister" in Spanish. *Chico* (chē´ kō) means "boy." If a father and son are calling each other *señor* and *chico*, which would be which?

The father would be señor and the son would be chico.

Word Power

rejected (ri jekt´ id) *adj.* unwanted; unaccepted

After the Chicano had left me, I thought that maybe these things which were happening to me in the town would all pass in a short time. The entire cotton crop would soon be harvested. Then the Chicanos would leave the north of Texas and journey back to their homes.

My town would be left alone for ten more months of the year, and in this time everything and everybody would be all right again. The Gringo barbers would maybe think twice before sending me to Mr. López's.

Early in November the last of the cotton around my town had been harvested. The people of South Texas climbed aboard their big trucks and they began their long journey to their homes in the border country.

The streets of the little town were now empty on Saturday. A few farmers came to town on Saturday and brought their families to do their shopping. Still the streets were quiet and empty.

In my home there was new excitement for me. Tobie considered leaving his newspaper route for another job, one that would pay more money. And I thought that maybe he would let me take over his route. By taking his route I would know all the Gringos of the town, and maybe . . .maybe then the barbers would invite me to their shops as they had invited Tobie.

At supper that night I asked Tobie if he would take me on his delivery for a few days, and then let me deliver the newspaper on my own.

Tobie said, "No, Joey. You're too young to handle money. Besides, the newspaper bag would be too heavy for you to carry on your shoulder all over town. No, I think I'll turn the route over to Red."

My father was quiet during this time, but soon he spoke, "Tobie, you give the route to Joey. He knows about money. And he needs to put a little muscle on his shoulders."

The issue was settled.

Reading Skill

Predict Reread the highlighted sentence. Predict what will happen after Tobie quits his job.

Possible response: Joey

will take over Tobie's paper

route.

The next day Tobie took me to the newspaper office. Tobie's boss studied me carefully, scratched his white head, and then asked Tobie, "Well, what do you think?"

"Oh," Tobie said, "I told him he was too young to handle this job, but he says he can do it."

"Yes, sir," I butted in excitedly.

Tobie's boss looked at me and chuckled, "Well, he's got enough spirit."

Tobie spoke, "I think he'll make you a good delivery boy, sir."

A short silence followed.

Finally, the boss said, "We'll give him a try, Tobie." He looked at me. "But, young 'un, you'd better be careful with that money. It's your responsibility."

"Yes, sir," I gulped.

"O.K., that's settled," the boss said.

I took his hand and shook it and promised him that I would do my extra best.

In a few days I was delivering the *Daily News* to all the Gringos of the town, and also to Mr. Brewer.

Each afternoon, during my delivery, I was careful not to go into Mr. Brewer's with the newspaper. I would carefully open the door and drop the paper in. I did this because I thought that maybe Mr. Brewer would remember me, and this might cause an embarrassing **incident.** One afternoon Mr. Brewer was standing at the door. He saw me. I opened the door and quickly handed him the newspaper. Before I could shut the door he said, "Say, sonny, aren't you the one I sent to Mr. López's a while back?"

"Yes, sir," I said.

Word Power

incident (in ′ sə dənt) *n.* an event that happens; an experience

English Coach

Tobie's boss studies Joey carefully. This means that the boss is carefully considering Joey's qualities. Write another meaning for the word *studied.*

Possible response: *Studied*

also means "applied oneself

to gain knowledge."

Comprehension Check

Reread the boxed paragraphs. What persuades the boss to give Joey the paper route? Check the correct response.

☐ Joey begs the boss for the job.

☑ Tobie says that Joey will do a good job.

☐ The boss thinks that Joey has delivered papers before.

Reading Skill

Predict What did you predict would happen after Tobie quit his job? Did your prediction match the story? What do you think will happen to Joey now that he has taken over the paper route?

Possible response: Joey

will be accepted by the

townspeople.

Literary Element

Point of View Reread the highlighted text. Underline the phrase that tells you which part of the conversation is being said by the first-person narrator. How do you know?

He uses the pronoun *I*.

Reading Skill

Cause and Effect Reread the highlighted sentences. What causes Mr. Brewer and the customer to be friendly with Joey?

Mr. Brewer learns that Joey is Tobie's brother. The other customer sees that he is a delivery boy, not a cotton picker. They see that he is a townsperson.

"Why'd you stay around here? Didn't your people go back home last week? You do belong to 'em, don't you?"

"No, sir," I said. "I live here in the town."

"You mean to say you're not one of those . . .?"

"No, sir."

He paused and thought. "You know, sonny, I have a young Meskin boy who lives here in town come to this here shop for haircuts every other Saturday. His name is . . . durn, can't think of his name to save my soul . . ."

"Tobie?"

"Yeah, yeah, that's his name. Fine boy. You know him?"

"Yes, sir. He's my older brother."

Then Mr. Brewer's eyes got bigger in **astonishment.** He paused and shook his head in disbelief. "And I told you to go to Mr. López's. Why didn't you speak up and tell me you was Tobie's brother? I woulda put you in that there chair and clipped you a pretty head of hair."

"Oh, I guess I forgot to tell you," I said.

"Well, from now on, sonny, you come to this here shop, and I'll cut your hair."

"But what about your customers? Won't they get mad?"

"Naw. I'll tell 'em you're Tobie's brother, and everything will be all right. Everybody in town knows Tobie, and everybody likes him."

Then a customer walked into the barbershop. He looked at Mr. Brewer, and then at me, and then at my newspaper bag. And then the Gringo customer smiled a nice smile at me.

"Well, excuse me, sonny, got a customer waitin'. Remember now, come Saturday, and I'll clip your hair."

"O.K., Mr. Brewer. Bye."

Mr. Brewer turned and said good-bye.

Word Power

astonishment (əs ton´ ish mənt) *n.* surprise; amazement

How does the scene in the picture reflect this story?

As I continued my delivery I began to chuckle small bits of satisfaction to myself because Mr. Brewer had invited me to his shop for haircuts. And because the Gringo customer had smiled at me. And because now all the Gringos of the town would know me and maybe accept me.

Those incidents which had happened to me during the cotton harvest in my town: Mr. Brewer sending me to Mr. López's for the haircut, and the Chicano cotton picker avoiding me after discovering that I was not one of his people, and the Gringo customers leaving Mr. Brewer's barbershop because of me; all seemed so **meaningless.** And now I felt that delivering the *Daily News* to the businessmen had given me a place among them, and all because of the fact that everybody in my town knew Tobie.

Word Power

meaningless (mē´ ning lis) *adj.* pointless; without importance

Respond to Literature

Everybody Knows Tobie

A Comprehension Check

Answer the following questions in the spaces provided.

1. How do the Gringos in Joey's town treat the cotton pickers?

   The barbers refuse to cut their hair. Some people curse at them.

2. What does Mr. Brewer say to Joey when he finds out Joey is Tobie's brother?

   Mr. Brewer says he would have cut Joey's hair before. He tells Joey to come

   to him for haircuts.

B Reading Skills

Complete the following activities in the spaces provided.

1. **Predict** Joey has the newspaper route at the end of the story. Predict how well he will do following in his brother's footsteps.

   Possible response: He will do well because he wants to be accepted by the

   townspeople.

2. **Cause and Effect** What happens when Joey goes to Mr. Brewer's barbershop to get a haircut?

   The Gringos all leave, and Mr. Brewer tells him he can't cut his hair.

3. **Cause and Effect** Once Joey takes over the newspaper route, what causes the Gringos to be nicer to him?

   They realize that Joey is part of their community and lives in the town.

   Joey also thinks they like him because they find out he is Tobie's brother.

C Word Power

Complete each sentence below, using one of the words in the box.

> **prejudiced**   **rejected**   **incident**
>
> **astonishment**   **meaningless**

1. Your words of apology are _____meaningless_____ if you continue to make the same mistakes over and over.

2. Mario felt hurt and _____rejected_____ when his sister would not let him come to the movies with her.

3. After hearing so many one-sided opinions on TV, the jury was _____prejudiced_____ against the accused.

4. The other player said he was sorry for his behavior, so the team soon forgot about the _____incident_____.

5. Imagine my _____astonishment_____ when I heard my name announced as the winner of the poetry contest.

Circle the word that best completes each sentence.

6. It is waste of time to do (incident, **meaningless**) work.

7. After the embarrassing (astonishment, **incident**) in the cafeteria, I hid in the library all afternoon.

8. The judge chose the small dog because he is (rejected, **prejudiced**) against big hunting dogs.

9. John gave up after six girls (**rejected**, prejudiced) his offer to dance.

10. You could see the (**astonishment**, meaningless) in the little boy's eyes when the clown gave him a balloon.

D Literary Element: Point of View

Read the passages below from "Everybody Knows Tobie." As you read, think about the point of view of the story. Then answer the questions that follow.

> Tears were welling in my eyes.[1] I felt a lump in my throat.[2] I was too choked up to tell him I was Tobie's brother, and that it was all right to cut my hair.[3] I only looked at him as he finished giving directions.[4]
>
> As I continued my delivery I began to chuckle small bits of satisfaction to myself because Mr. Brewer had invited me to his shop for haircuts.[5] And because the Gringo customer had smiled at me.[6] And because now all the Gringos of the town would know me and maybe accept me.[7]

1. In sentences 1 and 2, how do you know that the story is told in the first-person point of view?

   The sentences use the pronouns *I* and *my*.

   _____

2. In sentences 1–7, how does the first-person point of view help you understand how Joey feels?

   Joey tells us directly how he feels and what he is thinking, instead of having

   an outside narrator tell the story.

   _____

   _____

   _____

E An Editorial

An editorial is a part of a newspaper in which writers or editors of the newspaper express their opinions. Imagine that you are writing an editorial for a newspaper in Joey's town. You see how Joey is treated in the barbershop before he says that he is related to Tobie. Then you see him delivering papers and everybody waving to him. Write an editorial in which you express your opinions about the prejudices in your town.

Dear Readers:

There are many ways in which people can be unfair to others. The other day in the barbershop, Possible responses: a Mexican American boy came in and waited to get a haircut. Other customers got up and left. One customer called the boy a tamale. The barber refused to cut the boy's hair and told him to go to the other barber.

A few months later, I saw the boy delivering papers. Everyone was smiling at him. What does this say about our town? I think Possible responses: that the town should accept all people. It makes no difference that the boy is a Mexican American. He is a good boy. We should not judge people based on their backgrounds.

Thank you for reading.

Editor

Assessment

Fill in the circle next to each correct answer.

1. Why do the Chicanos from the Rio Grande Valley head north to Tobie's town in the fall?
   - ○ A. to sell food from the valley
   - ● B. to work in the cotton fields
   - ○ C. to sell their cotton
   - ○ D. to work in movie houses

2. Which sentence from the story **best** helps you predict that Mr. Brewer will not give Joey a haircut?
   - ● A. "Say, Tom, looks like you got yourself a little tamale to clip."
   - ○ B. I was convinced that I belonged in the Gringo barbershop.
   - ○ C. I thought about this new adventure for several days.
   - ○ D. "Really, kid-brother, that hair looks awful."

3. What happens when Tobie gives up his newspaper route?
   - ● A. Tobie recommends Joey for the job.
   - ○ B. His dad becomes angry that he quit a good job.
   - ○ C. Tobie gives the route to Red.
   - ○ D. Mr. Brewer does not allow Tobie in the barbershop anymore.

4. Which of the following sentences shows that the story is written from a first-person point of view?
   - ○ A. Yes, Tobie had it good.
   - ● B. I felt a lump in my throat.
   - ○ C. The barber would cut Tobie's hair.
   - ○ D. "You're too young to handle money."

5. Which of the following words means "having an unfair opinion"?
   - ○ A. incident
   - ○ B. meaningless
   - ● C. prejudiced
   - ○ D. rejected

Wrap-up

Compare and Contrast

Point of view is an important literary element in "Chanclas" and "Everybody Knows Tobie." Both selections are told from the first-person point of view. The main character in each story is the narrator. Because the narrators are telling the stories, we see events through their eyes.

In the Venn diagram below, describe how "Chanclas" and "Everybody Knows Tobie" are similar and different in the ways they are told. Write about the different ways the stories are told in the outer parts of the circles. Write about how the stories are told in similar ways in the overlapping part. Examples have been provided.

"Chanclas"

- The story does not include actual conversations.

- The story only focuses on the narrator's thoughts.

- The only change that takes place occurs completely in the narrator's mind.

Alike

- Both main characters describe how they feel about a personal experience.

- Both main characters use the pronouns *I*, *me*, and *my*.

- Both main characters go through a change in the way they are feeling.

"Everybody Knows Tobie"

- The narrator has conversations with other characters.

- The story also focuses on other characters.

- A change takes place in the character's mind, but also in his situation.

59

UNIT 2 Short Story

How is a Short Story Organized?

Now that you have read a few short stories, let's stop for a moment to take a closer look at how a short story is put together.

A **short story** always has a **beginning, middle,** and **end.**

Most stories also include a **conflict.** A conflict is a struggle between characters or a struggle between a character and nature or another outside force. A conflict can also be a struggle inside a character's mind.

What's the Plan?

Within the three parts of a story, there are five stages:

Exposition: The story is set up. Characters and places are introduced.
Rising Action: Conflicts or problems occur in the story.
Climax: The turning point in the story. This is the point of greatest interest or suspense.
Falling Action: The events following the climax.
Resolution: The final outcome.

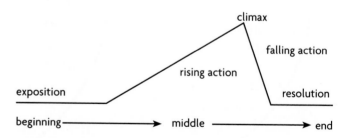

As you read the next four stories, try to find the five stages in each story. In the text, mark the places where each stage occurs.

Understanding the parts of a story can help you become a better reader.

How Do I Read Short Stories?

Focus on key **literary elements** and **reading skills** to get the most out of reading the four short stories in this unit. Here are two key literary elements and two key reading skills that you will practice in this unit.

Key Literary Elements

• Conflict

Conflict is a struggle between two opposing forces. There are two basic kinds of conflict. An external conflict is a struggle between a character and an outside force, such as another person, nature, or society. An internal conflict is a struggle in a character's mind. A character might be torn between opposing feelings, such as greed versus generosity.

• Theme

A **theme** of a story is its central message. To find the theme you might ask, "What message is the author trying to tell the readers?" Sometimes a theme is stated directly by the narrator or by a character. Sometimes, however, the reader must figure it out by looking carefully at the characters and the plot.

Key Reading Skills

• Question

Question yourself as you read. Ask yourself *who, what, where, when, why,* and *how* questions to make sure you understand what you are reading. Also ask yourself: Do I understand what is happening? Does this make sense based on what I have already read? What does this paragraph mean?

• Identifying Assumptions

Assumptions are beliefs that are based on experiences or opinions. An assumption may or may not be true. A character may believe that he or she is not smart. This may be a false assumption and in truth the character is very smart. Yet the character's behavior may be shaped by this assumption. Identifying the assumptions that characters make can help you understand why they act the way they do.

Get Ready to Read!

Raymond's Run

Meet Toni Cade Bambara

Toni Cade Bambara (kād´ bäm bä´ rä) was born in 1939. She wanted to make a difference in the lives of women and African Americans. She said by sharing through writing, she "might save somebody else some time, might lift someone's spirits, or might enable someone to see more clearly." Bambara wrote short stories, a novel, and several films. She was also a professor and a supporter of civil rights. She died in 1995. "Raymond's Run" was first published in 1972.

What You Know

How do you feel when people notice you or reward you for being good at something? Do you know someone who is really good at something? How do you treat him or her? Discuss your answers with a partner.

Reason to Read

Read to discover how one young person changes her view about life while doing what she loves best: running.

Background Info

In "Raymond's Run," the narrator is an expert at the fifty-yard dash. The fifty-yard dash is a sprint, or short running race. Right before the start of the race, the runners stoop at the starting line. As soon as the race begins, they run toward the finish line at top speed. Sprinters run with their knees high and arms swinging. They also lean forward. For longer races, runners must control their speed so that they do not tire too easily. They take shorter strides than sprinters, use less arm movement, and do not lean as far forward. Athletes usually train for races by performing a combination of exercises and keeping up good eating habits on a regular basis.

Word Power

fantasy (fan′ tə sē) *n.* expression of the imaginary; ideas about things that are not real; p. 65
My little sister has a *fantasy* in which she lives in a big castle.

liable (lī′ ə bəl) *adj.* likely; p. 65
If you walk on a steep roof, you are *liable* to fall.

psyching (sī′ king) *v.* making someone fearful or uneasy; p. 69
Before throwing a ball, the pitcher tries *psyching* the batter by glaring at him.

crouch (krouch) *v.* to stoop low with bent knees; p. 69
To see into the rabbit hole, you will have to *crouch.*

tradition (trə dish′ ən) *n.* a custom; a long-accepted practice; p. 72
It is a *tradition* that we sing songs before we open our birthday presents.

**Answer the following questions that contain the new words above.
Write your answers in the spaces provided.**

1. If you had to *crouch* to get through the passage, would the passage
   be high or low? _____ low _____

2. Would a *tradition* be something that has been handed down or something
   that is new? _____ something that has been handed down _____

3. Would a *fantasy* be realistic or fanciful? _____ fanciful _____

4. If you were *psyching* someone before playing basketball, would you be trying
   to make her calm or nervous? _____ nervous _____

5. If you were *liable* to win a baking contest, would you be a good baker
   or a bad one? _____ a good baker _____

Adapted from
Raymond's Run

Toni Cade Bambara

La Miranda 2, 1995. Robin Holder. Monotype with stencils and photo silkscreen, 18 x 14 in. Courtesy of the artist.

Background Info

Raymond's "big head" is probably the result of *hydrocephaly* (hī´ drə sef´ ə lē), a condition in which fluid is trapped around the brain. It damages the brain and enlarges the skull.

I don't have much work to do around the house like some girls. My mother does that. And anything else that's got to get done, my father does. All I have to do in life is mind my brother Raymond, which is enough.

Sometimes I slip and say my little brother Raymond. But as any fool can see he's much bigger and he's older too. But a lot of people call him my little brother cause he needs looking after cause he's not quite right. If anybody has anything to say to Raymond, anything to say about his big head, they have to come by me. And I don't believe in standing around with somebody in my face doing a lot of talking. I much rather just knock you down and take my chances even if I am a little girl with skinny arms and a squeaky voice, which is how I got the name Squeaky. And if things get too rough, I run. And as anybody can tell you, I'm the fastest thing on two feet.

There is no track meet that I don't win the first place medal. I used to win the twenty-yard dash when I was a little kid in kindergarten. Nowadays, it's the fifty-yard dash. And tomorrow I'm subject to run the quarter-meter relay all by myself and come in first, second, and third. I'm the swiftest thing in the neighborhood. Everybody knows that—except two people who know better, my father and me. He can beat me to Amsterdam Avenue with me having a two fire-hydrant head-start and him running with his hands in his pockets and whistling. But that's private information. So as far as everyone's concerned, I'm the fastest and that goes for Gretchen, too, who has put out the tale that she is going to win the first-place medal this year. Ridiculous.

I'm about to take a stroll down Broadway so I can practice my breathing exercises, and I've got Raymond walking on the inside close to the buildings, cause he's subject to fits of **fantasy** and starts thinking he's a circus performer and that the curb is a tightrope strung high in the air. So I keep Raymond on the inside of me, and he plays like he's driving a stage coach.

Now some people like to act like things come easy to them, won't let on that they practice. Not me. I'll high-prance down 34th Street like a rodeo pony to keep my knees strong even if it does get my mother uptight so that she walks ahead like she's not with me and I am somebody else's crazy child. I never walk if I can trot, and shame on Raymond if he can't keep up. But of course he does, cause if he hangs back someone's **liable** to walk up to him and get smart, or take his allowance from him, or ask him where he got that great big pumpkin head.

Literary Element

Conflict Reread the text highlighted in blue. One of Squeaky's conflicts is with another person. Whom is her conflict with and why?

Possible response: Her
conflict is with Gretchen.
Gretchen says she is
going to win the race, but
Squeaky doesn't agree.

English Coach

Squeaky describes how she walks down the street making her knees come up high. High-prance is what she calls it. Underline another word on the page that describes how she goes down the street.

Word Power

fantasy (fan´ tə sē) *n.* expression of the imaginary; ideas about things that are not real

liable (lī´ ə bəl) *adj.* likely

65

English Coach

Here, the word *salty* means "critical or sarcastic." Sometimes words that relate to the five senses (touch, taste, sight, smell, hearing) are used to describe people. For example, the word "bright" can be used to describe a person who is smart. What other words related to the five senses can you think of that can be used to describe people? Write at least two words below.

Possible responses: sweet,

rough, tender

Did You Know?

A *ventriloquist* is an entertainer who talks with a puppet by speaking both parts of the conversation.
. . . .

So I'm strolling down Broadway breathing out and breathing in on counts of seven, which is my lucky number, and here comes Gretchen and her sidekicks: Mary Louise, who talks about me like a dog; and Rosie, who is as fat as I am skinny and is too stupid to know that there is not a big deal of difference between herself and Raymond. So they are steady coming up Broadway and they're close to the buildings just as we are. As they get to me, they slow down. I'm ready to fight.

"You signing up for the May Day races?" smiles Mary Louise, only it's not a smile at all. A dumb question like that doesn't deserve an answer. Besides, there's just me and Gretchen standing there really, so no use wasting my breath talking to shadows.

"I don't think you're going to win this time," says Rosie, trying to signify with her hands on her hips all salty, completely forgetting that I have beat her behind many times for less salt than that.

"I always win cause I'm the best," I say straight at Gretchen who is, as far as I'm concerned, the only one talking in this ventriloquist-dummy routine. Then they all look at Raymond who has just brought his mule team to a standstill.

"What grade you in now, Raymond?"

"You got anything to say to my brother, you say it to me, Mary Louise Williams of Raggedy Town, Baltimore."

"What are you, his mother?" sasses Rosie.

"That's right, Fatso. And the next word out of anybody and I'll be their mother too." Then Gretchen walks around me looking me up and down but keeps walking up Broadway, and her sidekicks follow her. So me and Raymond smile at each other and he says, "Gidyap" to his team and I continue with my breathing exercises, strolling down Broadway toward the ice man on 145th.

I take my time getting to the park on May Day because the track meet is the last thing on the program. The biggest thing on the program is the May Pole dancing, which I can do without, even if my mother thinks it's a shame I don't take part and act like a girl for a change. You'd think she'd be glad her daughter ain't out there prancing around a May Pole getting the new clothes all dirty and sweaty and trying to act like a fairy or a flower or whatever you're supposed to be when you should be trying to be yourself, which is, as far as I am concerned, a poor Black girl who really can't afford to buy shoes and a new dress you only wear once a lifetime cause it won't fit next year.

I run. That is what I am all about. So I always come late to the May Day program, just in time to get my number pinned on and lay in the grass till they announce the fifty-yard dash.

I put Raymond in the little swings, which is a tight squeeze this year and will be impossible next year. Then I look around for Mr. Pearson, who pins the numbers on. I'm really looking for Gretchen if you want to know the truth, but she's not around. The park is jam-packed. Then here comes Mr. Pearson with his clipboard and his cards and pencils and whistles and safety pins and fifty million other things he's always dropping all over the place with his tall, clumsy self. We used to call him Jack and the Beanstalk to get him mad.

Literary Element

Conflict Reread the highlighted sentences. What is the cause of the conflict between Squeaky and Mr. Pearson?

Possible response: Mr.

Pearson suggests that

Squeaky let someone else

win the race. Squeaky gets

mad because she wants to

win the race.

"Well, Squeaky," he says, checking my name off the list and handing me number seven and two pins. And I'm thinking he's got no right to call me Squeaky, if I can't call him Beanstalk.

"Hazel Elizabeth Deborah Parker," I correct him and tell him to write it down on his board.

"Well, Hazel Elizabeth Deborah Parker, going to give someone else a break this year?" I squint at him real hard to see if he is seriously thinking I should lose the race on purpose just to give someone else a break. "Only six girls running this time," he continues, shaking his head sadly like it's my fault all of New York didn't turn out in sneakers. "That new girl should give you a run for your money. Wouldn't it be a nice gesture if you were . . . to ahhh . . . "

I give him such a look he couldn't finish putting that idea into words. I pin number seven to myself and stomp away, I'm so mad. And I go straight for the track and stretch out on the grass. I'm on my back looking at the sky, trying to pretend I'm in the country, but I can't, because even grass in the city feels hard as sidewalk, and there's just no pretending you are anywhere but in a "concrete jungle" as my grandfather says.

The twenty-yard dash takes all of two minutes cause most of the little kids don't know no better than to run off the track or run the wrong way or run smack into the fence and fall down and cry. Then the second-graders line up for the thirty-yard dash and I don't even bother to turn my head to watch cause Raphael Perez always wins.

He wins before he even begins by **psyching** the runners, telling them they're going to trip on their shoelaces and fall on their faces or lose their shorts or something, which he doesn't really have to do since he is very fast, almost as fast as I am. After that is the forty-yard dash which I used to run when I was in first grade. Raymond is hollering from the swings cause he knows I'm about to do my thing cause the man on the loudspeaker has just announced the fifty-yard dash, although he might just as well be giving a recipe for angel food cake cause you can hardly make out what he's sayin for the static. I get up and slip off my sweat pants and then I see Gretchen standing at the starting line, kicking her legs out like a pro. Then as I get into place I see that ole Raymond is on line on the other side of the fence, bending down with his fingers on the ground just like he knew what he was doing.

Every time, just before I take off in a race, I always feel like I'm in a dream, the kind of dream you have when you're sick with fever and feel all hot and weightless. I dream I'm flying over a sandy beach in the early morning sun, kissing the leaves of the trees as I fly by. And there's always the smell of apples, just like in the country when I was little and used to think I was a choo-choo train, running through the fields of corn and chugging up the hill to the orchard. And all the time I'm dreaming this, I get lighter and lighter until I'm flying over the beach again, getting blown through the sky like a feather that weighs nothing at all. But once I spread my fingers in the dirt and **crouch** over the Get on Your Mark, the dream goes and I am solid again and am telling myself, Squeaky you must win, you are the fastest thing in the world, you can even beat your father up Amsterdam if you really try.

Word Power
psyching (sī´ king) v. making someone fearful or uneasy
crouch (krouch) v. to stoop low with bent knees

Connect to the Text

Reread the boxed sentence. Have you ever been psyched out by someone? How did it feel?

Answers will vary.

Reading Skill
Identifying Assumptions Reread the highlighted sentence. What assumption does Squeaky make that helps her get ready for the race?

Possible response: Squeaky assumes that she is the fastest runner in the world and can even outrun her father.

Reading Skill

Question Reread the highlighted sentences. Which is the **best** question to ask yourself to get the most important information from this passage? Check the correct response.

☐ Where is Raymond during the race?

☐ How does Gretchen affect the way Squeaky runs?

☑ What does Squeaky experience as she runs?

And then I feel my weight coming back just behind my knees then down to my feet then into the earth and the pistol shot explodes in my blood and I am off and weightless again, flying past the other runners, my arms pumping up and down and the whole world is quiet except for the crunch as I zoom over the gravel in the track. I glance to my left and there is no one. To the right, a blurred Gretchen, who's got her chin jutting out as if it would win the race all by itself. And on the other side of the fence is Raymond with his arms down to his side and the palms tucked up behind him, running in his very own style, and it's the first time I ever saw that and I almost stop to watch my brother Raymond on his first run. But the white ribbon is bouncing toward me and I tear past it, racing into the distance till my feet with a mind of their own start digging up footfuls of dirt and brake me short. Then all the kids standing on the side pile on me, banging me on the back and slapping my head with their May Day programs, for I have won again.

Which runner reminds you of Squeaky? Why?
_____

"In the first place . . ." the man on the loudspeaker is clear as a bell now. But then he pauses and the loudspeaker starts to whine. And I lean down to catch my breath and here comes Gretchen walking back, for she's overshot the finish line too, huffing and puffing with her hands on her hips taking it slow, breathing in steady time like a real pro and I sort of like her a little for the first time. "In first place . . ." and then three or four voices get all mixed up on the loudspeaker and I dig my sneaker into the grass and stare at Gretchen who's staring back, we both wondering just who did win. Then I hear Raymond yanking at the fence to call me and I wave to shush him, but he keeps rattling the fence like a gorilla in a cage, but then like a dancer or something he starts climbing up nice and easy but very fast. And it occurs to me, watching how smoothly he climbs hand over hand and remembering how he looked running with his arms down to his side and with the wind pulling his mouth back and his teeth showing and all that Raymond would make a very fine runner. Doesn't he always keep up with me on my trots? And he surely knows how to breathe in counts of seven cause he's always doing it at the dinner table. And I'm smiling cause if I've lost this race, or tied, or even if I've won, I can always retire as a runner and begin a whole new career as a coach with Raymond as my champion. I've got a roomful of ribbons and medals and awards. But what has Raymond got to call his own?

Literary Element

Conflict Reread the sentence highlighted in blue. Is the conflict between Squeaky and Gretchen increasing or beginning to go away? How does Squeaky feel about Gretchen now?

Possible response: Their conflict is beginning to go away. Squeaky is starting to like Gretchen.

Reading Skill

Identifying Assumptions Reread the sentences highlighted in green. Squeaky has a new way of seeing her brother. What does she assume about his abilities as a runner?

Possible response: When she realizes that Raymond is a good runner, she assumes that he would be able to win races.

So I stand there with my new plans, laughing out loud by this time as Raymond jumps down from the fence and runs over with his teeth showing and his arms down to the side, which no one before him has quite mastered as a running style. And by the time he comes over I'm jumping up and down so glad to see him—my brother Raymond, a great runner in the family **tradition.** But of course everyone thinks I'm jumping up and down because the men on the loudspeaker are announcing "In first place—Miss Hazel Elizabeth Deborah Parker. In second place—Miss Gretchen P. Lewis." And I look over at Gretchen and I smile. And she nods to congratulate me and then she smiles. We stand there with this big smile of respect between us. It's about as real a smile as girls can do for each other, considering we don't practice real smiling every day, you know, cause maybe we too busy being flowers or fairies or strawberries instead of something honest and worthy of respect . . . you know . . . like being people.

Comprehension Check

Reread the boxed text. What do Squeaky and Gretchen do after the winners of the race are announced?

They smile sincerely at each

other.

What sports do you enjoy playing or watching?

Word Power

tradition (trə dish´ ən) *n.* a custom; a long-accepted practice

Respond to Literature

Raymond's Run

A Comprehension Check

Answer the following questions in the spaces provided.

1. What does Mr. Pearson ask Squeaky to do? He asks her to let someone else win the race.

2. What does Raymond do during the race? He starts to run along with Squeaky in his own style.

B Reading Skills

Answer the following questions in the spaces provided.

1. **Question** What is a good question to ask about the relationship between Squeaky and her brother after the race? Possible response: Will Squeaky give up running and help coach her brother?

2. **Identifying Assumptions** What assumptions does Squeaky make about Gretchen at the beginning of the story? How do her assumptions change at the end of the story? Possible response: Squeaky thinks Gretchen is just a braggart. Then she sees that Gretchen is a serious runner and gains respect for her by the end of the story.

3. **Identifying Assumptions** At the beginning of the story, Squeaky assumes that Raymond has no interest in running and could not keep up with her. How does that assumption change at the end of the story?

Possible response: She thinks that Raymond is a good runner and can win races.

C Word Power

Complete each sentence below, using one of the words in the box.

fantasy   liable   psyching
crouch   tradition

1. If you walk down the street with your purse open, someone is
   _____liable_____ to steal your wallet.

2. The door to the playhouse is so small that I have to ____crouch____
   to get in.

3. It is my ____fantasy____ to win the Indianapolis 500 race.

4. Did you see how the boxer was ____psyching____ his opponent?

5. A Thanksgiving ____tradition____ that has been handed down in
   my family is baking pumpkin pies.

Circle the word that best completes each sentence.

6. If you don't study, you are (**liable**, **psyching**) to get a bad grade on
   the test.

7. Keiko's (**tradition**, **fantasy**) is to be able to fly by flapping her arms.

8. Holding a class picnic at the end of the year is a (**liable**, **tradition**) at
   my school.

9. The champion was (**psyching**, **crouch**) her rival by staring at him without
   blinking.

10. The tall doctor had to (**fantasy**, **crouch**) to look at the child's face.

D Literary Element: Conflict

Read the passages below from "Raymond's Run." As you read, think about what the sentences reveal about Squeaky's conflict. Then answer the questions that follow.

So as far as everyone's concerned, I'm the fastest and that goes for Gretchen, too, who has put out the tale that she is going to win the first-place medal this year.[1] Ridiculous.[2]

And I look over at Gretchen and I smile.[3] And she nods to congratulate me and then she smiles.[4] We stand there with this big smile of respect between us.[5] It's about as real a smile as girls can do for each other, considering we don't practice real smiling every day. . .[6]

1. In sentences 1–2, what is the conflict that Squeaky has with Gretchen?

   Possible response: Squeaky is challenged by Gretchen, who says that she

   will win the race.

2. How do sentences 3–6 show that Squeaky no longer has a conflict with Gretchen?

   Possible response: Now Squeaky and Gretchen like and respect each other.

   They smile sincerely at each other.

E Victory Speech

Imagine that you are Squeaky and you have just won the fifty-yard dash. You are expected to make a victory speech. The speech should include descriptions of the race, details about how you train, and a message to your rival. The speech should also include what you plan to do in the future.

Thank you. I am so excited about winning the fifty-yard dash, even though I knew I was going to win.

A good runner always has to train. Even though I am better than just good, I train for the race by Possible responses: practicing breathing exercises; high-prancing.

As I run, I Possible responses: fly past the other runners; zoom over the track.

I would like to tell Gretchen that Possible response: I respect her; I think she's a good runner, too.

My plans for the future include Possible responses: winning more races; coaching my brother.

And don't forget to watch for Raymond, who will be a future star, because Possible response: he will be a great runner and has his own style; I will train him.

Enjoy the rest of your day and the flowers, fairies, and strawberries.

Assessment

Fill in the circle next to each correct answer.

1. What does Squeaky assume when she hears about Gretchen's bragging?
   - ○ A. Squeaky assumes that Gretchen is better than she is.
   - ○ B. Squeaky assumes that Gretchen is afraid of her.
   - ● C. Squeaky assumes that she is better than Gretchen.
   - ○ D. Squeaky assumes that Gretchen wants to be friends.

2. What does Raymond do while Squeaky runs the race?
   - ● A. He runs along with her in his own way.
   - ○ B. He follows Raphael Perez around the track.
   - ○ C. He waits for Squeaky outside of the park.
   - ○ D. He gets into a fight with Gretchen and her sidekicks.

3. Which is the **best** question to ask to determine what Squeaky's interests are?
   - ○ A. Where does Squeaky live?
   - ○ B. What does Squeaky's mother do?
   - ○ C. How does Squeaky get to the race?
   - ● D. How does Squeaky spend her time?

4. Which of the following describes a conflict in this story?
   - ○ A. Squeaky admits she has to practice to be a good runner.
   - ● B. Squeaky gets mad because Mr. Pearson wants her to let someone else win.
   - ○ C. Squeaky has a secret: her father is a better runner.
   - ○ D. Squeaky doesn't watch Raphael Perez run because he always wins.

5. Which of the following words means "likely"?
   - ○ A. fantasy
   - ○ B. crouch
   - ● C. liable
   - ○ D. tradition

Get Ready to Read!

Mother and Daughter

Meet Gary Soto

Gary Soto was born in 1952. He grew up in a Mexican American neighborhood in California. His father died in a factory accident when Gary was only five. As a child, Soto didn't dream of being a writer, but his life changed in college when he came across a book of poetry. "I discovered this poetry and thought, 'This is terrific: I'd like to do something like this.'" Soto has written more than thirty books. "Mother and Daughter" was first published in 1990.

What You Know

Think of a time when you couldn't get something you needed or wanted. Write a journal entry about how you reacted to this disappointment.

Reason to Read

As you read, think about the relationship between the mother and daughter and how they deal with hardship.

Background Info

In the past, a traditional family was commonly defined as including a mother, a father, and children. Today, however, the definition of family has widened. Many children are cared for by one parent, by other relatives, or by people to whom they are not related. The single-parent family is the fastest-growing type of family in the United States. Like the family in "Mother and Daughter," most single-parent families are headed by women. The most important thing about a family is not how it is made up, but how members of the family care for each other. It is possible for any type of family to be happy and healthy.

Word Power

grogginess (grog′ ē nis) *n.* a state of being sleepy or not fully alert; p. 81
The boy's *grogginess* made him stumble against the table.

gloated (glōt′ id) *v.* felt or expressed a greedy pleasure or satisfaction in one's own success or achievement, especially in a slightly nasty way; p. 81
When Lupe won the game, she *gloated* over her rival's loss.

meager (mē′ gər) *adj.* not enough in amount or quality; p. 83
I won't mow your lawn anymore because you paid me such a *meager* amount.

taunt (tônt) *v.* to make fun of in an insulting way; p. 83
Mike likes to *taunt* his younger brother when he tries to play the piano.

sophisticated (sə fis′ tə kā′ tid) *adj.* having or showing knowledge or experience of the world; p. 83
When Monica wore her pink silk prom dress, she looked very *sophisticated*.

tirade (tī′ rād) *n.* a long, angry or scolding speech; p. 86
When several players were late to practice, the coach went on a *tirade* about responsibility and discipline.

lurched (lurchd) *v.* moved suddenly in a jerky and uneven way; p. 88
I *lurched* across the counter to grab the dog before it knocked over the milk carton.

**Answer the following questions that contain the new words above.
Write your answers in the spaces provided.**

1. What kind of people would show *grogginess*, tired people or people who are wide awake? _____ tired people _____

2. If Maria *lurched* onto the stage when her name was called, was she graceful or awkward? _____ awkward _____

3. Who would go on a *tirade*, a calm person or an angry person? _____ an angry person _____

4. Would a *meager* diet have too much or not enough food? _____ not enough food _____

5. Would a child have *gloated* about her report card by showing everyone her grades or by hiding them? _____ by showing everyone her grades _____

6. Who would be more *sophisticated*, a world traveler or a baby? _____ a world traveler _____

7. If your classmates *taunt* you, would you be happy or upset? _____ upset _____

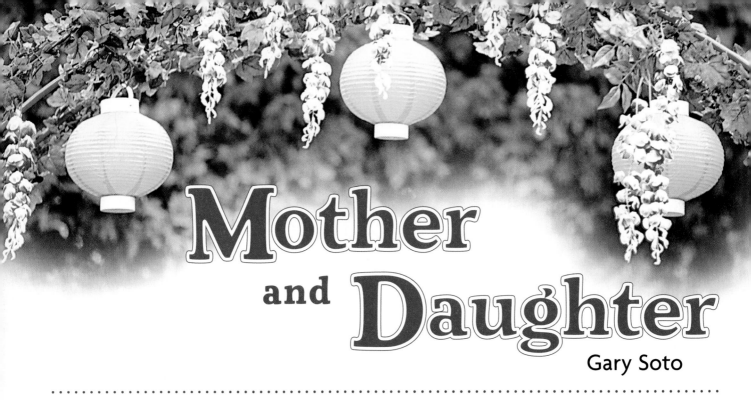

Mother and Daughter

Gary Soto

Yollie's mother, Mrs. Moreno, was a large woman who wore a muumuu and butterfly-shaped glasses. She liked to water her lawn in the evening and wave at low-riders, who would stare at her behind their smoky sunglasses and laugh. Now and then a low-rider from Belmont Avenue would make his car jump and shout "Mamacita!" But most of the time they just stared and wondered how she got so large.

Mrs. Moreno had a strange sense of humor. Once, Yollie and her mother were watching a late-night movie called "They Came to Look." It was about creatures from the underworld who had climbed through molten lava to walk the earth. But Yollie, who had played soccer all day with the kids next door, was too tired to be scared. Her eyes closed but sprang open when her mother screamed, "Look, Yollie! Oh, you missed a scary part. The guy's face was all ugly!"

But Yollie couldn't keep her eyes open. They fell shut again and stayed shut, even when her mother screamed and slammed a heavy palm on the arm of her chair.

"Mom, wake me up when the movie's over so I can go to bed," mumbled Yollie.

"OK, Yollie, I wake you," said her mother through a mouthful of popcorn.

But after the movie ended, instead of waking her daughter, Mrs. Moreno laughed under her breath, turned the TV and lights off, and tiptoed to bed. Yollie woke up in the middle of the night and didn't know where she was. For a moment she thought she was dead. Maybe something from the underworld had lifted her from her house and carried her into the earth's belly. She blinked her sleepy eyes, looked around at the darkness, and called, "Mom? Mom, where are you?" But there was no answer, just the throbbing hum of the refrigerator.

Finally, Yollie's **grogginess** cleared and she realized her mother had gone to bed, leaving her on the couch. Another of her little jokes.

But Yollie wasn't laughing. She tiptoed into her mother's bedroom with a glass of water and set it on the nightstand next to the alarm clock. The next morning, Yollie woke to screams. When her mother reached to turn off the alarm, she had overturned the glass of water.

Yollie burned her mother's morning toast and **gloated.** "Ha! Ha! I got you back. Why did you leave me on the couch when I told you to wake me up?"

Despite their jokes, mother and daughter usually got along. They watched bargain matinees together, and played croquet in the summer and checkers in the winter. Mrs. Moreno encouraged Yollie to study hard because she wanted her daughter to be a doctor. She bought Yollie a desk, a typewriter, and a lamp that cut glare so her eyes would not grow tired from hours of studying.

Yollie was slender as a tulip, pretty, and one of the smartest kids at Saint Theresa's. She was captain of crossing guards, an altar girl, and a whiz in the school's monthly spelling bees.

Word Power

grogginess (grog´ ē nis) *n.* a state of being sleepy or not fully alert
gloated (glōt´ id) *v.* felt or expressed a greedy pleasure or satisfaction in one's own success or achievement, especially in a slightly nasty way

English Coach

TV is an abbreviation for the word *television*. Abbreviations are the shortening of a word or a group of words. Think of two more abbreviations and write them below.

Possible responses: CD, DVD, ER

Literary Element

Conflict Reread the highlighted sentences. What causes the conflict between Mrs. Moreno and Yollie?

Possible response: Mrs. Moreno plays a trick on Yollie that makes Yollie mad.

81

Portrait, 1972. Eloy Blanco. Collection of El Museo del Barrio, New York.

What do you see in this young woman's face that reminds you of Yollie?

Reading Skill

Identifying Assumptions Reread the sentences highlighted in green. What does Mrs. Moreno assume will happen if Yollie does well in school?

Possible response: She assumes that Yollie will get a good job and be able to take care of her.

English Coach

Here, the word *riot* means "wildly funny." Write another meaning of the word *riot* below.

Possible response: A disturbance that is caused by a group of people that gets out of control

"*Tienes que estudiar mucho,*" Mrs. Moreno said every time she propped her work-weary feet on the hassock. "You have to study a lot, then you can get a good job and take care of me."

"Yes, Mama," Yollie would respond, her face buried in a book. If she gave her mother any sympathy, she would begin her stories about how she had come with her family from Mexico with nothing on her back but a sack with three skirts, all of which were too large by the time she crossed the border because she had lost weight from not having enough to eat.

Everyone thought Yollie's mother was a riot. Even the nuns laughed at her antics. Her brother Raul, a nightclub owner, thought she was funny enough to go into show business.

But there was nothing funny about Yollie needing a new outfit for the eighth-grade fall dance. They couldn't afford one. It was late October, with Christmas around the corner, and their dented Chevy Nova had gobbled up almost one hundred dollars in repairs.

"We don't have the money," said her mother, genuinely sad because they couldn't buy the outfit, even though there was a little money stashed away for college. Mrs. Moreno remembered her teenage years and her hardworking parents, who picked grapes and oranges, and chopped beets and cotton for **meager** pay around Kerman. Those were the days when "new clothes" meant limp and out-of-style dresses from Saint Vincent de Paul.

The best Mrs. Moreno could do was buy Yollie a pair of black shoes with velvet bows and fabric dye to color her white summer dress black.

"We can color your dress so it will look brand-new," her mother said brightly, shaking the bottle of dye as she ran hot water into a plastic dish tub. She poured the black liquid into the tub and stirred it with a pencil. Then, slowly and carefully, she lowered the dress into the tub.

Yollie couldn't stand to watch. She *knew* it wouldn't work. It would be like the time her mother stirred up a batch of molasses for candy apples on Yollie's birthday. She'd dipped the apples into the goo and swirled them and seemed to **taunt** Yollie by singing *"Las Mañanitas"* to her. When she was through, she set the apples on wax paper. They were hard as rocks and hurt the kids' teeth. Finally they had a contest to see who could break the apples open by throwing them against the side of the house. The apples shattered like grenades, sending the kids scurrying for cover, and in an odd way the birthday party turned out to be a success. At least everyone went home happy.

To Yollie's surprise, the dress came out shiny black. It looked brand-new and **sophisticated,** like what people in New York wear. She beamed at her mother, who hugged Yollie and said, "See, what did I tell you?"

Word Power

meager (mē´ gər) *adj.* not enough in amount or quality

taunt (tônt) *v.* to make fun of in an insulting way

sophisticated (sə fis´ tə kā´ tid) *adj.* having or showing knowledge or experience of the world

Reading Skill

Question Reread the highlighted paragraph. Which is the **best** question to ask to understand what Mrs. Moreno's childhood was like? Check the correct response.

- ☐ Why can't Mrs. Moreno buy a dress for Yollie?
- ☑ What kind of "new clothes" did Mrs. Moreno receive?
- ☐ Who founded Saint Vincent de Paul?

Connect to the Text

Reread the boxed text. Think of a time when something turned out differently from what you expected. How did you react?

Answers will vary.

_____

_____

_____

_____

83

Reading Skill
Identifying Assumptions Reread the highlighted paragraph. What assumptions do Yollie and Janice make about each other?

Possible response: Each thinks the other is the most beautiful and assumes that lots of boys will ask them to dance.

Connect to the Text

Reread the boxed sentences. Think about a time when you liked someone. How did you act around him or her?

Answers will vary.

The dance was important to Yollie because she was in love with Ernie Castillo, the third-best speller in the class. She bathed, dressed, did her hair and nails, and primped until her mother yelled, "All right already." Yollie sprayed her neck and wrists with Mrs. Moreno's Avon perfume and bounced into the car.

Mrs. Moreno let Yollie out in front of the school. She waved and told her to have a good time but behave herself, then roared off, blue smoke trailing from the tail pipe of the old Nova.

Yollie ran into her best friend, Janice. They didn't say it, but each thought the other was the most beautiful girl at the dance; the boys would fall over themselves asking them to dance.

The evening was warm but thick with clouds. Gusts of wind picked up the paper lanterns hanging in the trees and swung them, blurring the night with reds and yellows. The lanterns made the evening seem romantic, like a scene from a movie. Everyone danced, sipped punch, and stood in knots of threes and fours, talking. Sister Kelly got up and jitterbugged with some kid's father. When the record ended, students broke into applause.

Janice had her eye on Frankie Ledesma, and Yollie, who kept smoothing her dress down when the wind picked up, had her eye on Ernie. It turned out that Ernie had his mind on Yollie, too. He ate a handful of cookies nervously, then asked her for a dance.

"Sure," she said, nearly throwing herself into his arms.

They danced two fast ones before they got a slow one. As they circled under the lanterns, rain began falling, lightly at first. Yollie loved the sound of the raindrops ticking against the leaves. She leaned her head on Ernie's shoulder, though his sweater was scratchy. He felt warm and tender. Yollie could tell that he was in love, and with her, of course. The dance continued successfully, romantically, until it began to pour.

"Everyone, let's go inside—and, boys, carry in the table and the record player," Sister Kelly commanded.

The girls and boys raced into the cafeteria. Inside, the girls, drenched to the bone, hurried to the restrooms to brush their hair and dry themselves. One girl cried because her velvet dress was ruined. Yollie felt sorry for her and helped her dry the dress off with paper towels, but it was no use. The dress was ruined.

Yollie went to a mirror. She looked a little gray now that her mother's makeup had washed away but not as bad as some of the other girls. She combed her damp hair, careful not to pull too hard. She couldn't wait to get back to Ernie.

Yollie bent over to pick up a bobby pin, and shame spread across her face. A black puddle was forming at her feet. Drip, black drip. Drip, black drip. The dye was falling from her dress like black tears. Yollie stood up. Her dress was now the color of ash. She looked around the room. The other girls, unaware of Yollie's problem, were busy grooming themselves. What could she do? Everyone would laugh. They would know she dyed an old dress because she couldn't afford a new one. She hurried from the restroom with her head down, across the cafeteria floor and out the door. She raced through the storm, crying as the rain mixed with her tears and ran into twig-choked gutters.

When she arrived home, her mother was on the couch eating cookies and watching TV.

"How was the dance, m'ija? Come watch the show with me. It's really good."

Yollie stomped, head down, to her bedroom. She undressed and threw the dress on the floor.

Literary Element

Conflict Reread the highlighted sentences. In this passage, is Yollie struggling with an internal or external conflict? What is the conflict?

Possible responses: Internal.

She is embarrassed. She

thinks people will laugh at

her because she can't afford

a new dress.

Background Info

M'ija (mē´ hä) is a shortened form of mi hija (mē ē´ hä), which is Spanish for "my daughter."

Her mother came into the room. "What's going on? What's all the racket, baby?"

"The dress. It's cheap! It's no good!" Yollie kicked the dress at her mother and watched it land in her hands. Mrs. Moreno studied it closely but couldn't see what was wrong. "What's the matter? It's just a bit wet."

"The dye came out, that's what."

Mrs. Moreno looked at her hands and saw the grayish dye puddling in the shallow lines of her palms. Poor baby, she thought, her brow darkening as she made a sad face. She wanted to tell her daughter how sorry she was, but she knew it wouldn't help. She walked back to the living room and cried.

The next morning, mother and daughter stayed away from each other. Yollie sat in her room turning the pages of an old *Seventeen*, while her mother watered her plants with a Pepsi bottle.

"Drink, my children," she said loud enough for Yollie to hear. She let the water slurp into pots of coleus and cacti. "Water is all you need. My daughter needs clothes, but I don't have no money."

Yollie tossed her *Seventeen* on her bed. She was embarrassed at last night's **tirade.** It wasn't her mother's fault that they were poor.

When they sat down together for lunch, they felt awkward about the night before. But Mrs. Moreno had made a fresh stack of tortillas and cooked up a pan of *chile verde*, and that broke the ice. She licked her thumb and smacked her lips.

Did You Know?
Tortillas (tôr tē´ yäs) are made from cornmeal or wheat flour and baked on a griddle. They look like very flat pancakes.
. . . .

Reading Skill

Identifying Assumptions Reread the highlighted paragraph. Mrs. Moreno speaks loudly because she assumes something about Yollie. What does Mrs. Moreno assume?

Possible response: Mrs. Moreno assumes that Yollie can hear her and is listening to what she is saying.

Word Power

tirade (tī´rād) *n.* a long, angry or scolding speech

De la Corazón (From the Heart), 1973. Yreina D. Cervantes. Watercolor, 16 x 12 in. Collection of the artist.

How do the title of this painting and the expression on the woman's face reflect how Mrs. Moreno feels toward Yollie?

"You know, honey, we gotta figure a way to make money," Yollie's mother said. "You and me. We don't have to be poor. Remember the Garcias. They made this stupid little tool that fixes cars. They moved away because they're rich. That's why we don't see them no more."

"What can we make?" asked Yollie. She took another tortilla and tore it in half.

"Maybe a screwdriver that works on both ends? Something like that." The mother looked around the room for ideas, but then shrugged. "Let's forget it. It's better to get an education. If you get a good job and have spare time then maybe you can invent something." She rolled her tongue over her lips and cleared her throat. "The county fair hires people. We can get a job there. It will be here next week."

Reading Skill
Identifying Assumptions Reread the highlighted sentences. What does Mrs. Moreno assume Yollie will be able to do if she has a good job and spare time?

Possible response: Mrs. Moreno assumes that Yollie might be able to invent something and make money from it.

Comprehension Check

Reread the boxed paragraph. Who does Yollie assume is calling? Who is actually calling and why? Underline the answers to these questions in the text.

Literary Element

Conflict Reread the highlighted sentence and the following paragraph. How does using the money now help solve the conflict between mother and daughter?

Possible response: Mrs.

Moreno is able to buy an

outfit for Yollie that will

make Yollie feel better

about herself.

Yollie hated the idea. What would Ernie say if he saw her pitching hay at the cows? How could she go to school smelling like an armful of chickens? "No, they wouldn't hire us," she said.

The phone rang. Yollie **lurched** from her chair to answer it, thinking it would be Janice wanting to know why she had left. But it was Ernie wondering the same thing. When he found out she wasn't mad at him, he asked if she would like to go to a movie.

"I'll ask," Yollie said, smiling. She covered the phone with her hand and counted to ten. She uncovered the receiver and said, "My mom says it's OK. What are we going to see?"

After Yollie hung up, her mother climbed, grunting, onto a chair to reach the top shelf in the hall closet. She wondered why she hadn't done it earlier. She reached behind a stack of towels and pushed her chubby hand into the cigar box where she kept her secret stash of money.

"I've been saving a little money every month," said Mrs. Moreno. "For you, *m'ija*." Her mother held up five twenties, a blossom of green that smelled sweeter than flowers on that Saturday. They drove to Macy's and bought a blouse, shoes, and a skirt that would not bleed in rain or any other kind of weather.

Word Power

lurched (lurchd) *v.* moved suddenly in a jerky and uneven way

Respond to Literature

Mother and Daughter

A Comprehension Check

Answer the following questions in the spaces provided.

1. Why doesn't Mrs. Moreno buy Yollie a new dress for the dance? What does she do instead? Mrs. Moreno can't afford to buy a new dress, so she dyes a white dress black.

2. How is Mrs. Moreno able to buy Yollie clothes at Macy's? She uses the money she has been saving for Yollie.

B Reading Skills

Answer the following questions in the spaces provided.

1. **Question** What is a good question to ask to find out what happens between Yollie and Ernie after the dance? Possible response: Does Ernie ask Yollie to go out with him?

2. **Identifying Assumptions** What assumptions does Mrs. Moreno make about a good education? Possible response: She thinks that a good education will help Yollie get a good job and earn enough money to take care of her or invent something.

3. **Identifying Assumptions** What assumption does Yollie make about the girls in the restroom at the dance? Possible response: Yollie assumes that they will laugh at her because she cannot afford to buy a new dress.

C Word Power

Complete each sentence below, using one of the words in the box.

| grogginess | gloated | meager | taunt |
| sophisticated | tirade | lurched |

1. "Don't ___taunt___ your sister while she practices her speech," my mother said sharply.

2. When there was a sudden loud noise outside, the students ___lurched___ out of their chairs and ran to the window.

3. Kim ___gloated___ when she got the best part in the school play.

4. After my sister had gone on a ___tirade___ about knocking before entering her room, she walked into my room without knocking.

5. The students showed their ___grogginess___ by yawning and rubbing their eyes.

6. We all thought Maya was quite ___sophisticated___, because she had lived all over the world.

7. My allowance is so ___meager___ I can barely afford to buy a comic book!

D Literary Element: Conflict

Read the passage below from "Mother and Daughter." As you read, think about what the sentences reveal about the conflicts Yollie and her mother face. Then answer the questions that follow.

> Poor baby, she thought, her brow darkening as she made a sad face.[1] She wanted to tell her daughter how sorry she was, but she knew it wouldn't help.[2] She walked back to the living room and cried.[3]
>
> The next morning, mother and daughter stayed away from each other.[4] Yollie sat in her room turning the pages of an old *Seventeen*, while her mother watered her plants with a Pepsi bottle.[5]

1. In sentences 1–3, who is struggling with a conflict? What is the cause of this conflict? Possible responses: Mrs. Moreno is struggling with a conflict. She wants to tell her daughter that she is sorry about the dress, but she knows it won't help the situation. She feels powerless.

2. In sentences 4–5, is the conflict internal or external? How can you tell?

   Possible responses: The conflict is external. It is between the mother and the daughter, who are avoiding each other.

E An Essay

Imagine that you are Yollie and are asked to write an essay that describes the person you admire the most. You decide to write about your mother. What would you say about her? Would you mention some of her tricks? Complete your essay below.

Sometimes the people we admire most live with us. My mother deserves a medal for all she does for me. First of all, she is funny. She likes to Possible responses: wave at the low-riders; play practical jokes.

Second, she always tries to help me. When I needed a dress for the school dance, she Possible response: dyed a white dress black to make it look sophisticated.

Even though the dress was a disaster, she made me feel better by cooking my favorite meal. She wants me to study hard and become a doctor because Possible response: she thinks I could then make money and take care of myself and her.

To make me feel better about myself, she bought me

a blouse, shoes, and a skirt at Macy's.

I think my mom is the best mom in the world!

Assessment

Fill in the circle next to each correct answer.

1. What does Yollie assume when she sees that her dress is fading at the dance?
   - ○ A. Yollie assumes no one will notice her dress is gray.
   - ● B. Yollie assumes all the girls will laugh at her.
   - ○ C. Yollie assumes her dress must have stained Ernie's sweater.
   - ○ D. Yollie assumes her mother ruined her evening on purpose.

2. Which is the **best** question to ask to understand why Yollie gets upset at the dance?
   - ○ A. Why does Yollie dance with Ernie?
   - ○ B. What does Janice say to Yollie?
   - ○ C. How is the dance like a scene from a movie?
   - ● D. What happens to Yolllie's dress when it rains?

3. Which of the following sentences describes an internal conflict in this story?
   - ○ A. The black dress looks brand new after it is dyed.
   - ○ B. Mrs. Moreno wants Yollie to get a good education.
   - ● C. Yollie feels embarrassed for yelling at her mother.
   - ○ D. Ernie invites Yollie to go to the movies.

4. Where does Mrs. Moreno get the money to buy new clothes for Yollie?
   - ● A. She uses the money she has saved.
   - ○ B. She goes to work at the county fair.
   - ○ C. Yollie gives her the money.
   - ○ D. She earns the money with her new invention.

5. Which of the following words means "a long outburst"?
   - ○ A. gloated
   - ○ B. meager
   - ● C. tirade
   - ○ D. sophisticated

Get Ready to Read!

The Treasure of Lemon Brown

Meet Walter Dean Myers

Walter Dean Myers was born in 1937. He was ten years old when he started filling up notebooks with his stories and poems. "I wrote for years without getting published," he remembers. Myers later discovered that he could make a living at writing when he won a contest for picture-book writers. Today he is an award-winning author, recognized especially for young-adult fiction. "The Treasure of Lemon Brown" was first published in 1983.

What You Know

Think of objects you treasure most. They might include a letter, a ring, a picture, or a baseball. Bring in one of these objects to show the class and tell why you treasure it.

Reason to Read

Read "The Treasure of Lemon Brown" to find out how objects can be a reflection of a person's life.

Background Info

The blues is a type of folk music that was created by African Americans in the early 1900s. The words in blues songs often tell of hard times and sorrows. Many early blues songs were written and sung on the spot. Blues music led to the birth of jazz. It also served as the basis for rhythm and blues in the 1940s and rock-and-roll in the 1950s. The influence of blues can be heard in the popular music of today.

Word Power

tentatively (ten´ tə tiv lē) *adv.* in an uncertain way; hesitantly; p. 97 *tent + at + ive + ly*
Andrea *tentatively* approached my new beagle because she is afraid of dogs.

involuntary (in vol´ ən ter´ ē) *adj.* not done willingly or by choice; p. 98 *in + volunt + ary*
Ari gave an *involuntary* gasp of pain when the nurse gave him a shot.

eerie (ēr´ ē) *adj.* weird, especially in a frightening way; p. 103
The *eerie* light in the distance scared the hikers.

ominous (om´ ə nəs) *adj.* threatening harm or evil; p. 103 *om + ine + ous*
The snarling dog looked very *ominous,* so we crossed the street to avoid it.

exhaled (eks hāld´) *v.* breathed out; p. 103 *ex + hale + ed*
When I heard that I had made the team, I *exhaled* a sigh of relief.

Answer the following questions that contain the new words above.
Write your answers in the spaces provided.

1. If you *tentatively* tasted some soup, did you gulp it or sip it? _____ sip it _____

2. Would *eerie* music be strange and scary or sweet and soothing?

   _____ strange and scary _____

3. If you *exhaled,* did you take air in or let air out? _____ let air out _____

4. Would an *ominous* sky indicate that a storm or a sunny day was coming?

   _____ a storm _____

5. Is an *involuntary* movement something you do or do not have control over?

   _____ something you do not have control over _____

Adapted from

The Treasure of Lemon Brown

Walter Dean Myers

The dark sky, filled with threatening swirling clouds, reflected Greg Ridley's mood as he sat on the front stairs of his building. His father's voice came to him again, first reading the letter the principal had sent to the house, then lecturing endlessly about his poor efforts in math.

Greg had sat in the small, pale green kitchen listening, knowing the lecture would end with his father saying he couldn't play ball with the Scorpions. He had asked his father the week before, and his father had said it depended on his next report card. It wasn't often the Scorpions took on new players, especially 14-year-olds. This was a chance of a lifetime for Greg. Report cards were due in a week, and Greg had been hoping for the best. But the principal had ended the suspense early when she sent that letter saying Greg would probably fail math if he didn't spend more time studying.

There was a flash of nearby lightning. Soon large drops of rain splashed onto his jeans. He stood to go upstairs, thought of the lecture that probably awaited him if he did anything except shut himself in his room with his math book, and started walking down the street instead. Down the block there was an old building that had been abandoned for some months.

He reached the house just as another flash of lightning changed the night to day for an instant, then returned the graffiti-scarred building to the grim shadows. He jumped over the outer stairs and pushed **tentatively** on the door. It was open, and he let himself in.

The inside of the building was dark except for the dim light from the streetlamps that filtered through the dirty windows. There was a room a few feet from the door. From where he stood at the entrance, Greg could see a squarish patch of light on the floor. It was a large room that might have been where someone entertained guests at one time. Squinting, Greg could see an old table on its side against one wall, what looked like a pile of rags or a torn mattress in the corner, and a couch, with one side broken, in front of the window.

He went to the couch. From this spot he could see the blinking neon sign over the bodega on the corner. He sat awhile, watching the sign blink first green then red, allowing his mind to drift to the Scorpions, then to his father.

For a moment Greg thought he heard something that sounded like a scraping against the wall. He listened carefully, but it was gone.

There weren't any more scraping noises, but he was sure he had heard something in the darkness—something breathing!

Slowly he stood, tensing. As he turned, a flash of lightning lit up the room, frightening him with its sudden brilliance. He continued listening, but heard nothing and thought that it might have just been rats. He went to the window and was about to look out when he heard a voice behind him.

Reading Skill

Question Reread the highlighted sentences. Which is the **best** question to ask while reading to find out more about whom Greg might meet in the building? Check the correct question below.

- ☐ When was the building constructed?
- ☑ Who is living in this room?
- ☐ Where is the building located?

Background Info

Bodega (bō dā´gä) is the Spanish word for a store or bar.

Word Power

tentatively (ten´ tə tiv lē) *adv.* in an uncertain way; hesitantly

"Don't try nothin' 'cause I got a razor here sharp enough to cut a week into nine days!"

Greg, except for the **involuntary** shaking of his knees, stood stock still. The voice was high and brittle, like dry twigs being broken, surely not one he had ever heard before. Greg turned, holding his breath, his eyes straining to see in the dark room.

The upper part of the figure before him was still in darkness. The lower half was in the dim rectangle of light that fell unevenly from the window. There were two feet, in cracked, dirty shoes from which rose legs that were wrapped in rags.

"Who are you?" Greg hardly recognized his own voice.

"I'm Lemon Brown," came the answer. "Who're you?"

"Greg Ridley."

"What you doing here?" The figure shuffled forward again, and Greg took a small step backward.

"It's raining," Greg said.

"I can see that," the figure said.

The person who called himself Lemon Brown peered forward, and Greg could see him clearly. He was an old man. His black, heavily wrinkled face was surrounded by a halo of crinkly white hair and whiskers that seemed to separate his head from the layers of dirty coats piled on his smallish frame. His pants were bagged to the knee, where they were met with rags that went down to the old shoes. The rags were held on with strings, and there was a rope around his middle. Greg relaxed. He had seen the man before, picking through the trash on the corner and pulling clothes out of a Salvation Army box. There was no sign of the razor that could "cut a week into nine days."

"What are you doing here?" Greg asked.

"This is where I'm staying," Lemon Brown said. "What you here for?"

Word Power
involuntary (in vol´ ən ter´ ē) *adj.* not done willingly or by choice

"Told you it was raining out," Greg said, leaning against the back of the couch until he felt it give slightly.

"Ain't you got no home?"

"I got a home," Greg answered.

"You ain't one of them bad boys looking for my treasure, is you?" Lemon Brown cocked his head to one side and squinted one eye. "Because I told you I got me a razor."

"I'm not looking for your treasure," Greg answered, smiling. "*If* you have one."

"What you mean, *if* I have one," Lemon Brown said. "Every man got a treasure. You don't know that, you must be a fool!"

"Sure," Greg said as he sat on the sofa and put one leg over the back. "What do you have, gold coins?"

"Don't worry none about what I got," Lemon Brown said. "You know who I am?"

"You told me your name was orange or lemon or something like that."

"Lemon Brown," the old man said, pulling back his shoulders as he did so, "they used to call me Sweet Lemon Brown."

"Sweet Lemon?" Greg asked.

"Yessir. Sweet Lemon Brown. They used to say I sung the blues so sweet that if I sang at a funeral, the dead would start rocking with the beat. You mean you ain't never heard of Sweet Lemon Brown?"

"Afraid not," Greg said. "What . . . what happened to you?"

"Hard times, boy. One day I got tired, sat down to rest a while and felt a tap on my shoulder. Hard times caught up with me."

"Sorry about that."

"What you doing here? How come you didn't go home when the rain come?"

"Just didn't." Greg looked away.

Comprehension Check

Reread the boxed text. Why does Lemon Brown say he gave up singing the blues?

When things were going well, he felt as though he could not sing the blues anymore.

"I used to have a mixed up boy just like you. Had them big eyes like you got. I used to call them moon eyes. Look into them moon eyes and see anything you want."

"How come you gave up singing the blues?" Greg asked.

"Didn't give it up," Lemon Brown said. "You don't give up the blues; they give you up. After a while you do good for yourself, and it ain't nothing but foolishness singing about how hard you got it. Ain't that right?"

"I guess so."

Jim, 1930. William H. Johnson. Oil on canvas, 21⅝ x 18¼ in. Smithsonian American Art Museum, Washington, DC.

In what ways might the boy in the painting be similar to Greg?

 Stop here for **Break Time** on the next page.

100

Break Time

Asking questions that begin with *Why, Where, Who, What,* and *When* will help you understand a story. Ask yourself questions about the characters: Who are they? Why are they acting the way they do? You can also ask yourself: Where and when is the story taking place? In the chart below, write questions about "The Treasure of Lemon Brown" starting with these "W" words in the left-hand column. In the right-hand column, write the answers. A sample question and answer have been done for you.

Question	Answer
1. Why is Greg in a bad mood?	He has not been doing well in math, so his dad won't let him play with the Scorpions.
2. Where Possible response: does Greg go to escape the rain?	Possible response: Greg goes into an abandoned building.
3. Who Possible response: is staying in the building?	Possible response: Lemon Brown is staying in the building.
4. What Possible response: does Lemon Brown say every man has?	Possible response: Lemon Brown says that every man has a treasure.
5. When Possible response: does the story take place—during the day or during the night?	Possible response: The story takes place during the night.

 Turn the page to continue reading.

Comprehension Check

Reread the boxed sentences. Who is making the noise? What are they carrying?

Neighborhood thugs are

making the noise. They are

carrying a length of pipe.

Reading Skill

Identifying Assumptions Reread the highlighted paragraphs. What do the men assume about Lemon Brown's treasure?

They assume his treasure is

money.

"What's that noise?" Lemon Brown asked, suddenly sitting upright.

Greg went to the window and saw three men, neighborhood thugs, on the stairs. One was carrying a length of pipe. The old man looked out, then motioned frantically for Greg to follow him. They reached the top of the stairs, and Greg felt Lemon Brown's hand first lying on his shoulder, then probing down his arm. He finally took Greg's hand into his own as they crouched in the darkness.

"They's bad men," Lemon Brown whispered.

"Hey! Rag man!" A voice called. "We know you in here. What you got up under them rags? You got any money?"

Silence.

There was a banging downstairs and a light as the men entered.

"We heard you talking about your treasure," the voice was slurred. "We just want to see it, that's all."

Greg opened his mouth to quiet the sound of his breath as he sucked it in uneasily. A beam of light hit the wall a few feet opposite him, then went out.

"Ain't nobody in that room," a voice said. "You think he's gone or something?"

"I don't know," came the answer. "All I know is that I heard him talking about some kind of treasure.

"HEY, OLD MAN, ARE YOU UP THERE?"

Silence.

There was a footstep on the stairs. The beam from the flashlight danced crazily along the peeling wallpaper. Greg held his breath. There was another step and a loud crashing noise as the man banged the pipe against the wooden staircase. Greg thought about the pipe, wondering what he would do when the man reached them—what he *could* do.

Then Lemon Brown released his hand and moved toward the top of the stairs. Suddenly, Lemon Brown stood at the top of the stairs, both arms raised high above his head.

"There he is!" A voice cried from below.

"Throw down your money, old man, so I won't have to bash your head in!"

Lemon Brown didn't move. The steps came closer, and still Lemon Brown didn't move. He was an **eerie** sight. A bundle of rags standing at the top of the stairs, his shadow on the wall looming over him. Maybe, the thought came to Greg, the scene could be even eerier.

Greg wet his lips, put his hands to his mouth and tried to make a sound. Nothing came out. He swallowed hard, wet his lips once more and howled as evenly as he could.

"What's that?"

As Greg howled, the light moved away from Lemon Brown, but not before Greg saw him hurl his body down the stairs at the men who had come to take his treasure. There was a crashing noise, and then footsteps. A rush of warm air came in as the downstairs door opened, then there was only an **ominous** silence.

Greg stood on the landing. He listened, and after a while there was another sound on the staircase.

"Mr. Brown?" he called.

"Yeah, it's me," came the answer. "I got their flashlight."

Greg **exhaled** in relief as Lemon Brown made his way slowly back up the stairs.

"You O.K.?"

"Few bumps and bruises," Lemon Brown said.

"I think I'd better be going," Greg said, his breath returning to normal. "You'd better leave, too, before they come back."

Word Power

eerie (ēr′ ē) *adj.* weird, especially in a frightening way

ominous (om′ ə nəs) *adj.* threatening harm or evil

exhaled (eks hāld′) *v.* breathed out

Reading Skill

Question Reread the highlighted paragraph. Which is the **best** question to ask while reading to find out what Greg's plan is? Check the correct response.

- ☑ How does Greg think he can make the scene eerier?
- ☐ Why is Lemon Brown standing at the top of the stairs?
- ☐ When does Greg hear the steps coming closer?

Comprehension Check

Reread the boxed paragraph. What happens to the bad men?

Lemon Brown scares them away by throwing himself down the stairs. Greg helps Lemon Brown by howling.

Reading Skill

Identifying Assumptions Reread the highlighted sentences. What assumption does Lemon Brown make about the men?

Possible response: Lemon Brown assumes that the thugs will hang around, but will not come back inside.

English Coach

When Lemon Brown talks about his pain, he gives it human qualities by calling it "Mr. Pain." Which of the following sentences also give human qualities to something that is not a person? Check the correct responses.

- ☐ My computer is making me angry.
- ☑ The sun gently touched my face.
- ☑ His car was his baby.

"They may hang around outside for a while," Lemon Brown said, "but they ain't getting their nerve up to come in here again. Not with crazy old rag men and howling spooks. I'm heading out West tomorrow, out to east St. Louis."

"They were talking about treasures," Greg said. "You *really* have a treasure?"

"What I tell you? Didn't I tell you every man got a treasure?" Lemon Brown said. "You want to see mine?"

"If you want to show it to me," Greg shrugged.

"Let's look out the window first, see what them punks be doing," Lemon Brown said.

They saw the men who had tried to take the treasure sitting on the curb near the corner. One of them had his pants leg up, looking at his knee.

"You sure you're not hurt?" Greg asked Lemon Brown.

"Nothing that ain't been hurt before," Lemon Brown said. "When you get as old as me all you say when something hurts is, 'Howdy, Mr. Pain, sees you back again.'"

Greg smiled.

"Here, you hold this." Lemon Brown gave Greg the flashlight.

He sat on the floor near Greg and carefully untied the strings that held the rags on his right leg. When he took the rags away, Greg saw a piece of plastic. The old man carefully took off the plastic and unfolded it. He revealed some yellowed newspaper clippings and a battered harmonica.

"There it be," he said, nodding his head. "There it be."

Greg looked at the old man, saw the distant look in his eye, then turned to the clippings. They told of Sweet Lemon Brown, a blues singer and harmonica player who was appearing at different theaters in the South. All of the clippings were reviews of shows Lemon Brown had been in more than 50 years ago. Greg looked at the harmonica. It was dented badly on one side, with the holes on one end nearly closed.

"I used to travel around and make money for to feed my wife and Jesse—that's my boy's name. Then his mama died, and he stayed with his mama's sister. He growed up to be a man, and when the war come he saw fit to go off and fight in it. I didn't have nothing to give him except these things that told him who I was, and what he come from.

"Anyway, he went off to war, and I went off still playing and singing. 'Course by then I wasn't as much as I used to be, not without somebody to make it worth the while. I traveled around, and one time I come home, and there was this letter saying Jesse got killed in the war. Broke my heart, it truly did.

"They sent back what he had with him over there, and what it was is this old mouth fiddle and these clippings. Him carrying it around with him like that told me it meant something to him. That was my treasure, and when I give it to him he treated it just like that, a treasure. Ain't that something?"

"Yeah, I guess so," Greg said.

"You *guess* so?" Lemon Brown's voice rose as he started to put his treasure back into the plastic. "Well, you got to guess 'cause you sure don't know nothing. Don't know enough to get home when it's raining."

Why is Lemon Brown's harmonica part of his treasure?

_____

Literary Element

Theme Reread the highlighted paragraph. How does Lemon Brown's treasure help you understand the theme that a real treasure is what a person values, even though it may seem worthless to others?

Possible response: Even though the harmonica and clippings may seem worthless to others, Lemon Brown's son treated them as treasures. The treasure reflects who Lemon Brown is.

_____

_____

English Coach

Scalawags is a word used to describe troublemakers. What other words can you think of to describe troublemakers? Write two words below.

Possible responses: thugs,

punks, hoodlums

"I guess . . . I mean, you're right."

"You O.K. for a youngster," the old man said as he tied the strings around his leg, "better than those scalawags what come here looking for my treasure. That's for sure."

"You really think that treasure of yours was worth fighting for?" Greg asked. "Against a pipe?"

"What else a man got 'cepting what he can pass on to his son, or his daughter, if she be his oldest?" Lemon Brown said. "For a big-headed boy you sure do ask the foolishest questions."

Lemon Brown got up after patting his rags in place and looked out the window again.

"Looks like they're gone. You get on out of here and get yourself home."

"You sure you'll be O.K.?" Greg asked.

"Now didn't I tell you I was going to east St. Louis in the morning?" Lemon Brown asked. "Don't that sound O.K. to you?"

"Sure it does," Greg said. "And you take care of that treasure of yours."

"That I'll do," Lemon said, the wrinkles about his eyes suggesting a smile.

The night had warmed and the rain had stopped, leaving puddles at the curbs. Greg didn't even want to think how late it was. He thought ahead of what his father would say and wondered if he should tell him about Lemon Brown. He thought about it until he reached his home, and decided against it. Lemon Brown would be O.K., Greg thought, with his memories and his treasure.

Greg pushed the button over the bell marked Ridley, thought of the lecture he knew his father would give him, and smiled.

Reading Skill

Question Reread the highlighted sentence. Which is the **best** question to ask while reading to help you understand why Greg is smiling? Check the correct response.

- ☐ Will Lemon Brown be O.K. in St. Louis?
- ☑ What has Greg learned from Lemon Brown?
- ☐ Why will Greg's father lecture him?

Respond to Literature

The Treasure of Lemon Brown

A Comprehension Check

Answer the following questions in the spaces provided.

1. Why is Greg upset at the beginning of the story? Greg is upset because his father won't let him play ball due to his poor grades.

2. What is Lemon Brown's treasure? His treasure is a collection of newspaper clippings and an old harmonica.

B Reading Skills

Answer the following questions in the spaces provided.

1. **Question** What question can you ask yourself while reading that would help you get information about Lemon Brown's past? Possible responses: What did Lemon Brown used to do? Why would people know who he is? What happened to Lemon Brown's family?

2. **Identifying Assumptions** What assumptions does Lemon Brown first make about Greg? Lemon Brown thinks that Greg is one of the bad boys in the neighborhood. He thinks Greg is after his treasure.

3. **Identifying Assumptions** What assumptions does Greg first make about Lemon Brown? How do his assumptions change as he talks to Lemon Brown? At first Greg thinks Lemon Brown is dangerous. Then he sees that he is a harmless old man. Later, Greg is impressed with Lemon Brown's courage and moved by Lemon Brown's life story.

C Word Power

Complete each sentence below, using one of the words in the box.

tentatively	involuntary
eerie	ominous	exhaled

1. The shy child _____tentatively_____ reached for a glass of lemonade.

2. When four men walked into the restaurant looking mad, the mood became quiet and _____ominous_____.

3. Tiara blinks her eyes in an _____involuntary_____ manner when she is telling a lie.

4. As I ran, I breathed in through my nose and _____exhaled_____ through my mouth.

5. The shadows on my wall looked strange and _____eerie_____.

Circle the word that best completes each sentence.

6. After holding his breath underwater, Jose **(exhaled,** ominous) when he reached the surface.

7. My aunt told me that jumping when she sees a mouse is just an **(involuntary,** eerie) reaction.

8. Along the steep road, there were several **(exhaled,** **ominous)** signs of danger.

9. The **(tentatively,** **eerie)** sound of the howling wolves sent chills up and down our spines.

10. The rancher **(tentatively,** involuntary) approached the angry bull.

D Literary Element: Theme

Read the two passages below from "The Treasure of Lemon Brown." As you read, think about what the sentences reveal about the theme of the story that every person has a treasure and that different things can be treasures to different people. Then answer the questions that follow.

"He growed up to be a man, and when the war come he saw fit to go off and fight in it.[1] I didn't have nothing to give him except these things that told him who I was, and what he come from."[2]

"You really think that treasure of yours was worth fighting for?" Greg asked.[3] "Against a pipe?"[4]

"What else a man got 'cepting what he can pass on to his son, or his daughter, if she be his oldest?" Lemon Brown said.[5]

1. In sentences 1–2, what does Lemon Brown say his newspaper clippings and harmonica stand for? These are the only things that Lemon Brown was able to pass on to his son. They show who he was.

_____

_____

_____

2. Reread sentences 3–5. Why does Lemon Brown think his treasure is worth fighting for? Lemon Brown thinks his harmonica and clippings are worth fighting for because they are his treasure and that a person's treasure is the only thing he or she has to pass on to future generations.

_____

_____

E A Conversation

Imagine that you are Greg. You have just come home and have changed your mind about talking to your father about Lemon Brown. Write the conversation that Greg and his father might have.

Father: Where have you been?

Greg: I went for a walk. It started to rain, so I Possible response:

went into a building.

Then I saw an old man. His name was Lemon Brown.

Father: Son, don't you know that you might have been hurt or killed? Was Lemon Brown dangerous?

Greg: No, Dad, he was really nice. He used to be Possible response: a

traveling blues singer and harmonica player. He was famous.

He showed me his treasure, which is a harmonica and newspaper

clippings.

Father: Why does he call that a treasure?

Greg: Because Possible response: it was what he handed down to his son,

Jesse, to show Jesse who he was.

Jesse treated these things Possible response: as if they were valuable.

Lemon Brown made me think about you and me. I'm sorry that I
Possible responses: went against your wishes; got a bad grade in math.

Father: I may be hard on you, son. But you're *my* treasure. I want you to succeed.

Greg: Thanks, Dad.

Assessment

Fill in the circle next to each correct answer.

1. Why does Greg go into the abandoned building?
    - ○ A. He is running away from home.
    - ○ B. He wants to find a place to study.
    - ● C. He is trying to get out of the rain.
    - ○ D. He is hiding from the thugs.

2. Which is the **best** question to ask to learn about Lemon Brown's treasure?
    - ● A. What does the treasure mean to Lemon Brown and his son?
    - ○ B. What does Lemon Brown's treasure have to do with the blues?
    - ○ C. When did Lemon Brown get his treasure?
    - ○ D. What do the thugs think of Lemon Brown's treasure?

3. What does Greg assume about Lemon Brown at the end of the story?
    - ○ A. He will never move out of the building.
    - ● B. He will be O.K. with his treasure.
    - ○ C. Someone will steal his treasure.
    - ○ D. Someday he will get married again.

4. What does the theme of "The Treasure of Lemon Brown" reveal to us?
    - ● A. Treasures do not have to be expensive things.
    - ○ B. It is never too late to sing the blues.
    - ○ C. Memories are only temporary.
    - ○ D. Some parents have nothing to give their children.

5. Which of the following words means "scary or threatening"?
    - ○ A. tentatively
    - ○ B. exhaled
    - ○ C. involuntary
    - ● D. ominous

Get Ready to Read!

The Medicine Bag

Meet Virginia Driving Hawk Sneve

Virginia Driving Hawk Sneve (snā′vē) was born in South Dakota in 1933. Sneve, a member of the Rosebud Sioux tribe, grew up on the Rosebud Reservation. She went to college and became a writer, teacher, and school counselor. Sneve's goal as a writer is to teach others about her culture. She wants people to have a real picture of American Indian life. "The Medicine Bag" was first published in 1975.

What You Know

Think about a gift that you treasure because someone special gave it to you. What does it mean to you?

Reason to Read

As you read, think about why the two main characters in the story have different feelings toward the same object.

Background Info

Sioux is the name for groups of Native Americans also called *Lakota*, *Nakota*, and *Dakota*. They speak their own language and have a unique culture. They originally farmed, hunted, and fished in the forests and lakes of the north-central part of what is now the United States. Today they make up one of the largest Native American groups in the country.

A large number of Sioux live on reservations in Minnesota, Nebraska, North Dakota, South Dakota, and Montana. In the United States, an Indian reservation is land that is owned by the federal government, but is managed by Native American groups who live on the land. Native American groups make some of their own laws. There are about 300 Indian reservations in the United States.

Word Power

procession (prə sesh′ən) *n.* a march; people moving forward in an orderly way; p. 115
The parade included a *procession* of the winning basketball team.

fatigue (fə tēg′) *n.* weakness or tiredness; p. 115
The *fatigue* I felt was so strong that I decided to take a nap.

reluctantly (ri luk′tənt lē) *adv.* with hesitation; unwillingly; p. 116
I *reluctantly* ate the four-alarm chili that Joe had made.

descendants (di sen′dənts) *n.* people related to a person who lived in the past; p. 116
I am one of the *descendants* of a famous explorer.

sheepishly (shē′pish lē) *adv.* in an embarrassed way; shyly; p. 116
My sister *sheepishly* admitted that she wanted to sit next to me during the scary movie.

discomfort (dis kum′fərt) *n.* the state of being uncomfortable; a bother; p. 117
It is quite a *discomfort* to sit at this desk all day without taking a break.

sacred (sā′krid) *adj.* holy; worthy of great respect; p. 121
The ground where they buried the soldiers is *sacred.*

**Answer the following questions that contain the new words above.
Write your answers in the spaces provided.**

1. If I *reluctantly* accept an invitation, do I want to go or not want to go?

   I do not want to go.

2. Is the hot sun a *discomfort* because I like the heat or I do not like the heat?

   Because I do not like the heat.

3. Does a *procession* include one person or several people? ___several people___

4. Would *fatigue* cause someone to want to rest or run in a race? ___rest___

5. Are the *descendants* of a man younger or older than him? ___younger than him___

6. In a *sacred* place, should one be respectful or disrespectful? ___respectful___

7. Are people who act *sheepishly* usually confident or shy? ___shy___

Adapted from

The Medicine Bag

Virginia Driving Hawk Sneve

Reading Skill
Identifying Assumptions Reread the highlighted sentences. What assumptions does the narrator make about his friends and their ideas about Indians?

Possible response: The

narrator thinks his friends

would laugh if they saw his

Grandpa. He thinks they

would expect Grandpa to

look like Indians from TV.

My kid sister Cheryl and I always bragged about our Sioux grandpa, Joe Iron Shell. Maybe we exaggerated and made Grandpa and the reservation sound glamorous, but when we'd return home to Iowa after our yearly summer visit to Grandpa we always had some exciting tale to tell.

We never showed our friends Grandpa's picture. Our friends would have laughed at the picture, because Grandpa wasn't tall like TV Indians. His hair wasn't in braids, but hung in stringy, gray strands on his neck and he was old. He was our great-grandfather, and he didn't live in a tipi, but all by himself on the Rosebud Reservation in South Dakota. So when Grandpa came to visit us, I was so ashamed and embarrassed I could've died.

There are a lot of yippy poodles and other fancy little dogs in our neighborhood. They usually barked singly at the mailman from the safety of their own yards. Now it sounded as if a whole pack of mutts were barking together in one place.

I got up and walked to the curb to see what the commotion was. About a block away I saw a crowd of little kids yelling, with the dogs yipping and growling around someone who was walking down the middle of the street.

I watched the group as it slowly came closer and saw that in the center of the strange **procession** was a man wearing a tall black hat. I felt cold and hot at the same time as I recognized the man. "Oh, no!" I whispered. "It's Grandpa!"

I stood on the curb, unable to move even though I wanted to run and hide. The kids ran to the curb where they watched me and the old man.

"Grandpa," I said and felt pretty dumb when my voice cracked. I reached for his beat-up old tin suitcase, which was tied shut with a rope. But he set it down right in the street and shook my hand.

"Hau, Takoza, Grandchild," he greeted me formally in Sioux.

"Hi," I muttered with my head down. I tried to pull my hand away when I felt his bony hand trembling, and looked up to see **fatigue** in his face. I felt like crying. I couldn't think of anything to say so I picked up Grandpa's suitcase, took his arm, and guided him up the driveway to our house.

Mom was standing on the steps. I don't know how long she'd been watching, but her hand was over her mouth and she looked as if she couldn't believe what she saw. Then she ran to us.

"Grandpa," she gasped. "How in the world did you get here?"

She checked her move to embrace Grandpa and I remembered that such a display of affection is improper to the Sioux and would embarrass him.

"Hau, Marie," he said as he shook Mom's hand. She smiled and took his other arm.

Cheryl came bursting out of the house. She was all smiles and was so obviously glad to see Grandpa that I was ashamed of how I felt.

Reading Skill

Question Reread the highlighted sentences. What is the **best** question to ask while reading to understand how the narrator feels about his grandfather's arrival? Check the correct response.

- ☑ Why does the narrator keep his head down?
- ☐ How far did his grandfather travel?
- ☐ Does his grandfather speak English?

Connect to the Text

Reread the boxed paragraph. Think about a time when you were glad to see someone. How did you act toward him or her?

Answers will vary.

_____

_____

Word Power

procession (prə sesh′ən) *n.* a march; people moving forward in an orderly way

fatigue (fə tēg′) *n.* weakness or tiredness

115

"Grandpa!" she yelled happily. "You came to see us!"

Grandpa smiled and Mom and I let go of him as he stretched out his arms to my ten-year-old sister, who was still young enough to be hugged.

"*Wicincala*, little girl," he greeted her and then collapsed.

He had fainted. Mom and I carried him into her sewing room, where we had a spare bed.

"Shouldn't we call the doctor, Mom?"

"Yes," she agreed with a sigh.

I **reluctantly** moved to the bed. I knew Grandpa wouldn't want to have Mom undress him, but I didn't want to, either. When I loosened his tie and opened his shirt collar, I felt a small leather pouch that hung around his neck. I left it alone and moved to remove his boots.

I put the boots on the floor and saw why they fit so tight. Each one was stuffed with money. I looked at the bills that lined the boots and started to ask about them, but Grandpa's eyes were closed again.

Mom came back with a basin of water. "The doctor thinks Grandpa is suffering from heat exhaustion," she explained as she bathed Grandpa's face. Mom gave a big sigh, "*Oh hinh*, Martin. How do you suppose he got here?"

We found out after the doctor's visit. Grandpa was angrily sitting up in bed while Mom tried to feed him some soup.

Grandpa relaxed, and between sips of soup he told us of his journey. Soon after our visit to him Grandpa decided that he would like to see where his only living **descendants** lived. Besides, he admitted **sheepishly,** he was lonesome after we left.

Word Power

reluctantly (ri luk´ tənt lē) *adv.* with hesitation; unwillingly

descendants (di sen´ dənts) *n.* people related to a person who lived in the past

sheepishly (shē´ pish lē) *adv.* in an embarrassed way; shyly

I knew everybody felt as guilty as I did—especially Mom. Mom was all Grandpa had left. So even after she married my dad, who's a white man and teaches in the college in our city, and after Cheryl and I were born, Mom made sure that every summer we spent a week with Grandpa.

I never thought that Grandpa would be lonely after our visits, and none of us noticed how old and weak he had become. But Grandpa knew and so he came to us. He had ridden on buses for two and a half days. When he arrived in the city, tired and stiff from sitting for so long, he set out, walking, to find us.

I knew everybody felt as bad as I did. Yet I was proud of this 86-year-old man, who had never been away from the reservation, having the courage to travel so far alone.

"You found the money in my boots?" he asked Mom.

"Martin did," she answered, and roused herself to scold. "Grandpa, you shouldn't have carried so much money. What if someone had stolen it from you?"

Grandpa laughed. "I would've known if anyone tried to take the boots off my feet. The money is what I've saved for a long time—a hundred dollars—for my funeral. But you take it now to buy groceries so that I won't be a burden to you while I am here."

"That won't be necessary, Grandpa," Dad said. "We are honored to have you with us and you will never be a burden. I am only sorry that we never thought to bring you home with us this summer and spare you the **discomfort** of a long trip."

Grandpa was pleased. "Thank you," he answered. "But do not feel bad that you didn't bring me with you for I would not have come then. It was not time." To Grandpa and the Sioux, he once told me, a thing would be done when it was the right time to do it and that's the way it was.

Word Power

discomfort (dis kum´fərt) *n.* the state of being uncomfortable; a bother

Reading Skill
Identifying Assumptions Reread the highlighted sentences. Why does Martin assume his mother feels guilty?

Possible response: He assumes that she feels guilty because she is the only family Grandpa has left.

Connect to the Text
Reread the boxed sentence. Have you ever gone on a trip away from your home? Was it a good or bad experience? Why?

Answers will vary.

Literary Element

Theme Reread the highlighted sentences. The theme of the story is that people should accept their culture and keep it alive. Do you think Martin is ready to accept the fact that he is a Sioux? Why or why not?

Possible response: No.

Martin is embarrassed. He

does not want to wear the

bag and is afraid of what his

friends will think of him.

"Also," Grandpa went on, looking at me, "I have come because it is soon time for Martin to have the medicine bag."

We all knew what that meant. Grandpa thought he was going to die and he had to follow the tradition of his family to pass the medicine bag, along with its history, to the oldest male child.

"Even though the boy," he said still looking at me, "bears a white man's name, the medicine bag will be his."

I didn't know what to say. I had the same hot and cold feeling that I had when I first saw Grandpa in the street. The medicine bag was the dirty leather pouch I had found around his neck. "I could never wear such a thing," I almost said aloud. I thought of having my friends see it in gym class, at the swimming pool, and could imagine the smart things they would say. But I just swallowed hard and took a step toward the bed. I knew I would have to take it.

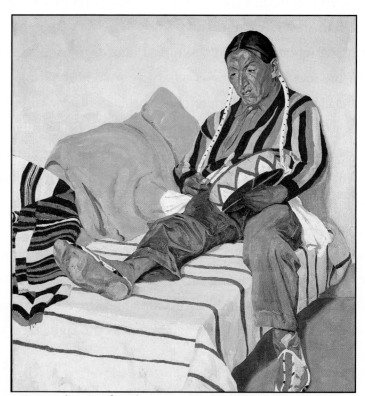

A Singing Indian. W. Ufer. Oil on canvas, 30 x 25¼ in.

What items in this painting represent the man's Native American background? What details about Grandpa reveal his background as a Sioux?

But Grandpa was tired. "Not now, Martin," he said, waving his hand in dismissal, "it is not time. Now I will sleep."

So that's how Grandpa came to be with us for two months. My friends kept asking to come see the old man, but I put them off. I told myself that I didn't want them laughing at Grandpa. But even as I made excuses I knew it wasn't Grandpa that I was afraid they'd laugh at.

Finally, one day after school, my friends came home with me because nothing I said stopped them. "We're going to see the great Indian of Bell View Drive," said Hank, who was supposed to be my best friend.

When we got to my house Grandpa was sitting on the patio. He had on his red shirt, but today he also wore a fringed leather vest that was decorated with beads. Instead of his usual cowboy boots he had beaded moccasins on his feet that stuck out of his black trousers. Of course, he had his old black hat on—he was seldom without it.

I stared just as my friends did and I heard one of them murmur, "Wow!"

Grandpa looked up and when his eyes met mine they twinkled as if he were laughing inside. He nodded to me and my face got all hot. I could tell that he had known all along I was afraid he'd embarrass me in front of my friends.

"*Hau, hoksilas,* boys," he greeted and held out his hand.

"You look fine, Grandpa," I said as the guys sat on the lawn chairs or on the patio floor.

"*Hanh,* yes," he agreed. "When I woke up this morning it seemed the right time to dress in the good clothes. I knew that my grandson would be bringing his friends."

Connect to the Text

Reread the boxed sentences. Martin thinks that he will be embarrassed by bringing his friends to meet his grandfather. Can you understand how he feels? What would you do if you were in this situation?

Answers will vary.

_____

_____

_____

_____

_____

Reading Skill

Identifying Assumptions Reread the highlighted paragraph. Why does Grandpa assume that Martin is afraid of being embarrassed by him? Check the correct response.

☐ Martin tells Grandpa that he doesn't want to wear the medicine bag.

☐ Martin feels badly about the money he found in Grandpa's shoes.

☑ Martin has not invited his friends over to meet Grandpa.

Reading Skill

Question Reread the highlighted sentences. What is the **best** question to ask while reading to understand the relationship between Grandpa and Martin's friends? Check the correct response.

- ☑ Does Grandpa impress Martin's friends?
- ☐ Does Grandpa say any words in Sioux?
- ☐ Why do Martin's friends have to leave?

Background Info

In Sioux tradition, a boy would become a man by going on a journey called a vision quest. His quest would show him his purpose in life. Many cultures have ceremonies to celebrate a child becoming an adult.

Grandpa did most of the talking while my friends were there. I was so proud of him and amazed at how respectfully quiet my buddies were. Mom had to chase them home at supper time. As they left they shook Grandpa's hand again and said to me:

"Martin, he's really great!"

"Can we come back?"

But after they left, Mom said, "No more visitors for a while, Martin. Grandpa won't admit it, but his strength hasn't returned."

That evening Grandpa called me to his room before he went to sleep. "Tomorrow," he said, "when you come home, it will be time to give you the medicine bag."

I felt a hard squeeze from where my heart is supposed to be and was scared, but I answered, "OK, Grandpa."

All night I had weird dreams about thunder and lightning on a high hill. From a distance I heard the slow beat of a drum. When I woke up in the morning I felt as if I hadn't slept at all. At school it seemed as if the day would never end and, when it finally did, I ran home.

Grandpa was in his room, sitting on the bed. "My father in his early manhood," Grandpa began, "made a vision quest to find a spirit guide for his life. You cannot understand how it was in that time, when the great Teton Sioux were first made to stay on the reservation. There was a strong need for guidance from *Wakantanka*, the Great Spirit. But too many of the young men were filled with despair and hatred. But my father held to the old ways.

"He carefully prepared for his quest with a purifying bath and then he went alone to a high butte top to fast and pray. After three days he received his **sacred** dream—in which he found the white man's iron. He did not understand his vision of finding something belonging to the white people, for in that time they were the enemy. When he came down from the butte to cleanse himself at the stream below, he found the remains of a campfire and the broken shell of an iron kettle. This was a sign which reinforced his dream. He took a piece of the iron for his medicine bag, which he had made of elk skin years before.

"He returned to his village, where he told his dream to the wise old men of the tribe. They gave him the name *Iron Shell,* but they did not understand the meaning of the dream. This first Iron Shell kept the piece of iron with him at all times and believed it gave him protection from the evils of those unhappy days.

"Then a terrible thing happened to Iron Shell. He and several other young men were taken from their homes by the soldiers and sent far away to a white man's boarding school. One day it was his turn to work in the school's blacksmith shop. As he walked into the place he knew that his medicine had brought him there to learn and work with the white man's iron.

"Iron Shell became a blacksmith and worked at the trade when he returned to the reservation. All of his life he treasured the medicine bag. When he was old, and I was a man, he gave it to me, for no one made the vision quest any more."

Word Power
sacred (sā′ krid) *adj.* holy; worthy of great respect

My Workspace

English Coach

Sage is a plant that has sweet-smelling leaves. The Sioux think the plant is sacred because of its healing powers. *Sage* can also mean "wise." Underline another word on this page with more than one meaning. Write the word and its definitions below.

Possible response: Right.

Opposite of left and

correct.

Connect to the Text

Reread the boxed paragraph. If you were Martin, how would you feel about wearing the medicine bag? Would you be proud? Why or why not?

Answers will vary.

Grandpa quit talking and I stared in disbelief as he covered his face with his hands. His shoulders were shaking with quiet sobs and I looked away until he began to speak again.

"I kept the bag until my son, your mother's father, was a man and had to leave us to fight in the war across the ocean. I gave him the bag, for I believed it would protect him in battle, but he did not take it with him. He was afraid that he would lose it. He died in a faraway place."

Again Grandpa was still and I felt his grief around me.

"My son," he went on after clearing his throat, "had only a daughter and it is not proper for her to know of these things."

He unbuttoned his shirt, pulled out the leather pouch, and lifted it over his head.

"In the bag," he said as he opened it and removed two objects, "is the broken shell of the iron kettle, a pebble from the butte, and a piece of the sacred sage."

"After the bag is yours you must put a piece of prairie sage within and never open it again until you pass it on to your son." He replaced the pebble and the piece of iron, and tied the bag.

I closed my eyes and waited for him to slip it over my head. But he spoke.

"No, you need not wear it." He placed the soft leather bag in my right hand and closed my other hand over it. "It would not be right to wear it in this time and place where no one will understand. Put it safely away until you are again on the reservation. Wear it then, when you replace the sacred sage."

"Go," he said, "I will sleep now."

"Thank you, Grandpa," I said softly and left with the bag in my hands.

That night Mom and Dad took Grandpa to the hospital. Two weeks later I stood alone on the lonely prairie of the reservation and put the sacred sage in my medicine bag.

Boy on Edge of Chasm, 1993 (detail). Kam Mak. Oil on panels, 14 x 10½ in. Collection of the artist.

What is the attitude of the boy in this painting? How is he like Martin at the end of the story?

Literary Element

Theme Reread the highlighted sentence. When Martin visits the reservation, he does what Grandpa told him to do and puts the sage in the bag. What does this say about Martin?

Possible responses: Martin finally accepts that he is a Sioux. He has become a man.

Respond to Literature

The Medicine Bag

A Comprehension Check

Answer the following questions in the spaces provided.

1. Why does Grandpa come to visit Martin's family?

   He is lonely. He wants to pass on the medicine bag before he dies.

2. How do Cheryl and Martin react when they see their grandfather?

   Cheryl is happy; Martin is embarrassed.

3. What does Grandpa want Martin to do with the medicine bag?

   Grandpa wants Martin to keep it safe and pass it on to his son.

B Reading Skills

Answer the following questions in the spaces provided.

1. **Question** What question can you ask yourself while reading that would help you understand Martin's attitude toward his grandfather?

   Possible response: When Martin sees his Grandpa arrive, why does Martin act ashamed rather than happy?

2. **Identifying Assumptions** What assumptions does Martin make about how his family feels when Grandpa says he is lonesome?

   Possible response: He assumes that his entire family, especially his mother, feels guilty.

3. **Identifying Assumptions** How does Martin assume his friends will respond toward Grandpa? Is he right? How do his friends react to Grandpa?

   Possible responses: He thinks they will laugh. No. Martin's friends are impressed by Grandpa.

C Word Power

Complete each sentence below, using one of the words in the box.

procession	fatigue	reluctantly	descendants
sheepishly	discomfort	sacred	

1. Many people come to pay their respects to the site because they believe
   it is ____sacred____.

2. After running in the marathon race, ____fatigue____ took over
   my body and I slept for nine hours.

3. The school band marched in the ____procession____ down
   Elm Street.

4. It was such a ____discomfort____ to sit in the car for five hours.

5. My sister ____reluctantly____ took the medicine, which tasted awful.

6. There are people who claim to be ____descendants____ of George
   Washington living in the United States today.

7. When I asked my brother if he had seen my backpack, he ____sheepishly____
   admitted that he had taken it.

D Literary Element: Theme

Read the passage below from "The Medicine Bag." As you read, think about what the sentences reveal about the theme of the story that people should respect their culture and try to preserve it. Then answer the questions that follow.

I closed my eyes and waited for him to slip it over my head.[1] But he spoke.[2]

"No, you need not wear it."[3] He placed the soft leather bag in my right hand and closed my other hand over it.[4] "It would not be right to wear it in this time and place where no one will understand.[5] Put it safely away until you are again on the reservation.[6] Wear it then, when you replace the sacred sage."[7]

1. How do sentences 1–5 show that Grandpa knows life is different away from the reservation?

   Possible responses: Grandpa knows that people who do not live on

   the reservation have different ways and beliefs. He knows they will not

   understand if they see Martin wearing the medicine bag.

2. How do sentences 6–7 show that Grandpa expects Martin to carry on the tradition of wearing the medicine bag?

   Possible responses: Grandpa asks Martin to keep the bag safe until he is

   on the reservation. He asks him to replace the sacred sage and wear the

   bag then.

E Journal Entry

Imagine that you are Martin. You keep a journal in which you write about things that have happened and how you feel. Write journal entries describing the day Grandpa gave you the medicine bag and the day you put the sacred sage in the medicine bag.

Tuesday:

Grandpa asked me to see him today. He wanted to give me the medicine bag. I ran home from school. When I entered Grandpa's room, Possible response: Grandpa told me about his father

and the medicine bag. Then he gave me the medicine bag.

I felt Possible response: proud and honored and also a

little scared because he has left me with a big responsibility.

Saturday:

It has been two weeks since Grandpa died. Today, we traveled to the reservation. When we got there, Possible response: I stood on the prairie and

put sacred sage into my medicine bag.

I felt Possible response: like I was doing a good thing. I

understood that I am a Sioux and now a man.

Assessment

Fill in the circle next to each correct answer.

1. Where does Grandpa live?
   - ● A. on a reservation
   - ○ B. in a big city
   - ○ C. in a hospital
   - ○ D. in a village

2. Why does Grandpa assume that he will be a burden on his family?
   - ○ A. He thinks he is going to die in their house.
   - ● B. He knows they will have to take care of him.
   - ○ C. He thinks his old ways will embarrass them.
   - ○ D. He thinks that Martin will have to give up his room.

3. What is the **best** question to ask while reading to understand what happens after Grandpa gives Martin the medicine bag?
   - ○ A. What is inside the bag?
   - ○ B. When does Grandpa die?
   - ● C. What does Martin do after Grandpa dies?
   - ○ D. How does Martin act around his friends?

4. What does the theme of "The Medicine Bag" reveal to us?
   - ○ A. Old things have no value.
   - ○ B. Things always change for the better.
   - ● C. We should be proud of our culture.
   - ○ D. Life is too short.

5. If you had taken a long, difficult trip, what would you feel?
   - ● A. fatigue
   - ○ B. sacred
   - ○ C. sheepishly
   - ○ D. procession

Wrap-up

Compare and Contrast

Theme is an important literary element in "The Treasure of Lemon Brown" and "The Medicine Bag." Although the themes in these two short stories are different, they both are about boys learning an important lesson about what is truly valuable in a person's life. Think about the themes in both stories. Think about what the characters value most. Finally, think about how these values influence the characters and their relationships with others.

In the left and right columns below, write the themes of "The Treasure of Lemon Brown" and "The Medicine Bag." In the middle column, explain what the themes have in common. An example has been provided.

"The Treasure of Lemon Brown"	Alike	"The Medicine Bag"
• The theme is that every person has a treasure and that different things can be treasures to different people.	• Both themes show that how a person lives and what a person respects are the most valuable "treasure" that a person owns. • A treasure or gift doesn't have to be expensive to be valuable. • Every person has something of value they can pass on to future generations.	• The theme is that people should respect their heritage and try to preserve their culture.

UNIT 3 Drama

What's Drama?

Have you ever acted out a scene from your favorite TV show or imitated a conversation to make someone laugh? If so, you were creating a drama.

A **drama,** also called a play, is a story that actors perform—most often on a stage or before a movie camera. A drama can also be read like a story or novel.

Understanding the elements of drama will help you appreciate plays.

- **Stage directions** tell the actors how to speak their lines and where they should move on the stage. They also describe the appearance of the stage. Stage directions are often printed in *italic* type.

- **Acts** divide long plays into shorter sections. **Scenes** break acts into even shorter sections.

- **Dialogue** is the conversation between characters. Most of the story and the personalities of the characters are revealed through dialogue.

Dramas take many forms, from television shows and movies to skits and stage plays. What types of dramas are you familiar with? **Put a check next to the types of dramas you have seen, heard, or performed in.**

_____ television show   _____ stage play

_____ movie   _____ radio play

Why Read Drama?

Dramas can entertain, inform, and inspire. They can give you an understanding of the way people live. Drama, like other kinds of literature, can give you a new view of the world.

How Do I Read Drama?

Focus on a key **literary element** and key **reading skills** to get the most out of reading the drama in this unit. Here are one key literary element and two key reading skills that you will practice in this unit.

Key Literary Element

Characterization

Characterization is the way an author reveals information about characters. Authors may provide direct information by describing a character's appearance and personality. A character's personality can also be revealed through his or her words and actions or through what others think and say about that character.

Key Reading Skills

• Respond

Active readers **respond** to what they are reading. When you stop and consider your thoughts and feelings about something you've read, you are responding. Think about what you've read and how you feel about it. You can ask yourself, "What does this mean to me?" and "How would I act in this situation?" You don't have to answer aloud. But thinking about and answering these questions will help you understand what you have read.

• Sequence

The order in which events occur—first, next, and last—is called **sequence.** Many stories tell events in the order in which they happen. For example, most mysteries begin with a crime and end with its being solved. Some stories tell about events out of order. A story may start in the present and go back to the past. As you read, look for clue, or signal, words like *first, then, meanwhile, after that,* and *later.* These words can help you figure out the sequence in which things happen.

Get Ready to Read!

The Diary of Anne Frank

Frances Goodrich has said that she was amazed by the liveliness of Anne Frank's diary. Inspired by *Anne Frank: The Diary of a Young Girl*, the authors, a husband and wife team, spent two years writing a play about Anne. They met with Anne's father, Otto Frank, and visited the building in which the Franks had hidden. The play, *The Diary of Anne Frank*, was first published in 1956. It has won many awards, including the Pulitzer Prize.

What You Know

Imagine having to hide with your family in a small living space. What are some of the day-to-day difficulties you might face?

Reason to Read

Read *The Diary of Anne Frank* to find out how a young girl deals with having to live in a harsh and dangerous place.

Background Info

During World War II, which lasted from 1939 to 1945, Jews in Europe were forced into hiding to avoid German labor and death camps. Most hiding places were tiny and uncomfortable: a barn, an attic, a basement, or even the space under the floorboards.

Anne Frank was born in Germany in 1929. Her family moved to the country of the Netherlands, which is sometimes called Holland, in the early 1930s. Anne's world changed in 1940, when Germany took control of the Netherlands. Two years later, Anne's family went into hiding on the top floor of the warehouse where her father had run his business. Despite her situation, Anne had many hopes and dreams for herself and a strong desire to be a writer.

When the Franks' hiding place was discovered, Anne and her family were sent to concentration camps. Anne died in a camp in early 1945, a few months before Germany surrendered and the war ended. This play is an adaptation of Anne Frank's diary, which she wrote from June 1942 to July 1944.

Word Power

sparsely (spärs′ lē) *adv.* in an uncrowded or thinly spread way; p. 135
A few trees were *sparsely* placed along the open city street.

compassionate (kəm pash′ ə nit) *adj.* kindhearted; concerned; p. 136
Ms. Smith was very *compassionate* as she comforted the lost child.

emigrated (em′ ə grāt′ id) *v.* left one's country to move to another; moved to another place; p. 137
Osman *emigrated* to the United States because he wanted to live in a democracy.

conspicuous (kən spik′ ū əs) *adj.* easily seen; obvious; p. 139
The scar on my face was quite *conspicuous*, although most people tried to ignore it.

mercurial (mər kyoor′ ē əl) *adj.* moody; quick to change; p. 140
Ginny's *mercurial* temper made the dinner party quite interesting.

interval (in′ tər vəl) *n.* a length of time between events; p. 143
The *interval* between classes is only five minutes, so I have to hurry to be on time.

reassuringly (rē′ ə shoor′ ing lē) *adv.* in a manner that restores confidence; p. 145
"I know you can pass your English test," my mother said *reassuringly*.

loathe (lō<u>th</u>) *v.* to consider with extreme disgust; hate; p. 152
There are many people who *loathe* hot weather, but I enjoy it.

**Answer the following questions, using one of the new words above.
Write your answers in the spaces provided.**

1. Which word goes with "in a way that supports"? _____ reassuringly _____

2. Which word goes with "moved to another country"? _____ emigrated _____

3. Which word goes with "having different moods"? _____ mercurial _____

4. Which word goes with "likely to be seen"? _____ conspicuous _____

5. Which word goes with "in a nearly empty way"? _____ sparsely _____

6. Which word goes with "the time in between"? _____ interval _____

7. Which word goes with "kind and giving"? _____ compassionate _____

8. Which word goes with "extreme dislike"? _____ loathe _____

The Diary of Anne Frank

Frances Goodrich and Albert Hackett

CHARACTERS

MR. FRANK E
MIEP L
MRS. VAN DAAN M
MR. VAN DAAN E
PETER VAN DAAN M

MRS. FRANK L
MARGOT FRANK E
ANNE FRANK M
MR. KRALER L

ACT 1, SCENE 1

[*The scene remains the same throughout the play. It is the top floor of a warehouse and office building in Amsterdam, Holland. The sharply peaked roof of the building is outlined against a sea of other rooftops, stretching away into the distance.* Nearby is the belfry of a church tower, the Westertoren, whose carillon *rings out the hours. Occasionally faint sounds float up from below: the voices of children playing in the street, the tramp of marching feet, a boat whistle from the canal. The three rooms of the top floor and a small attic space above are exposed to our view. The largest of the rooms is in the center, with two small rooms, slightly raised, on either side.*

Comprehension Check

Reread the text boxed in green. Underline the words that tell you where the play takes place.

Background Info

A *carillon* (kar´ ə lon´) is a set of bells sounded by machinery rather than rung by hand.

On the right is a bathroom, out of sight. A narrow steep flight of stairs at the back leads up to the attic. The rooms are **sparsely** furnished with a few chairs, cots, a table or two. The windows are painted over, or covered with makeshift blackout curtains. In the main room there is a sink, a gas ring for cooking and a wood-burning stove for warmth.

The room on the left is hardly more than a closet. There is a skylight in the sloping ceiling. Directly under this room is a small steep stairwell, with steps leading down to a door. This is the only entrance from the building below. When the door is opened we see that it has been concealed on the outer side by a bookcase attached to it.

The curtain rises on an empty stage. It is late afternoon, November, 1945. The rooms are dusty, the curtains in rags. Chairs and tables are overturned. The door at the foot of the small stairwell swings open. MR. FRANK comes up the steps into view. He is a gentle, cultured European in his middle years. There is still a trace of a German accent in his speech.

He stands looking slowly around, making a supreme effort at self-control. He is weak, ill. His clothes are threadbare.

After a second he drops his rucksack on the couch and moves slowly about. He opens the door to one of the smaller rooms, and then abruptly closes it again, turning away. He goes to the window at the back, looking off at the Westertoren as its carillon strikes the hour of six, then he moves restlessly on.

From the street below we hear the sound of a barrel organ and children's voices at play.

Background Info

Blackout curtains were used to hide room lights from enemy bombers during World War II.

Reading Skill

Sequence Reread the highlighted sentences. Clue words, such as *next* and *then*, can help you follow a sequence of events. Underline the clue words that help you picture the order in which Mr. Frank does things.

Word Power

sparsely (spärs´ lē) *adv.* in an uncrowded or thinly spread way

Comprehension Check

Reread the boxed sentences. What does Mr. Frank see that makes him start to cry?

He sees a woman's white

glove on the floor.

Reading Skill

Respond Reread the highlighted text. How would you respond to Mr. Frank if he were saying these words to you?

Possible response: I would

tell him not to be so hard

on himself.

There is a many-colored scarf hanging from a nail. MR. FRANK takes it, putting it around his neck. As he starts back for his rucksack, his eye is caught by something lying on the floor. It is a woman's white glove. He holds it in his hand and suddenly all of his self-control is gone. He breaks down, crying.

We hear footsteps on the stairs. MIEP GIES comes up, looking for MR. FRANK. MIEP is a Dutch girl of about twenty-two. She wears a coat and hat, ready to go home. She is pregnant. Her attitude toward MR. FRANK is protective, **compassionate.***]*

MIEP. Are you all right, Mr. Frank?

MR. FRANK. [*Quickly controlling himself.*] Yes, Miep, yes.

MIEP. Everyone in the office has gone home . . . It's after six. [*Then pleading.*] Don't stay up here, Mr. Frank. What's the use of torturing yourself like this?

MR. FRANK. I've come to say good-bye . . . I'm leaving here, Miep.

MIEP. What do you mean? Where are you going? Where?

MR. FRANK. I don't know yet. I haven't decided.

MIEP. Mr. Frank, you can't leave here! This is your home! Amsterdam is your home. Your business is here, waiting for you . . . You're needed here . . . Now that the war is over, there are things that . . .

MR. FRANK. I can't stay in Amsterdam, Miep. It has too many memories for me. Everywhere there's something . . . the house we lived in . . . the school . . . that street organ playing out there . . . I'm not the person you used to know, Miep. I'm a bitter old man. [*Breaking off.*] Forgive me. I shouldn't speak to you like this . . . after all that you did for us . . . the suffering . . .

MIEP. No. No. It wasn't suffering. You can't say we suffered. [*As she speaks, she straightens a chair which is overturned.*]

Word Power

compassionate (kəm pash´ ə nit) *adj.* kindhearted; concerned

MR. FRANK. I know what you went through, you and Mr. Kraler. I'll remember it as long as I live. [*He gives one last look around.*] Come, Miep.

[*He starts for the steps, then remembers his rucksack, going back to get it.*]

MIEP. [*Hurrying up to a cupboard.*] Mr. Frank, did you see? There are some of your papers here. [*She brings a bundle of papers to him.*] We found them in a heap of rubbish on the floor after... after you left.

MR. FRANK. Burn them.

[*He opens his rucksack to put the glove in it.*]

MIEP. But, Mr. Frank, there are letters, notes...

MR. FRANK. Burn them. All of them.

MIEP. Burn this?

[*She hands him a paperbound notebook.*]

MR. FRANK. [*Quietly.*] Anne's diary. [*He opens the diary and begins to read.*] "Monday, the sixth of July, nineteen forty-two." [*To MIEP.*] Nineteen forty-two. Is it possible, Miep?... Only three years ago. [*As he continues his reading, he sits down on the couch.*] "Dear Diary, since you and I are going to be great friends, I will start by telling you about myself. My name is Anne Frank. I am thirteen years old. I was born in Germany the twelfth of June, nineteen twenty-nine. As my family is Jewish, we **emigrated** to Holland when Hitler came to power."

[*As MR. FRANK reads on, another voice joins his, as if coming from the air. It is ANNE'S VOICE.*]

Connect to the Text

Reread the text boxed in purple. Have you ever kept a diary or journal? Do you think it's helpful to have a diary? Why or why not?

Answers will vary.

Background Info

Adolph Hitler, the head of the Nazi party, became the head of the German government in 1933. Thousands of German Jews left the country because they feared for their safety. The Nazis were also a threat to the people of surrounding countries, including the Netherlands.

Word Power

emigrated (em´ ə grāt´ id) *v.* left one's country to move to another; moved to another place

137

Background Info

Germany began the invasion of the Netherlands on May 10, 1940, and forced the surrender, or capitulation, of the country's army a few days later. Dutch is what the people of the Netherlands are called.

Reading Skill

Sequence Reread the highlighted text. Anne begins to tell the story of what happened to her and her family. Put the events below in the sequence in which they happened. Write 1 next to the first event, 2 next to the second event, and 3 next to the last event.

__2__ Anne's father says they are going into hiding.

__3__ Anne's mother tells her to hurry and get dressed.

__1__ Anne has fun even though she isn't allowed do many things.

MR. FRANK AND ANNE.   "My father started a business, importing spice and herbs. Things went well for us until nineteen forty. Then the war came, and the Dutch capitulation, followed by the arrival of the Germans. Then things got very bad for the Jews."

[*MR. FRANK'S VOICE dies out. ANNE'S VOICE continues alone. The lights dim slowly to darkness. The curtain falls on the scene.*]

Did You Know?

The six-pointed Star of David is a symbol of the religion of Judaism. During World War II, the Nazis ordered Jewish people to wear a yellow Star of David on their clothing at all times. This easily identified them as Jews.

ANNE'S VOICE.   You could not do this and you could not do that. They forced Father out of his business. We had to wear yellow stars. I had to turn in my bike. I couldn't go to a Dutch school any more. I couldn't go to the movies, or ride in an automobile, or even on a streetcar, and a million other things. But somehow we children still managed to have fun. Yesterday Father told me we were going into hiding. Where, he wouldn't say. At five o'clock this morning Mother woke me and told me to hurry and get dressed. I was to put on as many clothes as I could. It would look too suspicious if we walked along carrying suitcases. It wasn't until we were on our way that I learned where we were going. Our hiding place was to be upstairs in the building where Father used to have his business. Three other people were coming in with us . . . the Van Daans and their son Peter . . . Father knew the Van Daans but we had never met them . . .

[*During the last lines the curtain rises on the scene. The lights dim on. ANNE'S VOICE fades out.*]

SCENE 2

[*It is early morning, July, 1942. The rooms are bare, as before, but they are now clean and orderly.*

MR. VAN DAAN, a tall, portly man in his late forties, is in the main room, pacing up and down, nervously smoking a cigarette. His clothes and overcoat are expensive and well cut.

MRS. VAN DAAN sits on the couch, clutching her possessions, a hatbox, bags, etc. She is a pretty woman in her early forties. She wears a fur coat over her other clothes.

PETER VAN DAAN is standing at the window of the room on the right, looking down at the street below. He is a shy, awkward boy of sixteen. He wears a cap, a raincoat, and long Dutch trousers, like "plus fours." At his feet is a black case, a carrier for his cat. The yellow Star of David is **conspicuous** *on all of their clothes.*]

MRS. VAN DAAN. [*Rising, nervous, excited.*] Something's happened to them! I know it!

MR. VAN DAAN. Now, Kerli!

MRS. VAN DAAN. Mr. Frank said they'd be here at seven o'clock. He said . . .

MR. VAN DAAN. They have two miles to walk. You can't expect . . .

MRS. VAN DAAN. They've been picked up. That's what's happened. They've been taken . . .

[*MR. VAN DAAN indicates that he hears someone coming.*]

MR. VAN DAAN. You see?

[*PETER takes up his carrier and his schoolbag, etc., and goes into the main room as MR. FRANK comes up the stairwell from below. MR. FRANK looks much younger now. His movements are brisk, his manner confident. He wears an overcoat and carries his hat and a small cardboard box. He crosses to the VAN DAANS, shaking hands with each of them.*]

Word Power

conspicuous (kən spik′ ū əs) *adj.* easily seen; obvious

My Workspace

Reading Skill

Sequence Reread the highlighted text. Plays do not always show events in the order in which they happen. Which takes place earlier in time, scene 1 or scene 2?

scene 2

Background Info

Dutch trousers are loose pants gathered a few inches below the knees.

Reading Skill

Respond Reread the highlighted line and the rest of the conversation. Mr and Mrs. Van Daan react differently as they wait for the Franks. If you were in their place, would you respond more like Mr. Van Daan or Mrs. Van Daan? Why?

Answers will vary.

Background Info

One branch of the Nazi police force was called the Green Police because its members wore green uniforms.

Literary Element

Characterization Reread the highlighted sentences. We learn about characters by how they are described. Based on this description, what do you learn about Anne?

She is thirteen, emotional,

and curious, and she is a

student.

_____

_____

MR. FRANK. Mrs. Van Daan, Mr. Van Daan, Peter. [*Then, in explanation of their lateness.*] There were too many of the Green Police on the streets... we had to take the long way around.

[*Up the steps come MARGOT FRANK, MRS. FRANK, MIEP (not pregnant now), and MR. KRALER. All of them carry bags, packages, and so forth. The Star of David is conspicuous on all of the FRANKS' clothing. MARGOT is eighteen, beautiful, quiet, shy. MRS. FRANK is a young mother, gently bred, reserved. She, like MR. FRANK, has a slight German accent. MR. KRALER is a Dutchman, dependable, kindly. As MR. KRALER and MIEP go upstage to put down their parcels, MRS. FRANK turns back to call ANNE.*]

MRS. FRANK. Anne?

[*ANNE comes running up the stairs. She is thirteen, quick in her movements, interested in everything,* **mercurial** *in her emotions. She wears a cape, long wool socks and carries a schoolbag.*]

MR. FRANK. [*Introducing them.*] My wife, Edith. Mr. and Mrs. Van Daan [*MRS. FRANK hurries over, shaking hands with them.*] ... their son, Peter ... my daughters, Margot and Anne.

How do you think Anne is feeling at this moment? Why do you think so?

_____

Word Power

mercurial (mər kyoor′ ē əl) *adj.* moody; quick to change

[*ANNE gives a polite little curtsy as she shakes MR. VAN DAAN's hand. Then she immediately starts off on a tour of investigation of her new home, going upstairs to the attic room.*

MIEP and MR. KRALER are putting the various things they have brought on the shelves.]

MR. KRALER. I'm sorry there is still so much confusion.

MR. FRANK. Please. Don't think of it. After all, we'll have plenty of leisure to arrange everything ourselves.

MIEP. [*To MRS. FRANK.*] We put the stores of food you sent in here. Your drugs are here . . . soap, linen here.

MRS. FRANK. Thank you, Miep.

MIEP. I made up the beds . . . the way Mr. Frank and Mr. Kraler said. [*She starts out.*] Forgive me. I have to hurry. I've got to go to the other side of town to get some ration books for you.

MRS. VAN DAAN. Ration books? If they see our names on ration books, they'll know we're here.

MR. KRALER. There isn't anything . . .

MIEP. Don't worry. Your names won't be on them. } *Together* [*As she hurries out.*] I'll be up later.

MR. FRANK. Thank you, Miep.

MRS. FRANK. [*To MR. KRALER.*] It's illegal, then, the ration books? We've never done anything illegal.

MR. FRANK. We won't be living here exactly according to regulations.

[*As MR. KRALER reassures MRS. FRANK, he takes various small things, such as matches, soap, etc., from his pockets, handing them to her.*]

MR. KRALER. This isn't the black market, Mrs. Frank. This is what we call the white market . . . helping all of the hundreds and hundreds who are hiding out in Amsterdam.

Literary Element

Characterization Reread the highlighted sentences. What can you tell about what Miep is like from this text?

Possible response: She is

helpful and kind.

_____

Background Info

Ration books contained coupons that people used to buy a limited amount of food and supplies.

 Stop here for **Break Time** on the next page.

Break Time

As you read *The Diary of Anne Frank,* look for details describing each character. Details make the characters come to life. Complete the chart below to help you imagine and understand the characters in this drama and their behavior. Characters are listed in the left column. In the right column, list details that describe each character. Use information from the story to help you. An example has been provided.

Character	Description
Miep	A young Dutch woman; she is kind; she helps hide the families in the attic.
Mr. Frank	Possible responses: The father of Anne; he is gentle and cultured; he is in charge of the hiding place.
Mr. Van Daan	Possible responses: He is a tall, heavy man in his late forties; he wears expensive clothes.
Mrs. Van Daan	Possible responses: She is a pretty woman, in her early forties; she wears a fur coat.
Peter Van Daan	Possible responses: He is 16 years old, shy, awkward; he has a cat.
Mrs. Frank	Possible responses: She is Anne's mother; young, attractive, well bred, quiet, and reserved.
Margot	Possible responses: She is Anne's older sister; 18 years old; beautiful, quiet, and shy.
Anne	Possible responses: She is 13 years old, lively, energetic; full of curiosity.
Mr. Kraler	Possible responses: He is a Dutchman; kind and dependable; he helps hide the families.

 Continue reading on the next page.

[*The carillon is heard playing the quarterhour before eight. MR. KRALER looks at his watch. ANNE stops at the window as she comes down the stairs.*]

ANNE.   It's the Westertoren!

MR. KRALER.   I must go. I must be out of here and downstairs in the office before the workmen get here. [*He starts for the stairs leading out.*] Miep or I, or both of us, will be up each day to bring you food and news and find out what your needs are. Tomorrow I'll get you a better bolt for the door at the foot of the stairs. It needs a bolt that you can throw yourself and open only at our signal. [*To MR. FRANK.*] Oh . . . You'll tell them about the noise?

MR. FRANK.   I'll tell them.

MR. KRALER.   Good-bye then for the moment. I'll come up again, after the workmen leave.

MR. FRANK.   Good-bye, Mr. Kraler.

MRS. FRANK. [*Shaking his hand.*] How can we thank you? [*The others murmur their good-byes.*]

MR. KRALER.   I never thought I'd live to see the day when a man like Mr. Frank would have to go into hiding. When you think—[*He breaks off, going out. MR. FRANK follows him down the steps, bolting the door after him. In the **interval** before he returns, PETER goes over to MARGOT, shaking hands with her. As MR. FRANK comes back up the steps, MRS. FRANK questions him anxiously.*]

MRS. FRANK.   What did he mean, about the noise?

MR. FRANK.   First let us take off some of these clothes. [*They all start to take off garment after garment. On each of their coats, sweaters, blouses, suits, dresses, is another yellow Star of David. MR. and MRS. FRANK are underdressed quite simply. The others wear several things, sweaters, extra dresses, bathrobes, aprons, nightgowns, etc.*]

Word Power

interval (in´ tər vəl) *n.* a length of time between events

Comprehension Check

Reread the boxed sentences. What will Mr. Kraler do to help the families hiding in the warehouse?

He will bring them food and

news, and make sure that

their hiding place is secure.

_____

_____

Literary Element

Characterization Reread the highlighted line. We can learn about characters by what other characters say about them. What do you learn about Mr. Frank from Mr. Kraler's comment? Check the correct response.
☐ Nobody trusts him.
☑ He is well respected.
☐ He is very wealthy.

Reading Skill

Respond Reread the highlighted text. If you were in hiding with the Franks, how would you feel about having to keep completely quiet all day?

Answers will vary.

_____

_____

_____

_____

Background Info

The abbreviation *w.c.* is short for "water closet," which means a toilet.

English Coach

A *potato paring* is a thin strip of skin from a potato. What is a synonym, or another term that means the same as "potato paring"?

potato peel

MR. VAN DAAN.   It's a wonder we weren't arrested, walking along the streets . . . Petronella with a fur coat in July . . . and that cat of Peter's crying all the way.

ANNE.   [*As she is removing a pair of panties.*] A cat?

MRS. FRANK.   [*Shocked.*] Anne, please!

ANNE.   It's all right. I've got on three more.

[*She pulls off two more. Finally, as they have all removed their surplus clothes, they look to MR. FRANK, waiting for him to speak.*]

MR. FRANK.   Now. About the noise. While the men are in the building below, we must have complete quiet. Every sound can be heard down there, not only in the workrooms, but in the offices too. The men come at about eight-thirty, and leave at about five-thirty. So, to be perfectly safe, from eight in the morning until six in the evening we must move only when it is necessary, and then in stockinged feet. We must not speak above a whisper. We must not run any water. We cannot use the sink, or even, forgive me, the w.c. The pipes go down through the workrooms. It would be heard. No trash . . . [*MR. FRANK stops abruptly as he hears the sound of marching feet from the street below. Everyone is motionless, paralyzed with fear. MR. FRANK goes quietly into the room on the right to look down out of the window. ANNE runs after him, peering out with him. The tramping feet pass without stopping. The tension is relieved. MR. FRANK, followed by ANNE, returns to the main room and resumes his instructions to the group.*] . . . No trash must ever be thrown out which might reveal that someone is living up here . . . not even a potato paring. We must burn everything in the stove at night. This is the way we must live until it is over, if we are to survive.

[*There is silence for a second.*]

MR. FRANK.   Until it is over.

MR. FRANK. [*Reassuringly.*] After six we can move about . . . we can talk and laugh and have our supper and read and play games . . . just as we would at home. [*He looks at his watch.*] And now I think it would be wise if we all went to our rooms, and were settled before eight o'clock. Mrs. Van Daan, you and your husband will be upstairs. I regret that there's no place up there for Peter. But he will be here, near us. This will be our common room, where we'll meet to talk and eat and read, like one family.

MR. VAN DAAN. And where do you and Mrs. Frank sleep?

MR. FRANK. This room is also our bedroom.

MRS. VAN DAAN. That isn't right. We'll sleep here and you take the room upstairs. ⎫
                                    ⎬ *Together*

MR. VAN DAAN. It's your place. ⎭

MR. FRANK. Please. I've thought this out for weeks. It's the best arrangement. The only arrangement.

MRS. VAN DAAN. [*To MR. FRANK.*] Never, never can we thank you. [*Then to MRS. FRANK.*] I don't know what would have happened to us, if it hadn't been for Mr. Frank.

MR. FRANK. You don't know how your husband helped me when I came to this country . . . knowing no one . . . not able to speak the language. I can never repay him for that. [*Going to VAN DAAN.*] May I help you with your things?

MR. VAN DAAN. No. No. [*To MRS. VAN DAAN.*] Come along, liefje.

MRS. VAN DAAN. You'll be all right, Peter? You're not afraid?

PETER. [*Embarrassed.*] Please, Mother.

[*They start up the stairs to the attic room above. MR. FRANK turns to MRS. FRANK.*]

MR. FRANK. You too must have some rest, Edith. You didn't close your eyes last night. Nor you, Margot.

Word Power

reassuringly (rē´ ə shoor´ ing lē) *adv.* in a manner that restores confidence

Connect to the Text

Reread the boxed sentence. How do you spend your time in the evenings? What do you do?

Answers will vary.

_____

_____

_____

_____

Literary Element

Characterization Reread the highlighted text. Peter is embarrassed by his mother's questions. What does this tell you about Peter and his mother?

Possible responses: Peter

feels his mother babies

him. Mrs. Van Daan may be

overly protective of Peter.

He does not like to be

treated this way.

Reading Skill

Respond Reread the highlighted text. Do you think you would sleep well if you were in Anne's situation? Why or why not?

Answers will vary.

_____

_____

_____

_____

_____

English Coach

The word *carrier* is formed from the base word *carry* and the suffix *-er*, which means "a person or thing that does something." What is a person who worries called?

a worrier

ANNE.   I slept, Father. Wasn't that funny? I knew it was the last night in my own bed, and yet I slept soundly.

MR. FRANK.   I'm glad, Anne. Now you'll be able to help me straighten things in here. [*To MRS. FRANK and MARGOT.*] Come with me . . . You and Margot rest in this room for the time being.

[*He picks up their clothes, starting for the room on the right.*]

MRS. FRANK.   You're sure . . . ? I could help . . . And Anne hasn't had her milk . . .

MR. FRANK.   I'll give it to her. [*To ANNE and PETER.*] Anne, Peter . . . it's best that you take off your shoes now, before you forget.

[*He leads the way to the room, followed by MARGOT.*]

MRS. FRANK.   You're sure you're not tired, Anne?

ANNE. I feel fine. I'm going to help Father.

MRS. FRANK. Peter, I'm glad you are to be with us.

PETER. Yes, Mrs. Frank.

[*MRS. FRANK goes to join MR. FRANK and MARGOT. During the following scene MR. FRANK helps MARGOT and MRS. FRANK to hang up their clothes. Then he persuades them both to lie down and rest. The VAN DAANS in their room above settle themselves. In the main room ANNE and PETER remove their shoes. PETER takes his cat out of the carrier.*]

What do the expressions on Anne's and Peter's faces reveal about how they feel toward each other?

_____

ANNE. What's your cat's name?

PETER. Mouschi.

ANNE. Mouschi! Mouschi! Mouschi! [*She picks up the cat, walking away with it. To PETER.*] I love cats. I have one . . . a darling little cat. But they made me leave her behind. I left some food and a note for the neighbors to take care of her . . . I'm going to miss her terribly. What is yours? A him or a her?

PETER. He's a tom. He doesn't like strangers.

[*He takes the cat from her, putting it back in its carrier.*]

ANNE. [*Unabashed.*] Then I'll have to stop being a stranger, won't I? Is he fixed?

PETER. [*Startled.*] Huh?

ANNE. Did you have him fixed?

PETER. No.

ANNE. Oh, you ought to have him fixed—to keep him from— you know, fighting. Where did you go to school?

PETER. Jewish Secondary.

ANNE. But that's where Margot and I go! I never saw you around.

PETER. I used to see you . . . sometimes . . .

ANNE. You did?

PETER. . . . in the school yard. You were always in the middle of a bunch of kids. [*He takes a penknife from his pocket.*]

ANNE. Why didn't you ever come over?

PETER. I'm sort of a lone wolf. [*He starts to rip off his Star of David.*]

ANNE. What are you doing?

PETER. Taking it off.

ANNE. But you can't do that. They'll arrest you if you go out without your star. [*He tosses his knife on the table.*]

PETER. Who's going out?

Reading Skill

Respond Reread the highlighted conversation. Anne is not afraid to say what is on her mind. Would you feel comfortable having a conversation with her? Why or why not?

Answers will vary.

_____

_____

_____

_____

_____

Background Info

Wolves are social animals that tend to live in groups. The term *lone wolf* refers to someone who prefers to be alone.

Connect to the Text

Reread the boxed text. How do you spend your time after school? Do you see your friends like Anne does, or do you spend more time by yourself, like Peter?

Answers will vary.

_____

_____

_____

Reading Skill

Respond Reread the highlighted text. How do you feel about Peter burning his star? If you were Peter, what would you do?

Answers will vary.

_____

_____

_____

_____

_____

ANNE. Why, of course! You're right! Of course we don't need them any more. [*She picks up his knife and starts to take her star off.*] I wonder what our friends will think when we don't show up today?

PETER. I didn't have any dates with anyone.

ANNE. Oh, I did. I had a date with Jopie to go and play ping-pong at her house. Do you know Jopie de Waal?

PETER. No.

ANNE. Jopie's my best friend. I wonder what she'll think when she telephones and there's no answer? . . . Probably she'll go over to the house . . . I wonder what she'll think . . . we left everything as if we'd suddenly been called away . . . breakfast dishes in the sink . . . beds not made . . . [*As she pulls off her star, the cloth underneath shows clearly the color and form of the star.*] Look! It's still there! [*PETER goes over to the stove with his star.*] What're you going to do with yours?

PETER. Burn it.

ANNE. [*She starts to throw hers in, and cannot.*] It's funny, I can't throw mine away. I don't know why.

PETER. You can't throw . . . ? Something they branded you with . . . ? That they made you wear so they could spit on you?

ANNE. I know. I know. But after all, it is the Star of David, isn't it?

[*In the bedroom, right, MARGOT and MRS. FRANK are lying down. MR. FRANK starts quietly out.*]

PETER. Maybe it's different for a girl.

[*MR. FRANK comes into the main room.*]

MR. FRANK. Forgive me, Peter. Now let me see. We must find a bed for your cat. [*He goes to a cupboard.*] I'm glad you brought your cat. Anne was feeling so badly about hers. [*Getting a used small washtub.*] Here we are. Will it be comfortable in that?

PETER.   [*Gathering up his things.*] Thanks.

MR. FRANK.   [*Opening the door of the room on the left.*] And here is your room. But I warn you, Peter, you can't grow any more. Not an inch, or you'll have to sleep with your feet out of the skylight. Are you hungry?

PETER.   No.

MR. FRANK.   We have some bread and butter.

PETER.   No, thank you.

MR. FRANK.   You can have it for luncheon then. And tonight we will have a real supper . . . our first supper together.

PETER.   Thanks. Thanks.

[*He goes into his room. During the following scene he arranges his possessions in his new room.*]

MR. FRANK.   That's a nice boy, Peter.

ANNE.   He's awfully shy, isn't he?

MR. FRANK.   You'll like him, I know.

ANNE.   I certainly hope so, since he's the only boy I'm likely to see for months and months.

[*MR. FRANK sits down, taking off his shoes.*]

MR. FRANK.   Annele, there's a box there. Will you open it?

[*He indicates a carton on the couch. ANNE brings it to the center table. In the street below there is the sound of children playing.*]

ANNE.   [*As she opens the carton.*] You know the way I'm going to think of it here? I'm going to think of it as a boarding house. A very peculiar summer boarding house, like the one that we—[*She breaks off as she pulls out some photographs.*] Father! My movie stars! I was wondering where they were! I was looking for them this morning . . . and Queen Wilhelmina! How wonderful!

Connect to the Text

Reread the boxed paragraph. What gift have you received that made you especially happy? Why did it make you happy?

Answers will vary.

_____

_____

_____

_____

Literary Element

Characterization Reread the highlighted text. Anne finally realizes what it will be like to live in their new home. What does this new understanding tell you about her?

Possible response: It shows

that she is becoming more

serious.

_____

_____

MR. FRANK. There's something more. Go on. Look further.

[*He goes over to the sink, pouring a glass of milk from a thermos bottle.*]

> **ANNE.** [*Pulling out a pasteboard-bound book.*] A diary! [*She throws her arms around her father.*] I've never had a diary. And I've always longed for one. [*She looks around the room.*] Pencil, pencil, pencil, pencil. [*She starts down the stairs.*] I'm going down to the office to get a pencil.

MR. FRANK. Anne! No!

[*He goes after her, catching her by the arm and pulling her back.*]

ANNE. [*Startled.*] But there's no one in the building now.

MR. FRANK. It doesn't matter. I don't want you ever to go beyond that door.

ANNE. [*Sobered.*] Never...? Not even at nighttime, when everyone is gone? Or on Sundays? Can't I go down to listen to the radio?

MR. FRANK. Never. I am sorry, Anneke. It isn't safe. No, you must never go beyond that door.

[*For the first time ANNE realizes what "going into hiding" means.*]

ANNE. I see.

What does this scene tell you about the relationship between Anne and her father?

_____

MR. FRANK.   It'll be hard, I know. But always remember this, Anneke. There are no walls, there are no bolts, no locks that anyone can put on your mind. Miep will bring us books. We will read history, poetry, mythology. [*He gives her the glass of milk.*] Here's your milk. [*With his arm about her, they go over to the couch, sitting down side by side.*] As a matter of fact, between us, Anne, being here has certain advantages for you. For instance, you remember the battle you had with your mother the other day on the subject of overshoes? You said you'd rather die than wear overshoes? But in the end you had to wear them? Well now, you see, for as long as we are here you will never have to wear overshoes! Isn't that good? And the coat that you inherited from Margot, you won't have to wear that any more. And the piano! You won't have to practice on the piano. I tell you, this is going to be a fine life for you!

[*ANNE's panic is gone. PETER appears in the doorway of his room, with a saucer in his hand. He is carrying his cat.*]

PETER.   I...I...I thought I'd better get some water for Mouschi before...

MR. FRANK.   Of course.

[*As he starts toward the sink the carillon begins to chime the hour of eight. He tiptoes to the window at the back and looks down at the street below. He turns to PETER, indicating in pantomime that it is too late. PETER starts back for his room. He steps on a creaking board. The three of them are frozen for a minute in fear. As PETER starts away again, ANNE tiptoes over to him and pours some of the milk from her glass into the saucer for the cat. PETER squats on the floor, putting the milk before the cat. MR. FRANK gives ANNE his fountain pen, and then goes into the room at the right. For a second ANNE watches the cat, then she goes over to the center table, and opens her diary.*]

Literary Element

Characterization Reread the lines highlighted in blue. What does this passage reveal about Mr. Frank's view of the situation? Check the **best** response.

- ☑ He is positive and hopeful.
- ☐ He is scared of facing the truth.
- ☐ He is bitter and has no hope.

Reading Skill

Sequence Reread the text highlighted in green and the rest of the text on the page. Put the following events in the sequence in which they happen. Write 1 next to the first event, 2 next to the second event, and 3 next to the last event.

  2 Peter gives milk to his cat.
  1 The carillon chimes.
  3 Anne opens her diary.

In the room at the right, MRS. FRANK has sat up quickly at the sound of the carillon. MR. FRANK comes in and sits down beside her on the settee, his arm comfortingly around her. Upstairs, in the attic room, MR. and MRS. VAN DAAN have hung their clothes in the closet and are now seated on the iron bed. MRS. VAN DAAN leans back exhausted. MR. VAN DAAN fans her with a newspaper. ANNE starts to write in her diary. The lights dim out, the curtain falls.

In the darkness ANNE'S VOICE comes to us again, faintly at first, and then with growing strength.]

ANNE'S VOICE.   I expect I should be describing what it feels like to go into hiding. But I really don't know yet myself. I only know it's funny never to be able to go outdoors . . . never to breathe fresh air . . . never to run and shout and jump. It's the silence in the nights that frightens me most. Every time I hear a creak in the house, or a step on the street outside, I'm sure they're coming for us. The days aren't so bad. At least we know that Miep and Mr. Kraler are down there below us in the office. Our protectors, we call them. I asked Father what would happen to them if the Nazis found out they were hiding us. Pim said that they would suffer the same fate that we would . . . Imagine! They know this, and yet when they come up here, they're always cheerful and gay as if there were nothing in the world to bother them . . . Friday, the twenty-first of August, nineteen forty-two. Today I'm going to tell you our general news. Mother is unbearable. She insists on treating me like a baby, which I **loathe.** Otherwise things are going better. The weather is . . . [*As ANNE'S voice is fading out, the curtain rises on the scene.*]

Literary Element

Characterization Reread the highlighted text. According to Anne, what are Miep and Mr. Kraler like?

Possible responses: They

are brave; protectors of

families; always cheerful.

_____

_____

_____

Word Power

loathe (lōth) *v.* to consider with extreme disgust; hate

Respond to Literature

The Diary of Anne Frank

A Comprehension Check

Answer the following questions in the spaces provided.

1. In scene 1, what does Miep give Mr. Frank that he does not expect?

   Miep gives him Anne's diary.

2. Why do the Franks and the Van Daans go into hiding?

   The Franks and the Van Daans are Jewish. When the Nazis take over the

   Netherlands, the lives of all Jews are in danger.

B Reading Skills

Answer the following questions in the spaces provided.

1. **Respond** Imagine that you found Anne Frank's diary. Based on the parts of
   the diary included in this play, what would you think of Anne?

   Possible response: Anne is a good person. She is interesting and very aware.

   I would like to have known her.

2. **Sequence** Does scene 1 or 2 take place earlier in time? How are the scenes
   different? When does each scene take place?

   Scene 2 takes place earlier. In scene 1, the rooms are a mess and only Miep

   and Mr. Frank are onstage. In scene 2, the rooms are orderly and filled with

   the Franks, the Van Daans, Miep, and Mr. Kraler. Scene 1 takes place after

   the war, and Scene 2 takes place during the war.

C Word Power

Complete each sentence below, using one of the words in the box.

sparsely	compassionate	emigrated	conspicuous
mercurial	interval	reassuringly	loathe

1. In the 1800s, many people _____emigrated_____ from Europe to the United States.

2. Because Blake's personality is so _____mercurial_____, it's hard to guess what he is going to say next.

3. I absolutely _____loathe_____ brussel sprouts and refuse to eat them.

4. Because the Mojave Desert is a harsh environment in which to live, it is _____sparsely_____ populated.

5. In the long _____interval_____ between her arrival at the doctor's office and the time she saw him, Carmen read an entire book.

6. Mr. Achebe treats stray animals in a very kind and _____compassionate_____ way.

7. "Omar," I said _____reassuringly_____, "you must not forget that you are the best musician in the class."

8. Marla's _____conspicuous_____ purple hair made her stand out in the crowd.

D Literary Element: Characterization

You can learn about characters by how they are described in the text and also by what other characters say about them. Read the two passages below from *The Diary of Anne Frank*. As you read, think about what the sentences reveal about Anne. Then answer the questions that follow.

> *ANNE comes running up the stairs.*[1] *She is thirteen, quick in her movements, interested in everything, mercurial in her emotions.*[2]
>
> **MR. FRANK.** As a matter of fact, between us, Anne, being here has certain advantages for you.[3] For instance, you remember the battle you had with your mother the other day on the subject of overshoes?[4] You said you'd rather die than wear overshoes?[5] But in the end you had to wear them?[6] Well now, you see, for as long as we are here you will never have to wear overshoes![7] Isn't that good?[8]

1. Sentences 1–2 directly describe Anne. What do you learn about Anne from this passage?

   Possible response: Anne is a teenager, full of energy, curious, and lively.

2. Reread sentences 3–8. What do you learn about Anne from Mr. Frank's words?

   Possible response: Anne is stubborn. Anne argues with her mother, but does

   as she is told.

E A Letter to Anne

Imagine that you could write a letter to Anne. Tell her how you might feel if you had to go into hiding the way she did.

Dear Anne,

I think that you were very brave to go into hiding. I can't imagine living in such a small space. Your hiding space had only three small rooms and a tiny attic space. One room was no bigger than a closet.

For me, the most difficult part would be Possible responses: staying quiet all day and not moving; not using the water.

At least you had someone close to your age to talk to. You and Peter could talk about Possible responses: your friends at school and your hopes and dreams; his cat.

Like you, I would be afraid of every sound and creak in the house at night. It is easy to imagine Possible response: someone coming up the stairs and discovering your hiding place.

I think that if I were in your situation, I would feel Possible responses: frightened; sad; nervous.

I really admire you because Possible response: you handled such a difficult situation so well.

I am so glad your father kept your diary. Your words Possible response: are an inspiration to the entire world.

Sincerely,

_____

Assessment

Fill in the circle next to each correct answer.

1. Where do the Franks and the Van Daans hide?
   - ○ A. in the shed of the Franks' house
   - ○ B. in the basement of Miep's house
   - ● C. in the space above a warehouse
   - ○ D. in a barn near a church

2. Who gives Anne a diary?
   - ○ A. Mrs. Frank
   - ● B. Mr. Frank
   - ○ C. Peter Van Daan
   - ○ D. Miep

3. When does each scene in the selection take place?
   - ○ A. Scene 1 takes place at the beginning of the war, and scene 2 takes place one month later.
   - ○ B. Scene 1 takes place at the beginning of the war, and scene 2 takes place at the end of the war.
   - ○ C. Scene 1 takes place before the war starts, and scene 2 takes place at the beginning of the war.
   - ● D. Scene 1 takes place after the war, and scene 2 takes place three years earlier.

4. Which of the following words **best** describe Anne's character?
   - ● A. lively and emotional
   - ○ B. quiet and polite
   - ○ C. frightened and nervous
   - ○ D. shy and sensitive

5. Which of the following words means "obvious or visible"?
   - ○ A. compassionate
   - ○ B. sparsely
   - ● C. conspicuous
   - ○ D. loathe

UNIT 4

Folktale and Myth

What's a Folktale? What's a Myth?

Long before superheroes and animated troublemakers began entertaining people in comic books and movies, people amused themselves by telling stories. Stories were passed from generation to generation, helping to keep ideas and customs alive. Many of these stories are in the form of folktales and myths.

A **folktale** is a traditional story that entertains, amazes, or explains something. Many folktales are about larger-than-life characters, or animals that act like humans.

A **myth** is a story handed down from an ancient culture. Myths explain events in nature or the beliefs and customs of a people. Mythical characters include gods and goddesses, magical creatures, and heroes.

You probably have read a folktale or myth that included one of the following things. Circle one that you know about. Write the title of a folktale or myth it describes. For example, you might circle "talking animals" and write "The Three Little Pigs."

talking animals   people tricking others or getting tricked

a test of love   the wise against the unwise

three wishes

Answers will vary.

Why Read Folktales and Myths?

You can read a folktale or myth to enjoy a good story. But folktales and myths provide more than entertainment. They often include a lesson or an explanation of something in the world. Through these stories, readers learn about the values and concerns of different cultures.

How Do I Read Folktales and Myths?

Focus on key **literary elements** and **reading skills** to get the most out of reading the folktales and myths in this unit. Here are two key literary elements and two key reading skills that you will practice in this unit.

Key Literary Elements

• Tone = *word choices*

Tone is the attitude taken by a writer toward the subject. The tone can vary from gloomy and ominous to cheerful and hopeful. To identify the tone, look at the writer's word choices. For example, the writer might describe a dark forest as lush and magical or as eerie and menacing. The first description has an admiring tone. The second has a fearful tone.

• Symbol

A **symbol** is an object, person, place, or experience that also stands for something else. Symbols can stand for big ideas, like love, wealth, and death. A tree might be a symbol for life. A flowing river might be a symbol for time passing. Symbols can add an extra layer of meaning to a story.

Key Reading Skills

• Visualize

When you picture in your mind what you are reading, you are **visualizing.** As you read, visualize the characters and events in your mind. Use the details and exact words in the story to help you create mental pictures. For example, the writer might include a description of the wrinkles on an old person's face. Also use your own experiences to help you understand as well as imagine the scene.

• Infer

When you **infer,** you are making an educated guess about information that is not directly stated in what you are reading. A good reader connects his or her own knowledge with details in the story to figure out what the writer is hinting at. You must "read between the lines" to figure it out. For example, if a character says that he is the best in his class, you can infer that he is proud of himself.

Get Ready to Read!

The Wise Old Woman

Meet Yoshiko Uchida

Yoshiko Uchida (yō shē´ kō ū´ chē dä) was born in California in 1921. Uchida liked to write retellings of old Japanese folktales. She hoped that the folktales would teach young Americans about Japanese culture. She also liked to retell folktales to inspire in children a "love of fun and a good story." Yoshiko Uchida died in 1992. "The Wise Old Woman" was first published in 1965.

What You Know

The number three often appears in folktales. What folktales or stories do you know that have three main characters, wishes, or tasks? With a partner, make a list of the tales and stories. Tell how three comes up in each story. Share your list with the class.

Reason to Read

Read this folktale to learn what happens when a village faces three difficult challenges.

Background Info

Folktales are popular all over the world. They often follow a similar pattern. They begin with a dreamlike "once upon a time" or "in a land far away." Then listeners or readers are carried away by the magical events of the story. There are usually three wishes, characters, or tasks in the tale. The main characters often are opposites of each other, with one being very, very good and the other being terribly evil. The evil characters are punished or they change for the better. The good characters are rewarded. In the end, everyone lives "happily ever after."

Word Power

arrogant (ar´ə gənt) *adj.* full of undeserved pride; p. 162
Amanda is *arrogant* because she thinks she is the best student in the class.

banished (ban´ishd) *v.* forced to leave a country or a community; p. 162
After the man was caught setting fires, he was *banished* from town.

commotion (kə mō´shən) *n.* noise and confusion; a noisy uproar; p. 164
Because of the car accident, there was a big *commotion* in the street.

conquer (kong´kər) *v.* to take over, usually by force; p. 164
Napoleon said he was going to *conquer* all of Europe and take over the world.

commended (kə men´did) *v.* gave approval of; gave praise; p. 167
My teacher *commended* me for writing such a beautiful poem.

**Answer the following questions that contain the new words above.
Write your answers in the spaces provided.**

1. Did Alexander the Great *conquer* his enemies by avoiding them or by fighting them?

   _____ by fighting them _____

2. If you are *commended*, did you do a good job or a bad job? _____ a good job _____

3. Would a *commotion* be silent and orderly or loud and full of chaos?

   _____ loud and full of chaos _____

4. What kind of a student would be *banished* from the cafeteria, one who is

   well-behaved or one who causes trouble? _____ one who causes trouble _____

5. Would someone *arrogant* brag or be humble? _____ brag _____

Adapted from

The Wise Old Woman

Yoshiko Uchida

Background Info

Japan used to have a government run by an emperor. Each village also had its own ruler, called a *lord*, who owned the land and made the laws. The people who lived in the village worked for the lord.

Many long years ago, there lived an **arrogant** and cruel young lord who ruled over a small village in Japan. "I have no use for old people in my village," he said. "They are neither useful nor able to work for a living. Therefore anyone over seventy-one must be **banished** from the village and left in the mountains to die."

"What a cruel and unreasonable lord we have," the people of the village murmured. But the lord punished anyone who disobeyed him, and so villagers who turned seventy-one were tearfully carried into the mountains, never to return.

Gradually there were fewer and fewer old people in the village and soon they disappeared altogether. Then the young lord was pleased.

"What a fine village of young, healthy and hardworking people I have," he bragged. "Soon it will be the finest village in all of Japan."

Now there lived in this village a kind young farmer and his aged mother. They were poor, but the farmer was good to his mother, and the two of them lived happily together. However, as the years went by, the mother grew older, and before long she reached the terrible age of seventy-one.

Word Power
arrogant (ar′ ə gənt) *adj.* full of undeserved pride
banished (ban′ ishd) *v.* forced to leave a country or a community

"If only I could somehow fool the cruel lord," the farmer thought. But there were records in the village books and everyone knew that his mother had turned seventy-one.

Each day the son put off telling his mother that he must take her into the mountains to die, but the people of the village began to talk. The farmer knew that if he did not take his mother away soon, the lord would send his soldiers and throw them both into a dark dungeon to die.

"Mother—" he would begin, as he tried to tell her what he must do, but he could not go on.

Then one day the mother herself spoke. "Well, my son," she said, "the time has come for you to take me to the mountains. We must hurry before the lord sends his soldiers for you." And she did not seem worried at all that she must go to the mountains to die.

"Forgive me, dear mother, for what I must do," the farmer said sadly, and the next morning he lifted his mother to his shoulders and set off toward the mountains. Up and up he climbed, until the trees clustered close and the path was gone. There was no longer even the sound of birds. The son walked slowly, for he could not bear to think of leaving his old mother in the mountains. On and on he climbed, not wanting to stop and leave her behind. Soon, he heard his mother breaking off small twigs from the trees that they passed.

"Mother, what are you doing?" he asked.

"Do not worry, my son," she answered gently. "I am just marking the way so you will not get lost returning to the village."

The son stopped. "Even now you are thinking of me?" he asked.

The mother nodded. "Of course, my son," she replied. "You will always be in my thoughts. How could it be otherwise?"

At that, the young farmer could bear it no longer. "Mother, I cannot leave you in the mountains to die all alone," he said. "We are going home and no matter what the lord does to punish me, I will never leave you again."

Connect to the Text

Reread the boxed sentences. The son must take his mother to the mountains. How would you feel if you had to send your mother away? Write words to describe your emotions.

Possible responses: sad, filled with grief, torn, guilty

Reading Skill

Visualize Reread the highlighted sentences. When the son carries his mother up the mountain, what do you think his face looks like?

Possible response: The son's eyes are sad, he may be crying.

Reading Skill

Infer Reread the sentence highlighted in green. Do you think Lord Higa believes the village will be able to make one thousand ropes of ash? Why does he ask for this?

Possible response: No. He

gives them an impossible

task so he can conquer their

village.

Literary Element

Tone Reread the paragraph highlighted in blue. First the young lord asks his wise men for help. Then he yells at them and calls them fools. What is the tone of this passage? Check the correct response.

☐ humorous
☐ eerie
☑ tense

So they waited until the sun had set and a lone star crept into the silent sky. Then in the dark shadows of night, the farmer carried his mother down the hill and they returned quietly to their little house. The farmer dug a deep hole in the floor of his kitchen and made a small room where he could hide his mother. From that day, she spent all her time in the secret room and the farmer carried meals to her there. The rest of the time, he was careful to work in the fields and act as though he lived alone. In this way, for almost two years, he kept his mother safely hidden and no one in the village knew that she was there.

Then one day there was a terrible **commotion** among the villagers for Lord Higa of the town beyond the hills threatened to **conquer** their village and make it his own.

"Only one thing can spare you," Lord Higa announced. "Bring me a box containing one thousand ropes of ash and I will spare your village."

The cruel young lord quickly gathered together all the wise men of his village. "You are men of wisdom," he said.

"Surely you can tell me how to meet Lord Higa's demands so our village can be spared."

But the wise men shook their heads. "It is impossible to make even one rope of ash, sire," they answered. "How can we ever make one thousand?"

"Fools!" the lord cried angrily. "What good is your wisdom if you cannot help me now?"

And he posted a notice in the village square offering a great reward of gold to any villager who could help him save their village.

But all the people in the village whispered, "Surely, it is an impossible thing, for ash crumbles at the touch of the finger. How could anyone ever make a rope of ash?" They shook their heads and sighed, "Alas, alas, we must be conquered by yet another cruel lord."

Word Power

commotion (kə mō′ shən) *n.* noise and confusion; a noisy uproar
conquer (kong′ kər) *v.* to take over, usually by force

The young farmer wondered what would happen to his mother if a new lord even more terrible than their own came to rule over them.

When his mother saw the troubled look on his face, she asked, "Why are you so worried, my son?"

So the farmer told her of the impossible demand made by Lord Higa. But his mother did not seem troubled at all. Instead she laughed softly and said, "Why, that is not such an impossible task. All one has to do is soak ordinary rope in salt water and dry it well. When it is burned, it will hold its shape and there is your rope of ash! Tell the villagers to hurry and find one thousand pieces of rope."

The farmer shook his head in amazement. "Mother, you are wonderfully wise," he said, and he rushed to tell the young lord what he must do.

"You are wiser than all the wise men of the village," the lord said when he heard the farmer's solution, and he rewarded him with many pieces of gold. The thousand ropes of ash were quickly made and the village was spared.

In a few days, however, there was another great commotion in the village as Lord Higa sent another threat. This time he sent a log with a small hole that curved and bent seven times through. And he demanded that a single piece of thread be threaded through the hole. "If you cannot perform this task," the lord threatened, "I shall come to conquer your village."

Reading Skill

Infer Reread the highlighted sentences. The mother does not think the request is impossible. What can you infer about the mother from this passage?

Possible response: She is

wise and knows more than

the other villagers.

Comprehension Check

Reread the boxed sentences. Lord Higa has given the villagers a second task. What does he want the villagers to do?

Weave a piece of thread

through a twisting hole in

a log.

Connect to the Text

Reread the boxed paragraph. Have you ever encountered a problem that seemed difficult to solve? What did you do? Was the problem solved?

Answers will vary.

_____

_____

_____

_____

> The young lord hurried once more to his wise men, but they all shook their heads in confusion. "A needle cannot bend its way through such curves," they moaned. "Again we are faced with an impossible demand."

"And again you are stupid fools!" the lord said, stamping his foot. He then posted a second notice in the village square asking the villagers for their help.

Once more the young farmer hurried with the problem to his mother in her secret room.

"Why, that is not so difficult," his mother said with a quick smile. "Put some sugar at one end of the hole. Then, tie an ant to a piece of thread and put it in at the other end. He will weave his way in and out of the curves to get to the sugar and he will take the thread with him."

Standing Beauty, 1851. Ando Hiroshige. Hanging scroll, ink and color on paper, 91.5 x 27.7 cm. The British Museum, London.

Notice the way the woman is standing and her expression. What might she have in common with the old woman in this story?

"Mother, you are remarkable!" the son cried, and he hurried off to the lord with the solution to the second problem.

Once more the lord **commended** the young farmer and rewarded him with many pieces of gold. "You are a brilliant man and you have saved our village again," he said.

But the lord's troubles were not over even then, for a few days later Lord Higa sent still another demand. "This time you will fail and then I shall conquer your village," he threatened. "Bring me a drum that sounds without being beaten."

"But that is not possible," sighed the people of the village. "How can anyone make a drum sound without beating it?"

This time the wise men held their heads in their hands and moaned, "It is hopeless. It is hopeless. This time Lord Higa will conquer us all."

The young farmer hurried home breathlessly. "Mother, Mother, we must solve another terrible problem or Lord Higa will conquer our village!" And he quickly told his mother about the impossible drum.

His mother, however, smiled and answered, "Why, this is the easiest of them all. Make a drum with sides of paper and put a bumblebee inside. As it tries to escape, it will buzz and beat itself against the paper and you will have a drum that sounds without being beaten."

The young farmer was amazed at his mother's wisdom. "You are far wiser than any of the wise men of the village," he said, and he hurried to tell the young lord how to meet Lord Higa's third demand.

When the lord heard the answer, he was greatly impressed. "Surely a young man like you cannot be wiser than all my wise men," he said. "Tell me honestly, who has helped you solve all these difficult problems?"

Word Power

commended (kə men′ did) v. gave approval of; gave praise

English Coach

Characters in folktales are often extremely good or extremely bad. One word used to describe a good character in this story is *remarkable*. Underline another word in the next paragraph that describes a good person.

Reading Skill

Visualize Reread the highlighted paragraph. The mother describes a drum that will beat on its own. What do you imagine a drum with a bumblebee inside looks like? Draw a picture of it below.

Your Sketch

English Coach

The term *law of the land* originally referred to the laws of a kingdom. Today, one example of the law of the land is our constitution. In the case of our constitution, what does the word *land* mean?

our country, the United

States

Literary Element

Tone Reread the highlighted sentences. The story ends with the young lord respecting old people and Lord Higa allowing the village to live in peace. What is the tone at the end of the story?

Possible response: The tone

is happy and hopeful.

The young farmer could not lie. "My lord," he began slowly, "for the past two years I have broken the law of the land. I have kept my aged mother hidden beneath the floor of my house. She solved each of your problems and saved the village from Lord Higa."

He trembled as he spoke, for he feared the lord's rage. Surely now the soldiers would be called to throw him into the dark dungeon. But when he glanced at the lord, he saw that the young ruler was not angry at all. Instead, he was silent and thoughtful, for at last he realized how much wisdom and knowledge old people possess.

"I have been very wrong," he said finally. "And I must ask the forgiveness of your mother and of all my people. Never again will I demand that the old people of our village be sent to the mountains to die. Instead, they will be treated with the respect and honor they deserve and share with us the wisdom of their years."

And so it was. From that day, the villagers were no longer forced to take their parents to the mountains. The village became once more a happy, cheerful place to live. The terrible Lord Higa stopped sending his impossible demands and no longer threatened to conquer them, for he too was impressed. "Even in such a small village there is much wisdom," he declared, "and its people should be allowed to live in peace."

And that is exactly what the farmer and his mother and all the people of the village did for all the years thereafter.

Respond to Literature

The Wise Old Woman

A Comprehension Check

Answer the following questions in the spaces provided.

1. What does the young lord decide to do at the beginning of this folktale?

   He decides to banish all of the old people from the village.

2. What three tasks does Lord Higa demand from the village?

   Lord Higa demands that the village make one thousand ropes of ash, weave
   a thread through a twisting hole in a log, and make a drum that sounds
   without beating it.

B Reading Skills

Answer the following questions in the spaces provided.

1. **Visualize** Picture in your mind what the village looks like. What are three
   features in the village? Possible response: mountains, village square, farms

2. **Infer** What can you infer about the young farmer when he decides to hide
   his mother? Possible response: He loves his mother so much that he risks
   punishment to save her.

3. **Infer** When the young lord admits his mistake, what can you infer about
   him? Possible response: He is strong and humble enough to admit his
   mistakes.

C Word Power

Complete each sentence below, using one of the words in the box.

> arrogant   banished
> commotion   conquer   commended

1. Lisa was ___commended___ for getting good grades on her report card.

2. After the big ___commotion___ in the hallway, the teachers told the students to go back to their classes.

3. The queen was so ___arrogant___ she thought she was the fairest in the kingdom.

4. The leader's plan was to ___conquer___ all his neighbors so he would rule the entire land.

5. Some fans were ___banished___ from the game after they threw tomatoes.

Circle the word that best completes each sentence.

6. The president was too (commended, **arrogant**) to be a good leader.

7. Fireworks during the parade always cause a huge (**commotion**, conquer).

8. The general (banished, **commended**) his troops for their bravery.

9. The large country wanted to (**conquer**, arrogant) the small island.

10. A long time ago, villages (commotion, **banished**) thieves to the forest.

D Literary Element: Tone

Read the passage below from "The Wise Old Woman." As you read, think about the tone the writer creates. Then answer the questions that follow.

> This time the wise men held their heads in their hands and moaned, "It is hopeless.[1] It is hopeless.[2] This time Lord Higa will conquer us all."[3]
>
> The young farmer hurried home breathlessly.[4] "Mother, Mother, we must solve another terrible problem or Lord Higa will conquer our village!"[5] And he quickly told his mother about the impossible drum.[6]
>
> His mother, however, smiled and answered, "Why, this is the easiest of them all.[7] Make a drum with sides of paper and put a bumblebee inside."[8]

1. What do the characters say in sentences 1–6 to show that the tone of the story at this point is serious and tense? Possible responses:

   The wise men say they feel hopeless. The young farmer tells his mother

   that the village will be conquered if they don't solve the problem.

   _____

   _____

2. Reread sentences 7–8. How do the wise woman's words change the tone in the story? Possible response: The story becomes calmer and happier when

   she smiles and says this task is the easiest of all.

   _____

   _____

   _____

A Newspaper Article

Imagine that you are writing a newspaper article about the events from this tale. You want readers who do not live in the village to be able to picture what happened. You talk to both the young farmer and the wise old woman. Now make their story come alive for your readers.

Headline: Answers will vary.

Last week, a village was in trouble. An evil lord planned to conquer the village unless his demands were met. But a wise old woman saved the day.

The old woman and her son lived in Possible response: a house with a

secret room to hide the woman.

The old woman had a solution for each of the lord's demands. Her solution for making ropes of ash was to soak the ropes in salt water, dry

them well, and burn them.

Her solution for threading a hole in a log was to put sugar at one end of

the hole and tie a thread to an ant.

She said the last problem was the easiest. These are her instructions for making a drum that sounds without beating it: Make a drum with paper

sides and put a bee in it.

In the end, Possible response: the lord did not attack and all the villagers

were left in peace.

Assessment

Fill in the circle next to each correct answer.

1. What reason does the young lord give for banishing the old people in the village?
   - ○ A. He says they remind him of his cruel parents.
   - ○ B. He says young people will make the village richer.
   - ○ C. He says they are too wise and hardworking.
   - ● D. He says they are useless and cannot work.

2. Why does the farmer disobey the young lord's rule?
   - ○ A. His mother tells him the law is foolish.
   - ● B. He is too caring and can't leave his mother to die.
   - ○ C. He has never liked the young lord.
   - ○ D. He does not think anything will happen if he disobeys.

3. Which phrase from the story describes the hiding place of the wise old woman?
   - ● A. a deep hole in the floor of his kitchen
   - ○ B. the finest village in all of Japan
   - ○ C. a log with a small hole
   - ○ D. a box containing one thousand ropes

4. At the very end of the folktale, what is the tone?
   - ○ A. scary
   - ○ B. sad
   - ● C. happy
   - ○ D. funny

5. Which of the following words means "full of undeserved pride"?
   - ○ A. commotion
   - ○ B. banished
   - ○ C. conquer
   - ● D. arrogant

Get Ready to Read!

Racing *the* Great Bear

Meet
Joseph Bruchac

Joseph Bruchac (brōō´ shak) was born in 1942. As a member of the Abenaki tribe, he has drawn on his own life and Native American legends for many of his books. He writes, "One of the reasons I have devoted so much of my own life to the understanding and the respectful telling of traditional Native stories is my strong belief that now, more than ever, these tales have much to teach us." "Racing the Great Bear" was first published in 1993.

What You Know

How do people become leaders? Should leaders be intelligent, determined, caring, and brave? As a class, make a list of qualities that make some men and women stand out as leaders.

Reason to Read

Read "Racing the Great Bear" to learn about how a boy becomes a leader.

Background Info

When early Europeans came to the Americas, the Iroquois (ir´ ə kwoi´) Indians were living in what is today the northeastern United States. Around 1570, the Iroquois formed the Iroquois Confederacy, or League of Five Nations. It united the Mohawk (mō´ hôk), Oneida (ō nī´ də), Onondaga (on´ ən dô´ ga), Cayuga (kā ū´ gə), and Seneca (sen´ ə kə) nations. When the United States was founded, the Iroquois Confederacy served as a model for the new country's government and constitution. The Confederacy is also known as the Great Peace.

Word Power

clan (klan) *n.* a group of families that have a common ancestor; p. 177
The Moreno *clan* can trace their roots back to the Aztecs.

keen (kēn) *adj.* highly sensitive; sharp; p. 179
The firefighter's *keen* instincts helped determine the cause of the blaze.

pursue (pər sōo′) *v.* to chase; to seek; p. 182
The screaming fans will *pursue* the rock star if his destination is revealed.

spare (spār) *v.* to treat with mercy; to hold back from harming or injuring; p. 184
To *spare* her from the pain, the dentist gave Lin some laughing gas.

sinewy (sin′ ū ē) *adj.* physically tough or powerful; p. 184
After lifting weights for several months, John was beginning to look *sinewy*.

embraced (em brāsd′) *v.* hugged or held in the arms; p. 186
Tyrone *embraced* his lost puppy and said he would never let him out of his sight again.

**Answer the following questions, using one of the new words above.
Write your answers in the spaces provided.**

1. Which word goes with "to not hurt"? _____ spare _____

2. Which word goes with "a large group of people who are related"? _____ clan _____

3. Which word goes with "to hunt or follow"? _____ pursue _____

4. Which word goes with "very aware"? _____ keen _____

5. Which word goes with "held someone tightly"? _____ embraced _____

6. Which word goes with "mighty and strong"? _____ sinewy _____

Racing the Great Bear

Retold by Joseph Bruchac

Background Info

A *longhouse* is the traditional dwelling of the Iroquois people. Each longhouse would serve as the home for an extended family.

Literary Element

Tone Reread the highlighted text. The tone of a passage or story shows how the author feels about what he or she is writing about. What is the tone of this passage? Check the correct response.

- ☑ The tone is serious. The author believes the Great Peace is important.
- ☐ The tone is lighthearted. The author thinks the Great Peace is funny.
- ☐ The tone is scary. The author thinks the Great Peace is dangerous.

NE ONENDJI. Hear my story, which happened long ago. For many generations, the five nations of the Haudenosaunee, the People of the Longhouse, had been at war with one another. No one could say how the wars began, but each time a man of one nation was killed, his relatives sought revenge in the blood feud, and so the fighting continued. Then the Creator took pity on his people and sent a messenger of peace. The Peacemaker traveled from nation to nation, convincing the people of the Five Nations—the Mohawk, the Oneida, the Onondaga, the Cayuga, and the Seneca—that it was wrong for brothers to kill one another. It was not easy, but finally the nations agreed and the Great Peace began. Most welcomed that peace, though there were some beings with bad hearts who wished to see the return of war.

One day, not long after the Great Peace had been established, some young men in a Seneca village decided they would pay a visit to the Onondaga people.

"It is safe now to walk the trail between our nations," the young men said. "We will return after the sun has risen and set seven times."

Then they set out. They walked toward the east until they were lost from sight in the hills. But many more than seven days passed, and those young men never returned. Now another group of young men left, wanting to find out where their friends had gone. They, too, did not return.

The people grew worried. Parties were sent out to look for the vanished young men, but no sign was found. And the searchers who went too far into the hills did not return, either.

The old chief of the village thought long and hard. He asked the **clan** mothers, those wise women whose job it was to choose the chiefs and give them good advice, what should be done.

"We must find someone brave enough to face whatever danger is out there," the clan mothers said.

So the old chief called the whole village to a council meeting. He held up a white strand of wampum beads made from quahog clamshells as he spoke.

"Hear me," he said. "I am of two minds about what has happened to our people. It may be that the Onondaga have broken the peace and captured them. It may be there is something with an evil mind that wishes to destroy this new peace and so has killed our people. Now someone must go and find out. Who is brave enough? Who will come and take this wampum from my hand?"

Many men were gathered in that council. Some were known to speak of themselves as brave warriors. Still, though they muttered to one another, no man stepped forward to take the strand of wampum. The old chief began to walk about the circle, holding the wampum in front of each man in turn. But each man only lowered his eyes to the ground. No man lifted his hand to take the wampum.

Did You Know?

Wampum is a shortened form of the word *wampumpeag*, or *wampumpeake*, which means "a string of white shell beads." These small, polished beads were used to decorate headbands, belts, collars, and necklaces. They were used to record history and in ceremonies.

. . . .

Word Power

clan (klan) *n.* a group of families that have a common ancestor

Comprehension Check

Reread the boxed paragraph. To whom does the chief go for advice? Why?

He goes to the clan

mothers for advice. These

women are wise, and it

is their job to give good

advice.

Reading Skill

Infer Reread the highlighted sentences. What can you infer about why the warriors are behaving this way?

Possible response: They

lower their eyes and don't

take the wampum because

they are scared of what

might have caused the men

to disappear and they are

ashamed of being afraid.

Reading Skill

Visualize Reread the highlighted sentences. Think about how the details help you picture what Swift Runner looks like. Draw a picture of Swift Runner in the box below.

Your Sketch

Connect to the Text

Reread the boxed paragraph. Think of a time when you accepted a challenge. What made you decide to face it? How did you feel?

Answers will vary.

_____

_____

_____

_____

_____

Just outside the circle stood a boy who had not yet become a man. His parents were dead, and he lived with his grandmother in her old lodge at the edge of the village. His clothing was always torn and his face dirty because his grandmother was too old to care for him as a mother would. The other young men made fun of him, and as a joke they called him Swift Runner—even though no one had ever seen him run and it was thought that he was weak and lazy. All he ever seemed to do was play with his little dog or sit by the fire and listen when the old people were talking.

"Our chief has forgotten our greatest warrior," one of the young men said to another, tilting his head toward Swift Runner.

"*Nyoh*," the other young man said, laughing. "Yes. Why does he not offer the wampum to Swift Runner?"

The chief looked around the circle of men, and the laughing stopped. He walked out of the circle to the place where the small boy in torn clothes stood. He held out the wampum and Swift Runner took it without hesitating.

"I accept this," Swift Runner said. "It is right that I be the one to face the danger. In the eyes of the people I am worthless, so if I do not return, it will not matter. I will leave when the sun rises tomorrow."

When Swift Runner arrived home at his grandmother's lodge, the old woman was waiting for him.

"Grandson," she said, "I know what you have done. The people of this village no longer remember, but your father was a great warrior. Our family is a family that has power."

Then she reached up into the rafters and took down a heavy bow. It was blackened with smoke and seemed so thick that no man could bend it.

"If you can string this bow, Grandson," the old woman said, "you are ready to face whatever waits for you on the trail."

Swift Runner took the bow. It was as thick as a man's wrist, but he bent it with ease and strung it.

"Wah-hah!" said his grandmother. "You are the one I knew you would grow up to be. Now you must sleep. At dawn we will make you ready for your journey."

It was not easy for Swift Runner to sleep, but when he woke the next morning, he felt strong and clearheaded. His grandmother was sitting by the fire with a cap in her hand.

"This was your grandfather's cap," she said. "I have sewed four hummingbird feathers on it. It will make your feet more swift."

Swift Runner took the cap and placed it on his head.

His grandmother held up four pairs of moccasins.

"Carry these tied to your waist. When one pair wears out, throw them aside and put on the next pair."

Swift Runner took the moccasins and tied them to his belt.

Next his grandmother picked up a small pouch. "In this pouch is cornmeal mixed with maple sugar," she said. "It is the only food you will need as you travel. It will give you strength when you eat it each evening."

Swift Runner took the pouch and hung it from his belt by the moccasins.

Did You Know?

Moccasins are soft shoes made of leather. Moccasins were originally worn by North American Indians. Different groups decorated these shoes with symbols important to their cultures.

. . . .

"The last thing I must give you," said the old woman, "is this advice. Pay close attention to your little dog. You have treated him well and so he is your great friend. He is small, but his eyes and nose are **keen.** Keep him always in front of you. He will warn you of danger before it can strike you."

 Stop here for **Break Time** on the next page.

Word Power

keen (kēn) *adj.* highly sensitive; sharp

Reading Skill

Infer Reread the highlighted paragraphs. Swift Runner's grandmother gives him many things to take with him on his journey. What can you infer about the grandmother from her actions? Check the correct response.

☐ She is sad and lonely.

☑ She is wise and caring.

☐ She is mean and hateful.

Break Time

As you read, visualizing the characters and events helps you understand what you are reading. You can use the details the author includes, as well as your imagination, to picture the story. Complete the chart below to help you visualize the characters in this story. Characters are listed in the left column. In the right column, describe what you think they look like and how they act. An example has been provided.

Character	What I Picture
Chief	He is old, but he probably stands tall and proud because he is a leader of the village.
Swift Runner before he leaves the village	Possible responses: He is small and his clothes are torn. He wears moccasins and a cap with feathers.
Grandmother	Possible response: She is old and weak, but might have a wise-looking face.
Swift Runner's dog	Possible response: He is small, but his eyes are alert.

After you have finished reading the story, come back to this page to complete the final two descriptions below. You can also add to the descriptions in the four rows above.

Character	What I Picture
The Nyagwahe	Possible responses: It looks like a giant bear with huge teeth. It can look like a man with glowing eyes.
Swift Runner after he returns to the village.	Possible response: He is a tall and strong man.

 Continue reading on the next page.

Then Swift Runner set out on his journey. His little dog stayed ahead of him, sniffing the air and sniffing the ground. By the time the sun was in the middle of the sky, they were far from the village. The trail passed through deep woods, and it seemed to the boy as if something was following them among the trees. But he could see nothing in the thick brush.

The trail curved toward the left, and the boy felt even more the presence of something watching. Suddenly his little dog ran into the brush at the side of the trail, barking loudly. There were the sounds of tree limbs breaking and heavy feet running. Then out of the forest came a Nyagwahe, a monster bear. Its great teeth were as long as a man's arm. It was twice as tall as a moose. Close at its heels was Swift Runner's little dog.

"I see you," Swift Runner shouted. "I am after you. You cannot escape me."

Swift Runner had learned those words by listening to the stories the old people told. They were the very words a monster bear speaks when it attacks, words that terrify anyone who hears them. On hearing those words, the great bear turned and fled from the boy.

"You cannot escape me," Swift Runner shouted again. Then he ran after the bear.

The Nyagwahe turned toward the east, with Swift Runner and his dog close behind. It left the trail and plowed through the thick forest, breaking down great trees and leaving a path of destruction like that of a whirlwind. It ran up the tallest hills and down through the swamps, but the boy and the dog stayed at its heels. They ran past a great cave in the rocks. All around the cave were the bones of people the bear had caught and eaten.

Reading Skill

Visualize Reread the sentences highlighted in green. Underline the details in the text that help you visualize what the monster bear looks like. What other details from your imagination can you add to this description?

Answers will vary.

_____

_____

English Coach

Words can have more than one meaning. The word _plowed_ can mean "broke up the soil," but here it means "forced a way through something." Use the word in a sentence as it is used in the story.

Possible response: I plowed

through the crowd to see

what was going on.

_____

Reading Skill

Infer Reread the highlighted paragraph. What can you infer about Swift Runner from this passage? Check the correct response.

- ☑ He is determined to catch the bear.
- ☐ He is as weak and lazy as the villagers think.
- ☐ He does not think his dog will be loyal.

Comprehension Check

Reread the boxed paragraph. Why does Swift Runner wake up? What does he see?

Swift Runner's dog growls

and wakes him up. He sees

a tall figure with glowing

green eyes.

_____

_____

"My relatives," Swift Runner called as he passed the cave, "I will not forget you. I am after the one who killed you. He will not escape me."

Throughout the day, the boy and his dog chased the great bear, growing closer bit by bit. At last, as the sun began to set, Swift Runner stopped at the head of a small valley and called his small dog to him.

"We will rest here for the night," the boy said. He took off his first pair of moccasins, whose soles were worn away to nothing. He threw them aside and put on a new pair. Swift Runner made a fire and sat beside it with his dog. Then he took out the pouch of cornmeal and maple sugar, sharing his food with his dog.

"Nothing will harm us," Swift Runner said. "Nothing can come close to our fire." He lay down and slept.

In the middle of the night, he was awakened by the growling of his dog. He sat up with his back to the fire and looked into the darkness. There, just outside the circle of light made by the flames, stood a dark figure that looked like a tall man. Its eyes glowed green.

"I am Nyagwahe," said the figure. "This is my human shape. Why do you **pursue** me?"

"You cannot escape me," Swift Runner said. "I chase you because you killed my people. I will not stop until I catch you and kill you."

The figure faded back into the darkness.

"You cannot escape me," Swift Runner said again. Then he patted his small dog and went to sleep.

Word Power
pursue (pər soo´) v. to chase; to seek

182

As soon as the first light of the new day appeared, Swift Runner rose. He and his small dog took the trail. It was easy to follow the monster's path, for trees were uprooted and the earth torn by its great paws. They ran all through the morning. When the sun was in the middle of the sky, they reached the head of another valley. At the other end they saw the great bear running toward the east. Swift Runner pulled off his second pair of moccasins, whose soles were worn away to nothing. He put on his third pair and began to run again.

All through that day, they kept the Nyagwahe in sight, drawing closer bit by bit. When the sun began to set, Swift Runner stopped to make camp. He took off the third pair of moccasins, whose soles were worn away to nothing, and put on the last pair.

"Tomorrow," he said to his small dog, "we will catch the monster and kill it." He reached for his pouch of cornmeal and maple sugar, but when he opened it, he found it filled with worms. The magic of the Nyagwahe had done this. Swift Runner poured out the pouch and said in a loud voice, "You have spoiled our food, but it will not stop me. I am on your trail. You cannot escape me."

That night, once again, he was awakened by the growling of his dog. A dark figure stood just outside the circle of light. It looked smaller than the night before, and the glow of its eyes was weak.

"I am Nyagwahe," the dark figure said. "Why do you pursue me?"

"You cannot escape me," Swift Runner said. "I am on your trail. You killed my people. You threatened the Great Peace. I will not rest until I catch you."

Reading Skill

Visualize Reread the highlighted sentence. Use the details to help you picture what this landscape looks like. In the box below, draw a picture of the scene described in the text.

Your Sketch

My Workspace

Comprehension Check

Reread the boxed paragraph. What does the Nyagwahe offer to do if Swift Runner does not kill him?

It offers Swift Runner its

teeth to use for healing.

It says it will go away and

never return.

English Coach

The prefix *un-* can mean "reverse action of." When Swift Runner *unslung* the bow, he did the reverse of slinging the bow over his shoulder. Write two other words that use this prefix to mean "reverse action of."

Possible responses: unfold,

unlock, undo

"Hear me," said the Nyagwahe. "I see your power is greater than mine. Do not kill me. When you catch me, take my great teeth. They are my power, and you can use them for healing. **Spare** my life and I will go far to the north and never again bother the People of the Longhouse."

"You cannot escape me," Swift Runner said. "I am on your trail."

The dark figure faded back into the darkness, and Swift Runner sat for a long time, looking into the night.

At the first light of day, the boy and his dog took the trail. They had not gone far when they saw the Nyagwahe ahead of them. Its sides puffed in and out as it ran. The trail was beside a big lake with many alder trees close to the water. As the great bear ran past, the leaves were torn from the trees. Fast as the bear went, the boy and his dog came closer, bit by bit. At last, when the sun was in the middle of the sky, the giant bear could run no longer. It fell heavily to the earth, panting so hard that it stirred up clouds of dust.

Swift Runner unslung his grandfather's bow and notched an arrow to the **sinewy** string.

"Shoot for my heart," said the Nyagwahe. "Aim well. If you cannot kill me with one arrow, I will take your life."

"No," Swift Runner said. "I have listened to the stories of my elders. Your only weak spot is the sole of your foot. Hold up your foot and I will kill you."

Word Power

spare (spâr) *v.* to treat with mercy; to hold back from harming or injuring
sinewy (sin′ ū ē) *adj.* physically tough or powerful

184

Grizzly Bear in a Mountainous Landscape (detail). Carl Rungius (1869–1959). Oil on canvas, 47 x 52 in. Private collection.

How is the Nyagwahe similar to the bear in this painting? How is it different?

The great bear shook with fear. "You have defeated me," it pleaded. "Spare my life and I will leave forever."

"You must give me your great teeth," Swift Runner said. "Then you must leave and never bother the People of the Longhouse again."

"I shall do as you say," said the Nyagwahe. "Take my great teeth."

Swift Runner lowered his bow. He stepped forward and pulled out the great bear's teeth. It rose to its feet and walked to the north, growing smaller as it went. It went over the hill and was gone.

Carrying the teeth of the Nyagwahe over his shoulder, Swift Runner turned back to the west, his dog at his side. He walked for three moons before he reached the place where the bones of his people were piled in front of the monster's empty cave. He collected those bones and walked around them four times. "Now," he said, "I must do something to make my people wake up." He went to a big hickory tree and began to push it over so that it would fall on the pile of bones.

Background Info

It takes about 30 days, or approximately one month, for the moon to go through its cycle of orbiting the earth. Swift Runner walked for *three moons*, or about three months, to get back to the place where his people had died.

185

Reading Skill

Visualize Reread the paragraph highlighted in green. Picture in your mind what the people look like when they come back to life. Write two words below to describe how they might look.

Possible responses: healthy, smiling, lively, surprised

Literary Element

Tone Reread the paragraph highlighted in blue. Think about how the author feels about the Great Peace and about Swift Runner. What is the tone of this passage? Check the correct response.

- ☑ The tone is uplifting because Swift Runner heals people and keeps the peace.
- ☐ The tone is sad because there is sickness and fighting in the world.
- ☐ The tone is tense because the author worries about keeping the Great Peace.

"My people," he shouted, "get up quickly or this tree will land on you."

The bones of the people who had been killed all came together and jumped up, alive again and covered with flesh. They were filled with joy and gathered around Swift Runner.

"Great one," they said, "who are you?"

"I am Swift Runner," he said.

"How can that be?" one of the men said. "Swift Runner is a skinny little boy. You are a tall, strong man."

Swift Runner looked at himself and saw that it was so. He was taller than the tallest man, and his little dog was bigger than a wolf.

"I am Swift Runner," he said. "I was that boy and I am the man you see before you."

Then Swift Runner led his people back to the village. He carried with him the teeth of the Nyagwahe, and those who saw what he carried rejoiced. The trails were safe again, and the Great Peace would not be broken. Swift Runner went to his grandmother's lodge and **embraced** her.

"Grandson," she said, "you are now the man I knew you would grow up to be. Remember to use your power to help the people."

So it was that Swift Runner ran with the great bear and won the race. Throughout his long life, he used the teeth of the Nyagwahe to heal the sick, and he worked always to keep the Great Peace.

Da neho. I am finished.

Word Power

embraced (em brāsd´) *v.* hugged or held in the arms

Respond to Literature

Racing the Great Bear

A Comprehension Check

Answer the following questions in the spaces provided.

1. Why is the chief looking for a brave person?

   The chief wants a brave person to find out what happened to the young

   men who did not return to the village.

2. How is Swift Runner changed when he returns from his journey?

   He has grown from a small boy into a strong and powerful man.

B Reading Skills

Answer the following questions in the spaces provided.

1. **Visualize** The author describes the Nyagwahe as a monster bear. What do you think a monster bear would look like? Describe it below.

   Possible responses: A monster bear would be huge, look mean and scary,

   have big sharp teeth and claws, have eerie eyes.

2. **Infer** Swift Runner knows what to say to the bear and how to defeat it because he has listened to the old people tell their stories. What inference can you make about Swift Runner based on this fact?

   Possible responses: Swift Runner respects his elders. He is probably very

   smart and observant.

C Word Power

Complete each sentence below, using one of the words in the box.

clan	keen	pursue	spare
	sinewy	embraced	

1. Although the rope looked worn and thin, it was actually strong and
   _____ sinewy _____.

2. The raccoon's _____ keen _____ sense of smell drew him to our
   remote campsite.

3. The sheriff had to _____ pursue _____ the thief for many miles
   before she finally caught him.

4. The families who are part of the Macintosh _____ clan _____ meet
   every year in Scotland.

5. Hector kissed and _____ embraced _____ his grandmother when she got
   off the airplane.

6. The king showed mercy and decided to _____ spare _____ the
   outlaw's life.

D Literary Element: Tone

Read the passages below from "Racing the Great Bear." As you read, think about the tone of the passages. Then answer the questions that follow.

> "Our chief has forgotten our greatest warrior," one of the young men said to another, tilting his head toward Swift Runner.[1]
>
> "*Nyoh*," the other young man said, laughing.[2] "Yes.[3] Why does he not offer the wampum to Swift Runner?"[4]
>
> So it was that Swift Runner ran with the great bear and won the race.[5] Throughout his long life, he used the teeth of the Nyagwahe to heal the sick, and he worked always to keep the Great Peace.[6]

1. Reread sentences 1–4. What is the tone of the warriors' conversation?

   Possible response: The tone is sarcastic and lacking in respect.

   _____

   _____

   _____

2. In sentences 5–6, Swift Runner has solved the village's problem. What is the tone of this passage? How does it compare with the tone of the first passage?

   Possible responses: The tone is serious and respectful. It is the opposite of

   the tone taken by the warriors in the first passage.

   _____

   _____

E Interview

Imagine that you are Swift Runner and are being interviewed. Write answers that Swift Runner might give to the questions the interviewer asks.

Interviewer: Swift Runner, why did you take the wampum when the chief offered it to you?

Swift Runner: I took the wampum because I thought no one would miss me if I did not return from the journey.

But I went home and my grandmother said that my father was a great warrior. She knew that I would succeed in my task.

Interviewer: How did your dog help you hunt the Nyagwahe?

Swift Runner: He is a keen dog. At night, he guarded me and the fire. He growled and woke me up when the great bear came to see me. He barked and warned me of danger.

Interviewer: How did you defeat the Nyagwahe?

Swift Runner: I was ready to kill it, but the Nyagwahe said it would give me its teeth and that it would go away if I did not kill it.

Interviewer: What are you doing with your life now?

Swift Runner: These days, I heal the sick. I have worked to keep the Great Peace.

Interviewer: Thank you, Swift Runner. You are quite an inspiration.

Assessment

Fill in the circle next to each correct answer.

1. What items does Swift Runner's grandmother give him for his journey?
   - ○ A. some food, a wampum, and a blanket
   - ○ B. food, a dog, a cap, a necklace, and a prayer
   - ● C. a bow, a cap, moccasins, food, and advice
   - ○ D. some teeth, a weapon, and several pairs of moccasins

2. What can you infer about Swift Runner when he starts chasing the monster bear?
   - ○ A. He is terrified that he will lose his life.
   - ○ B. He thinks he has special powers.
   - ○ C. He doesn't care if he catches the bear or not.
   - ● D. He is brave and determined.

3. Which of the following phrases describes Swift Runner at the end of his journey?
   - ● A. a strong man, taller than the tallest man
   - ○ B. a skinny little boy in torn clothes
   - ○ C. a dark figure with eyes that glowed green
   - ○ D. a weak and lazy boy with a dirty face

4. What is the tone of this story?
   - ○ A. funny
   - ● B. serious
   - ○ C. happy
   - ○ D. gloomy

5. Which of the following words means "to follow or chase"?
   - ● A. pursue
   - ○ B. spare
   - ○ C. embraced
   - ○ D. keen

Get Ready to Read!

Icarus and Daedalus

Meet Josephine Preston Peabody

Josephine Preston Peabody was born in New York in 1874. She grew up reading and writing all the time. Peabody published her first poem when she was only fourteen years old. Six years later, the publication of her poems in magazines helped her to attend Radcliffe College. Peabody's retelling of "Icarus and Daedalus" is part of a collection called *Old Greek Folk Stories Told Anew*, which was first published in 1897. Peabody died in 1922.

What You Know

Have you ever known someone who ignored warnings and did something dangerous? What happened to him or her? Share your story with the class.

Reason to Read

Read this story to find out what happens to a father and son when they try to escape from an island.

Background Info

The story of Icarus (ik ′ ər əs) and Daedalus (ded ′ əl əs) takes place on the island of Crete in the legendary time when both humans and gods lived in ancient Greece. This story is a myth. The word myth comes from *mythos*, a Greek word meaning "story." A *myth* is a special kind of story that often involves gods and goddesses. No one knows where myths first came from. It is likely that they were passed from generation to generation over hundreds of years of oral retellings before the Greeks began writing. They were already very old by around 850 B.C., when the Greek writer Homer referred to them in his poems. Greek myths tell stories of gods and goddesses, their lives on Mount Olympus, and their relationships with the people on Earth.

Word Power

cunning (kun´ing) *adj.* skillful and clever; sly; p. 194
He was *cunning* enough to get himself out of trouble.

captive (kap´tiv) *adj.* imprisoned; kept within bounds; p. 194
The *captive* soldiers were locked in cells.

glimpse (glimps) *n.* a very quick look; a peek; p. 195
While shopping at the mall, I caught a *glimpse* of the movie star.

quench (kwench) *v.* to satisfy; to put an end to a need or desire; p. 196
Do you have any lemonade to *quench* my thirst?

offering (ô´fər ing) *n.* a gift, often given for a religious purpose; p. 196
We gave an *offering* of money to our church.

**Answer the following questions that contain the new words above.
Write your answers in the spaces provided.**

1. How would you *quench* a thirst, by drinking water or by avoiding water?

   _____ by drinking water _____

2. How would you catch a *glimpse* of something, by staring at it a long time or by

   glancing briefly at it?_____ by glancing briefly at it _____

3. Would someone *cunning* be clever or unskilled? _____ clever _____

4. Would someone spend or give an *offering*? _____ give _____

5. Is a *captive* free to leave or forced to stay? _____ forced to stay _____

Adapted from
Icarus and Daedalus

Josephine Preston Peabody

Background Info

Crete is a Greek island in the Mediterranean Sea. The Minoan culture, named after King Minos, may have begun on Crete as early as 3000 B.C. This culture was the first major civilization in ancient Greece. It flourished between 1700 and 1400 B.C. Minoans were known for their cleverness.

Literary Element

Symbol Reread the highlighted text. When Daedalus looks at the sea gulls, he sees more than the birds. What do they symbolize to Daedalus?

The birds symbolize liberty

or freedom.

Among all those humans who became so wise that they learned the secrets of the gods, none was more **cunning** than Daedalus.

He once built, for King Minos of Crete, a wonderful Labyrinth of winding ways. It was so cunningly tangled up and twisted around that, once inside, you could never find your way out again without a magic clue. But the king's friendship changed with the wind, and one day he had his master architect imprisoned in a tower. Daedalus managed to escape, but it seemed impossible to leave the island. Every ship that came or went was well guarded by order of the king.

After watching the sea gulls in the air—the only creatures that were sure of liberty—Daedalus thought of a plan for himself and his young son Icarus, who was **captive** with him.

Did You Know?

The *Labyrinth* (lab´ ə rinth´) was a huge maze. Its complicated and twisted path enclosed by high walls made it impossible for people to find their way out once they had entered it.

Word Power

cunning (kun´ing) *adj.* skillful and clever; sly
captive (kap´tiv) *adj.* imprisoned; kept within bounds

Little by little, Daedalus gathered a supply of feathers large and small. He fastened them together with thread, molded them in with wax, and so created two great wings like those of a bird. When they were done, Daedalus fitted them to his own shoulders. After one or two tries, he found that by waving his arms to fan the air he could move through it, as a swimmer moves through the sea. He managed to stay aloft, swaying this way and that with the wind. At last, like a great young bird, he learned to fly.

Without delay, he began to work on a pair of wings for the boy Icarus. He taught him carefully how to use them and gave him a warning. "Remember," said the father, "never to fly very low or very high. The fogs that circle the earth can weigh you down, but the blaze of the sun will surely melt your feathers apart if you go too near."

For Icarus, this warning went in one ear and out the other. Who could remember to be careful when he was to fly for the first time? Are birds careful? Not they! Only one idea remained in the boy's head—the joy of escape.

Finally, a day came with the perfect wind that was to set them free. The father bird put on his wings. He waited to see that all was well with Icarus, because the two could not fly hand in hand. Up they rose, the boy after his father. The hated ground of Crete sank beneath them. Country folk, who caught a **glimpse** of them when they were high above the treetops, thought that they were seeing the gods—perhaps Apollo with Cupid after him.

At first there was terror in their joy. The wide emptiness of the sky dazed them—a glance downward made their brains spin. But when a great wind filled their wings and Icarus felt himself supported, like a child lifted up by his mother, he forgot everything in the world but joy. He forgot Crete and the other islands that he had passed over. He hardly noticed that winged thing in the distance that was his father Daedalus.

Word Power

glimpse (glimps) *n.* a very quick look; a peek

Reading Skill

Visualize Reread the highlighted sentence. Do you think these wings would look like those of a bird? Describe how they would look similar to or different from a bird's wings.

Possible responses: They are similar because they have feathers. They are different because they are also made of thread and wax.

English Coach

The phrase *in one ear and out the other* means that Icarus did not listen to his father's advice. The words did not actually travel in and out of his head. Which of the following phrases about speaking or listening does **not** actually mean what it says? Check the correct response.

- ☑ The word is on the tip of my tongue.
- ☐ I listened carefully as he spoke.
- ☐ They could clearly hear what I said.

Icarus, 1947. Henri Matisse. From the *Jazz* **series.** Gouache on paper, 42 x 32.5 cm. COPYRIGHT ARS, New York, Ecole des Beaux Arts, Paris.

How is the flight of Icarus, as described in the myth, like the Icarus painted by Matisse?

Reading Skill

Infer Reread the highlighted sentence. Why would being held captive make Icarus want to fly?

Possible response: As a prisoner he was unable to go where he wanted or to escape. Flying makes those things possible.

Reading Skill

Visualize Reread the highlighted sentence. Picture the scene described here. What is happening to Icarus? Where are the sun and ocean? Sketch the scene below.

Your Sketch

He longed for one taste of flight to **quench** the thirst for freedom created by his being held captive. He stretched out his arms to the sky and flew toward the highest heavens.

Poor Icarus! Warmer and warmer grew the air. Those arms, that had seemed to support him earlier, relaxed. His wings hesitated, drooped. He fluttered his young hands uselessly—he was falling—and in his terror he remembered his father's warning. The heat of the sun had melted the wax from his wings. The feathers were falling, one by one, like snowflakes. And there was no one to help.

Icarus fell like a leaf tossed down the wind—down, down—with one cry that reached his father far away. When Daedalus returned, he looked high and low for the poor boy. He saw nothing but the bird-like feathers floating on the water, and he knew that Icarus was drowned.

Daedalus named the nearest island Icaria in memory of the child. In heavy grief, he went to the temple of Apollo in Sicily, where he hung up his wings as an **offering.** Never again did he attempt to fly.

Word Power

quench (kwench) *v.* to satisfy; to put an end to a need or desire
offering (ô′ fər ing) *n.* a gift, often given for a religious purpose

Respond to Literature

Icarus and Daedalus

A Comprehension Check

Answer the following questions in the spaces provided.

1. What does King Minos do to keep Daedalus and Icarus from escaping?

   King Minos locks them in a tower and guards all the ships.

2. What happens to Icarus? Icarus flies too close to the sun, melting his wings.

   He drowns in the sea.

B Reading Skills

Answer the following questions in the spaces provided.

1. **Visualize** What do you think the wings Daedalus builds look like?

   Answers will vary. Students should mention that he builds the wings from

   feathers, thread, and wax.

2. **Infer** The writer tells you that Icarus longs for a taste of freedom and forgets everything else. What does the writer want you to figure out about Icarus from this description? Possible responses: Icarus is too hungry for

   freedom. He is more interested in flying and does not listen to his father's

   advice, resulting in his death.

C Word Power

Complete each sentence below, using one of the words in the box.

cunning	captive	glimpse	quench	offering

1. The car was going so fast that I caught only a ___glimpse___ of the driver.

2. Alfonso read four books to ___quench___ his curiosity about ancient Greece.

3. The man who owned the chickens was more ___cunning___ than the fox that could not figure out how to get into the cage.

4. The men were held ___captive___ after they were caught stealing.

5. The visitors to the temple left an ___offering___ of flowers.

Circle the word that best completes each sentence.

6. His (**cunning**, **offering**) mind helped him find an exit from the maze.

7. I got a (**glimpse**, **captive**) of the president before he jumped into his limousine.

8. Even a big bar of chocolate could not (**cunning**, **quench**) Lee's desire for candy.

9. After getting caught, she felt as if she were being kept (**glimpse**, **captive**) in the principal's office.

10. The branch was left on the table as an (**offering**, **glimpse**) of peace.

D Literary Element: Symbol

Read the passages below from "Icarus and Daedalus." As you read, think about how some elements in the story also stand for something else. Then answer the questions that follow.

He once built, for King Minos of Crete, a wonderful Labyrinth of winding ways.[1] It was so cunningly tangled up and twisted around that, once inside, you could never find your way out again without a magic clue.[2]

Finally, a day came with the perfect wind that was to set them free.[3]

Up they rose, the boy after his father.[4] The hated ground of Crete sank beneath them.[5]

1. In sentences 1–2, how does the Labyrinth represent Daedalus's cunning?

   Possible response: The Labyrinth is so cleverly built that no one can find

   the way out without help.

2. In sentences 3–5, what does the ability to fly symbolize? Why?

   Possible response: Flying symbolizes freedom for Icarus and Daedalus

   because they are able to escape from being held captive.

E Words of Wisdom

Imagine that you saw young Icarus fall to his death. You learned the story about Daedalus and now you want to advise others. You will write words of wisdom on stone tablets for people to see. Write your answers to the following questions on the stone tablets below.

SHOULD PEOPLE FLY?

Possible responses: Yes,

especially if they are

trapped and denied their

freedom. No; if people were

meant to fly they would be

born with wings.

SHOULD PEOPLE NOT TRY TO "FLY TOO HIGH"? WHY? FUTURE GENERATIONS WILL READ AND HEED YOUR ADVICE.

Possible responses: People should

not fly too high because they

may end up like Icarus. People

should be careful when they try

something new.

SHOULD CHILDREN LISTEN TO THEIR PARENTS?

Possible response: Yes.

Parents have more life

experience than children and

are wiser.

Assessment

Fill in the circle next to each correct answer.

1. What does Daedalus build for King Minos?
   - ○ A. a tower
   - ● B. a labyrinth
   - ○ C. a boat
   - ○ D. wings

2. What do the sea gulls symbolize for Daedalus?
   - ○ A. death
   - ○ B. imprisonment
   - ● C. freedom
   - ○ D. life

3. Which phrase from the story **does not** help the reader to visualize what Daedalus and Icarus look like when they are flying?
   - ● A. cunningly tangled up and twisted around
   - ○ B. high above the treetops, [they] thought that they were seeing the gods
   - ○ C. like a great young bird
   - ○ D. as a swimmer moves through the sea

4. What causes Icarus to fly too close to the sun?
   - ○ A. He is looking for his father.
   - ○ B. He misunderstands what his father says.
   - ○ C. He wants to get away from his father.
   - ● D. He does not listen to his father's advice.

5. Which of the following words means "clever and skillful"?
   - ○ A. glimpse
   - ● B. cunning
   - ○ C. quench
   - ○ D. captive

The People Could Fly

Meet Virginia Hamilton

Virginia Hamilton was born in 1936. Her writing celebrates her African American heritage and culture. She says, "In the background of much of my writing is the dream of freedom." But this freedom is out of reach for many of her characters. The dream of freedom and her interest in African folklore are the sources of many of her folktales. "The People Could Fly" is a folktale that had been told orally for two hundred years before Hamilton retold it in 1985.

What You Know

Where could someone who is treated unfairly go for help? Think of ways that people can escape a bad situation. As a class, make a list of ideas.

Reason to Read

Read this folktale to discover how a group of people deal with unfairness and cruelty.

Background Info

This story takes place on a plantation, or large farm, in North America during the 1700s.

When Europe was struggling through the Dark Ages (A.D. 476 to 1000), Africa had thriving kingdoms and talented artists. Then, in 1619, Africans began to be kidnapped and brought to North America for slave labor. Slavery was allowed to continue in parts of the United States until the end of the Civil War in 1865. It was only at this point that all enslaved people in the United States were freed.

Word Power

scorned (skôrnd) *v.* treated with dislike or disrespect; p. 205
The people in the village *scorned* those who did not work hard all day.

bawling (bôl´ ing) *v.* crying loudly; p. 205
I was *bawling* so hard at the sad movie that I ran out of tissues.

croon (kro̅o̅n) *v.* to gently sing or hum; p. 205
The singer promised to *croon* a romantic song for my mother.

scrunched (skrunchd) *v.* crouched; squatted; p. 205
The little boy who was playing hide and seek *scrunched* behind the bush.

seize (sēz) *v.* to grab and take hold of someone or something, possibly by force; p. 207
The officer tried to *seize* the thief who was running away from the bank.

Answer the following questions, using one of the new words above.
Write your answers in the spaces provided.

1. Which word goes with "to capture"? _____ seize _____

2. Which word goes with "sat on one's heels or bent low"? _____ scrunched _____

3. Which word goes with "showed disapproval"? _____ scorned _____

4. Which word goes with "sobbing or wailing"? _____ bawling _____

5. Which word goes with "to softly sing a song"? _____ croon _____

The People Could Fly

Told by Virginia Hamilton

The People Could Fly, 1985. Leo & Diana Dillon. Pastel and watercolor. Private collection.

Background Info

Slavery refers to the practice of keeping people as property. From the 1500s through the 1800s, more than 10 million Africans were enslaved and brought to the Americas. They traveled across the Atlantic Ocean in overcrowded slave ships and had to stay in hot, airless spaces below deck. Many died during the journey.

They say the people could fly. Say that long ago in Africa, some of the people knew magic. And they would walk up on the air like climbin up on a gate. And they flew like blackbirds over the fields. Black, shiny wings flappin against the blue up there.

Then, many of the people were captured for Slavery. The ones that could fly shed their wings. They couldn't take their wings across the water on the slave ships. Too crowded, don't you know.

The folks were full of misery, then. Got sick with the up and down of the sea. So they forgot about flyin when they could no longer breathe the sweet scent of Africa.

Say the people who could fly kept their power, although they shed their wings. They kept their secret magic in the land of slavery. They looked the same as the other people from Africa who had been coming over, who had dark skin. Say you couldn't tell anymore one who could fly from one who couldn't.

One such who could was an old man, call him Toby. And standin tall, yet afraid, was a young woman who once had wings. Call her Sarah. Now Sarah carried a babe tied to her back. She trembled to be so hard worked and **scorned.**

The slaves labored in the fields from sunup to sundown. The owner of the slaves callin himself their Master. Say he was a hard lump of clay. A hard, glinty coal. A hard rock pile, wouldn't be moved. His Overseer on horseback pointed out the slaves who were slowin down. So the one called Driver cracked his whip over the slow ones to make them move faster. That whip was a slice-open cut of pain. So they did move faster. Had to.

Sarah hoed and chopped the row as the babe on her back slept.

Say the child grew hungry. That babe started up **bawling** too loud. Sarah couldn't stop to feed it. Couldn't stop to soothe and quiet it down. She let it cry. She didn't want to. She had no heart to **croon** to it.

> "Keep that thing quiet," called the Overseer. He pointed his finger at the babe. The woman **scrunched** low. The Driver cracked his whip across the babe anyhow. The babe hollered like any hurt child, and the woman fell to the earth.

The old man that was there, Toby, came and helped her to her feet.

"I must go soon," she told him.

"Soon," he said.

Sarah couldn't stand up straight any longer. She was too weak. The sun burned her face. The babe cried and cried, "Pity me, oh, pity me," say it sounded like.

English Coach

Reread the words highlighted in pink. This description is a *metaphor*. A metaphor is a comparison of two unlike things without clue words such as *like* or *as*. Here, the Master is being compared to *a hard lump of clay*. Underline two more metaphors in the paragraph that describe the Master.

Comprehension Check

Reread the boxed paragraph. What does the Overseer do when Sarah's baby does not stop crying?
Driver
The Overseer whips Sarah
and her baby.

Word Power

scorned (skôrnd) *v.* treated with dislike or disrespect

bawling (bôl´ ing) *v.* crying loudly

croon (kro͞on) *v.* to gently sing or hum

scrunched (skrunchd) *v.* crouched; squatted

Reading Skill

Infer Reread the highlighted text. What can you infer about what Sarah thinks will happen to her if she does not leave? Check the correct response.

- ☐ She thinks she will be able to escape.
- ☑ She thinks she will die.
- ☐ She thinks she will be rewarded.

Sarah was so sad and starvin, she sat down in the row.

"Get up, you black cow," called the Overseer. He pointed his hand, and the Driver's whip snarled around Sarah's legs. Her sack dress tore into rags. Her legs bled onto the earth. She couldn't get up.

Toby was there where there was no one to help her and the babe.

"Now, before it's too late," panted Sarah. "Now, Father!"

"Yes, Daughter, the time is come," Toby answered. "Go, as you know how to go!"

He raised his arms, holding them out to her. "*Kum ... yali, kum buba tambe,*" and more magic words, said so quickly, they sounded like whispers and sighs.

Alexander Chandler, 1955. Andrew Wyeth. Drybrush, 21¼ x 14½ in. Private collection. Photograph courtesy of the Wyeth Collection. © Andrew Wyeth.

What qualities might the man in the painting have in common with Toby?

_____

The young woman lifted one foot on the air. Then the other. She flew clumsily at first, with the child now held tightly in her arms. Then she felt the magic, the African mystery. Say she rose just as free as a bird. As light as a feather.

The Overseer rode after her, hollerin. Sarah flew over the fences. She flew over the woods. Tall trees could not snag her. Nor could the Overseer. She flew like an eagle now, until she was gone from sight. No one dared speak about it. Couldn't believe it. But it was, because they that was there saw that it was.

Say the next day was dead hot in the fields. A young man slave fell from the heat. The Driver come and whipped him. Toby come over and spoke words to the fallen one. The words of ancient Africa once heard are never remembered completely. The young man forgot them as soon as he heard them. They went way inside him. He got up and rolled over on the air. He rode it awhile. And he flew away.

Another and another fell from the heat. Toby was there. He cried out to the fallen and reached his arms out to them. "*Kum kunka yali, kum … tambe!*" Whispers and sighs. And they too rose on the air. They rode the hot breezes. The ones flyin were black and shinin sticks, wheelin above the head of the Overseer. They crossed the rows, the fields, the fences, the streams, and were away.

"**Seize** the old man!" cried the Overseer. "I heard him say the magic *words*. Seize him!"

Word Power

seize (sēz) *v.* to grab and take hold of someone or something, possibly by force

Literary Element

Symbol Reread the sentences highlighted in blue. What does flying symbolize to the enslaved men and women?

Possible responses: It symbolizes freedom from slavery. It could symbolize a return to Africa.

Reading Skill

Visualize Reread the sentences highlighted in green. In the frame below, draw a picture of what you think the flying people look like. If you have room, you can add the fields, fences, streams, or the Overseer.

Your Sketch

The one callin himself Master come runnin. The Driver got his whip ready to curl around old Toby and tie him up. The slaveowner took his hip gun from its place. He meant to kill old, black Toby. But Toby just laughed. Say he threw back his head and said, "Hee, hee! Don't you know who I am? Don't you know some of us in this field?" He said it to their faces. "We are ones who fly!"

And he sighed the ancient words that were a dark promise. He said them all around to the others in the field under the whip, "...*buba yali* ... *buba tambe*...."

There was a great outcryin. The bent backs straighted up. Old and young who were called slaves and could fly joined hands. Say like they would ring-sing. But they didn't shuffle in a circle. They didn't sing. They rose on the air. They flew in a flock that was black against the heavenly blue. Black crows or black shadows. It didn't matter, they went so high. Way above the plantation, way over the slavery land. Say they flew away to *Free-dom*.

Background Info

A *ring-sing*, or ring shout, is a custom that was performed after a long day of work on the plantation. Singers and dancers would form a circle. Then they would shuffle their feet on the ground, move their bodies, clap their hands, and sing. Ring-sings are still performed today in some parts of the United States.

The People Could Fly, 1985. Leo & Diana Dillon. Pastel and watercolor. Private collection.

Do you think this picture is a good illustration of what is happening in the story? Why?

And the old man, old Toby, flew behind them, takin care of them. He wasn't cryin. He wasn't laughin. He was the seer. His gaze fell on the plantation where the slaves who could not fly waited.

"*Take us with you!*" Their looks spoke it but they were afraid to shout it. Toby couldn't take them with him. Hadn't the time to teach them to fly. They must wait for a chance to run.

"Goodie-bye!" The old man called Toby spoke to them, poor souls! And he was flyin gone.

So they say. The Overseer told it. The one called Master said it was a lie, a trick of the light. The Driver kept his mouth shut.

The slaves who could not fly told about the people who could fly to their children. When they were free. When they sat close before the fire in the free land, they told it. They did so love firelight and *Free-dom*, and tellin.

They say that the children of the ones who could not fly told their children. And now, me, I have told it to you.

Reading Skill

Infer Reread the highlighted paragraph. Why do you think the Master says that the people didn't fly? Why does the Driver say nothing?

Possible responses: They don't believe what they saw. They don't want other slaves to know it has happened.

209

Respond to Literature

The People Could Fly

A Comprehension Check

Answer the following questions in the spaces provided.

1. Why are the people who are captured unable to take their wings with them? They are not able to take their wings because the ships are too crowded.

2. How do the enslaved people who cannot fly react to the amazing flight of the others? They are afraid to shout, but they want to go along.

B Reading Skills

Complete the following activities in the spaces provided.

1. **Visualize** The following passage describes how the people who could not fly react: " *'Take us with you!'* Their looks spoke it but they were afraid to shout it." Describe what you think their faces look like.

   Possible responses: They have sad expressions; some of them are crying.

   Their eyes are pleading, but their mouths are closed because they are

   afraid to say anything.

2. **Infer** The men want to kill Toby for saying the magic words. But Toby laughs at them while he flies away. What can you infer about how Toby feels? Possible responses: He is not afraid of the men who want to kill him.

   He is happy that he is free and that he has helped some people escape.

Respond to Literature

C Word Power

Complete each sentence below, using one of the words in the box.

| scorned | bawling | croon | scrunched | seize |

1. The little boy started _____bawling_____ when he accidentally let go of his balloon.

2. Jill _____scrunched_____ to look under the bed for her slippers.

3. The birds will _____seize_____ the fish from the water and fly away.

4. The long, dull movie was _____scorned_____ by film critics.

5. The baby will fall asleep if you _____croon_____ a lullaby to her.

Circle the word that best completes each sentence.

6. Amy (**scorned**, **scrunched**) her friends after they lied to her.

7. The clown was supposed to be funny, but all the children were (**seize**, **bawling**) when he left the party.

8. The plumber (**bawling**, **scrunched**) down to work on the pipes under the sink.

9. Carlos tried to (**croon**, **seize**) the ball from Edgar, but Edgar held on tightly to it.

10. The glee club will softly (**croon**, **scorned**) our school song as the audience watches the slide show.

D Literary Element: Symbol

Read the passages below from "The People Could Fly." As you read, think about how some of the elements in the story also stand for something else. Then answer the questions that follow.

> Say the people who could fly kept their power, although they shed their wings.[1] They kept their secret magic in the land of slavery.[2] They looked the same as the other people from Africa who had been coming over, who had dark skin.[3]
>
> So the one called Driver cracked his whip over the slow ones to make them move faster.[4] The whip was a slice-open cut of pain.[5]
>
> He said them all around to the others in the field under the whip, "... *buba yali* ... *buba tambe*...."[6]

1. In sentences 1–3, what do the wings and the power to fly symbolize?

   Possible responses: The wings are a symbol of power and freedom. The

   ability to fly is a secret that can be used to help the enslaved people

   escape one day.

2. In sentences 4–6, what does the whip symbolize?

   Possible responses: It symbolizes slavery, the cruelty of working under such

   harsh conditions, the unfairness of the situation, suffering.

E Late-Edition Scoop

Imagine that you are a newspaper reporter. Your boss wants you to cover a late-breaking story about the unusual events happening on the plantation. Write your report below.

ESCAPE TO FREEDOM

Reported by _____

What looked like an ordinary scene this evening was anything but ordinary earlier today.

Said one witness, "An old man called Toby whispered

ancient African words to the men and women.

The next thing I saw was people flying away. "

Another witness said that as the people flew they Possible responses:

rode the breezes; looked like black sticks; crossed many parts of the land

and disappeared.

When asked about this strange event, the Master of the plantation said,

"It was a trick. It didn't happen."

But what many people said happened was that Possible response: the

workers were treated so badly, they finally found a way to escape.

Only time will tell what happened to those who flew away and what will happen to those who remain behind.

Assessment

Fill in the circle next to each correct answer.

1. Why can't the people who are captured take their wings with them?
   - ● A. The ships do not have room for wings.
   - ○ B. The wings are never supposed to leave Africa.
   - ○ C. The people do not have time to get their wings.
   - ○ D. The wings would not work where the people are going.

2. Which of the following sentences from the story helps the reader visualize what the Master is like?
   - ○ A. Got sick with the up and down of the sea.
   - ○ B. Black, shiny wings flappin against the blue up there.
   - ○ C. Say the next day was dead hot in the fields.
   - ● D. A hard rock pile, wouldn't be moved.

3. Which sentence **best** describes why Toby finally says the magic words for the first time?
   - ○ A. He gets tired of listening to Sarah and her baby.
   - ● B. He cannot bear to see Sarah and the baby getting whipped.
   - ○ C. He is being chased by the Overseer and the Driver.
   - ○ D. He is afraid that he will be killed for not helping Sarah.

4. What does flying symbolize for the enslaved people?
   - ○ A. death
   - ○ B. forgetting
   - ● C. freedom
   - ○ D. slavery

5. Which of the following words means "loud crying"?
   - ● A. bawling
   - ○ B. scorned
   - ○ C. scrunched
   - ○ D. seize

Wrap-up

Compare and Contrast

Both "Icarus and Daedalus" and "The People Could Fly" include **symbols**. This is an important literary element in both stories. Although the setting and the characters of the stories are very different, a symbol in both stories—the ability to fly—stands for similar ideas. Think about the symbols in these stories. Think about what the symbols stand for. Finally, think about how the symbols reflect the meanings of the stories.

In the Venn diagram below, describe how the symbols of flying in "Icarus and Daedalus" and "The People Could Fly" are alike and how they are different. Write about how the symbols are different in the outer parts of the circles. Write about how the symbols are alike in the overlapping part of the circles. Examples have been provided.

"Icarus and Daedalus"

- Flying ends in tragedy.

- A character loses his wings and can no longer fly.

- Flying teaches a lesson about the importance of listening to wisdom and experience.

Alike

- Flying means freedom.

- Flying enables characters to escape from harsh treatment.

- A central character helps another or others to fly.

"The People Could Fly"

- Enslaved people successfully fly to their freedom.

- Some characters are not able to fly.

- Flying is a message of hope.

UNIT 5 Nonfiction

What's Nonfiction?

Pick up a newspaper or magazine, or check out many Web sites, and you will find writing that is nonfiction.

Nonfiction is the name for writing that is about real people and real events. Many types of nonfiction are meant to inform or to relate experiences. Nonfiction can go beyond just telling facts to include the use of vivid descriptions. Sometimes nonfiction writing also tries to influence the reader's opinion. There are many kinds of nonfiction. Essays, biographies, and autobiographies are popular types of this kind of writing.

- An **essay** is a short piece of nonfiction about a single topic.
- A **biography** is the story of a person's life written by someone other than that person.
- An **autobiography** is the story of a person's life written by that person.

Nonfiction can deal with many topics—the life of a famous person, historical events, or observations about a place.

On the line below, write a nonfiction subject that you would like to read about.

Sample response: the Civil War

Why Read Nonfiction?

Read nonfiction to learn about new places, new people, and new ideas. By reading nonfiction and learning new things, you can better understand the world around you. Nonfiction can even help you better understand yourself.

How Do I Read Nonfiction?

Focus on key **literary elements** and **reading skills** to get the most out of reading the four nonfiction selections in this unit. Here are two key literary elements and two key reading skills that you will practice in this unit.

Key Literary Elements

• Setting

Setting is the time and place in which a work of nonfiction takes place. The setting includes elements such as time period, location, or weather. A culture described by the author is also part of the setting.

• Author's Purpose

The **author's purpose** is his or her reason for writing a piece of nonfiction. It can be to inform, to persuade, or to entertain—or a combination of all three. Many nonfiction authors attempt to capture the emotion and significance of world events. Other writers may want to educate the public, build support for a cause, honor a group of people, or simply tell a story.

Key Reading Skills

• Evaluate

To **evaluate** is to make a judgment about what you are reading and how it is presented. Think about your reaction to the writer's words. Evaluate what you read by asking yourself questions: Does what is happening make sense? How do I feel about this character's thoughts and actions? Does the writer make her thoughts and ideas clear? Does the writer succeed in his purpose?

• Paraphrase

When you **paraphrase** a part or all of a nonfiction selection, you are restating the text in your own words. Paraphrasing can help you simplify text to make it clearer to yourself and others. For example, you can replace large words with smaller ones and leave out unnecessary details. Paraphrasing also helps you understand what you have read and what the author means.

Thank You in Arabic

Meet Naomi Shihab Nye

Naomi Shihab Nye (nā ō´mē shi häb nī) was born in Missouri in 1952. She is an Arab American. In 1992, after the Persian Gulf War, she published a book that includes poems by Iraqi writers. She wanted American children to see that Iraqis are very similar to Americans, with "the same daily needs, the same inner lives." "Thank You in Arabic" is from her book called *Going Where I'm Coming From*. It was first published in 1995.

What You Know

Think of a situation in which you couldn't make people understand you, or you couldn't understand others. Share this experience with a classmate. As a class, discuss things that can be done to help people understand each other better.

Reason to Read

Read to find out how a teenage girl deals with a new situation that she does not fully understand.

Background Info

In "Thank You in Arabic," the narrator and her family move to Jerusalem for a year. Jerusalem is a sacred city to the followers of the religions of Judaism, Christianity, and Islam. For hundreds of years, people have disagreed over borders in the Middle East, especially Jerusalem. When the country of Israel was established in 1948, Jerusalem was divided into an Israeli section and an Arab section. Since 1967, the city has been united under Israeli rule. This has caused many conflicts between Israel and its Arab neighbors.

Word Power

underestimated (un´ dər es´ tə māt´ id) *v.* placed too low a value on; guessed too low; p. 220
I *underestimated* how much paper we would need, so we had to get some more.

insolence (in´ sə ləns) *n.* a lack of respect; rudeness; p. 224
Because of my *insolence*, the teacher made me stay after class.

uninhabited (un´ in hab´ it id) *adj.* not lived in or on; p. 227
With only cactuses and lizards, the Arizona desert looked nearly *uninhabited*.

refugee (ref´ ū jē´) *n.* a person who leaves his or her home or country to escape or seek protection; p. 227
The *refugee* lived in a camp until he could move to the United States.

pilgrims (pil´ grəmz) *n.* people who travel to a holy place for a religious purpose; p. 229
The *pilgrims* traveled all the way from New York City to see the temple in Israel.

infamous (in´ fə məs) *adj.* well-known for being bad; p. 229
The robbers were *infamous* for stealing money from old people.

**Answer the following questions, using one of the new words above.
Write your answers in the spaces provided.**

1. Which word goes with "believers who visit a religious site"? _____ pilgrims _____

2. Which word goes with "a place that is empty and deserted"? _____ uninhabited _____

3. Which word goes with "thought something was going to be less than it was"?
   _____ underestimated _____

4. Which word goes with "a person who leaves home because of danger"?
   _____ refugee _____

5. Which word goes with "a bad reputation"? _____ infamous _____

6. Which word goes with "no respect"? _____ insolence _____

Adapted from

"Thank You in Arabic

Naomi Shihab Nye

أشكرك

....

Reading Skill

Paraphrase Reread the highlighted sentence. Which statement best paraphrases this sentence? Check the response that correctly completes the following sentence.

We left our home after my mother found out

- ☑ my brother threw away his pills.
- ☐ my brother got good grades on his test.
- ☐ my brother was younger than his classmates.

Shortly after my mother discovered my brother had been pitching his vitamin C tablets behind the stove for years, we left the country. Her sharp alert, "Now the truth be known!" startled us at the breakfast table as she poked into the dim space with the nozzle of her vacuum. We could hear the pills go click, click, up the long tube.

My brother, an obedient child, a bright-eyed, dark-skinned charmer who scored high on all his tests and sang a boy's sweet soprano, stared down at his oatmeal. Four years younger than I, he was also the youngest and smallest in his class.

The pills episode was really a pleasant surprise to me. Companions in mischief are not to be **underestimated,** especially when everything else in your life is about to change.

We sold everything we had and left the country. The move had been in the works for months.

Word Power

underestimated (un´ dər es´ tə māt´ id) v. placed too low a value on; guessed too low

220

Our parents had closed their imported-gifts stores. Our mother ran a little shop in our neighborhood in St. Louis and our father ran a bigger one in a hotel downtown. For years my brother and I had been sitting with them behind the counters after school, guessing if people who walked through the door would buy something or only browse. My brother and I helped unpack the crates. Something wonderful was always on its way.

But there were problems too. Sometimes whole days passed and nobody came in. Then the stockroom filled with pre-Christmas items caught on fire and burned up, right when our father was between insurance policies. We could hear our parents in the living room, worrying and arguing after we went to bed at night. Finally they had to give the business up.

Our father had also been attending the Unity School for Christianity for a few years, but decided not to become a minister after all. We were relieved, having felt like fakes the whole time he was enrolled. He wasn't even a Christian, to begin with, but a gently nonpracticing Muslim. Our mother had given up the glare of her Lutheran ancestors, raising my brother and me in the Vedanta Society of St. Louis. When anyone asked what we were, I said, "Hindu."

Did You Know?

A *keffiyah* (usually spelled *kaffiyah*) is a type of Arab headdress consisting of folded cloth and a cord.
....

Now and then, just to keep things balanced, we attended the Unity Sunday School. My teacher invited me to bring artifacts for Show and Tell. I wrapped a red and white *keffiyah* around my friend Jimmy's curly blond head while the girls in lacy socks giggled behind their hands. I told about my father coming to America from Palestine on the boat and throwing his old country clothes overboard before docking at Ellis Island. I felt relieved he'd kept a few things, like the *keffiyah* and its black braided band.

English Coach

When the author writes, "that language had never lived in our mouths," she means that she and her brother do not speak Arabic. The language did not actually inhabit their mouths. Check the phrases below that don't actually mean what they say.

- ☑ He was on her mind.
- ☑ My lips are sealed.
- ☐ Her eyes hurt from the strain.

Connect to the Text

Reread the boxed sentences. *Shookrun* is Arabic for "thank you." Do you know how to say "thank you" in more than one language? Why is "thank you" an important phrase to learn?

Answers will vary. Possible

response: Because it is a

polite thing to say when

someone helps you.

We had never met our Palestinian grandmother, Sitti Khadra, or seen Jerusalem, where our father had grown up. Our mother hadn't either. We did not speak Arabic, though the sound of the language was familiar to us—our father's musical blessings before meals. But that language had never lived in our mouths.

And that's where we were going, to Jerusalem.

The first plane flight of my whole life was the night flight out of New York City across the ocean. I was fourteen years old.

We stopped in Portugal for a few weeks. We were making a slow change. We stopped in Spain and Italy and Egypt, where the pyramids shocked me by sitting right on the edge of the giant city of Cairo. While we waited for our baggage to clear customs, I stared at six tall African men in a discussion with an Egyptian customs agent and realized I did not even know how to say "thank you" in Arabic. How was this possible? The most elemental and important of human phrases in my father's own tongue had been unknown to me till now. "Daddy," I said. "Daddy, I have to know. Daddy, tell me. Daddy, why didn't we ever *learn?*" Always thereafter, the word *shookrun*, so simple, would remind me of the vast African baggage.

We stayed one or two nights at the old Shepheard's Hotel downtown but couldn't sleep due to the heat and honking traffic beneath our windows. So our father moved us to the famous Mena House Hotel next to the pyramids.

That night, my brother and I both awakened burning with fever. We lay in bed for a week. An aged doctor tripped over my suitcase every time he entered to take our temperatures. We smothered our laughter. "*Shookrun*," I would say. But as soon as he left, to my brother, "I feel bad. How do you feel?"

222

"I feel really, really bad."

"I think I'm dying."

"I think I'm already dead."

Finally, finally, we appeared in the restaurant, thin and weakly smiling, and ordered the famous Mena House *shorraba*, lentil soup.

In those days Jerusalem, which was then a divided city, had an operating airport on the Jordanian side. The airport had just two runways, and the first thing I observed as we climbed down slowly from the stuffy plane was all my underwear strewn across one of them. Somehow my suitcase had popped open in the hold and dropped its contents the minute the men opened the cargo door. So the first thing I did on the home soil of my father was re-collect my underwear, down on my knees, the posture of prayer over that ancient holy land.

Our relatives came to see us at a hotel. Our grandmother was very short. She kept touching our heads and faces as if she couldn't believe we were there. I had not yet fallen in love with her. Sometimes you don't fall in love with people immediately, even if they're your own grandmother.

How is the place in this picture similar to and different from where you live?

Reading Skill

Evaluate Reread the highlighted conversation. Is it effective in telling how sick the narrator and her brother feel? Why or why not?

Possible response: It is effective because it is realistic. Many people exaggerate how bad they feel when they are sick.

Connect to the Text

Reread the boxed paragraph. Think of a time when you met someone new. What did you think of him or her? What do you think of this person now?

Answers will vary.

Reading Skill

Paraphrase Reread the text highlighted in green and the rest of the paragraph. Paraphrase the text by completing this sentence: I went to the Friends Boy School because

Possible response: I was

in high school and classes

would be taught in English.

_____

_____

_____

Literary Element

Setting Reread the sentences highlighted in blue. The narrator is experiencing a new culture. How is it different from what she has experienced until now?

Possible responses: She is

not allowed to talk with

boys. She is kicked out of

school for disagreeing with

the counselor.

_____

_____

We moved into a stone house eight miles north of the city. My brother was enrolled in the Friends Girls School and I was enrolled in the Friends Boys School in the town of Ramallah a few miles farther north. It all was a little confused. But the Girls School offered grades one through eight in English. High school continued at the Boys School. Most local girls went to Arabic-speaking schools after eighth grade.

I was one of seven girl students among two hundred boys, which would cause me problems a month later. I was called in from the schoolyard at lunchtime, to the office of our counselor who wore shoes so pointed and tight her feet bulged out pinkly on top.

"You will not be talking to them anymore," she said. She hit on the desk with a pencil for emphasis.

"To whom?"

"All the boy students at this institution. It is inappropriate behavior. From now on, you will speak only with the girls."

"But there are only six other girls! And I like only one of them!"

"No, thank you," I said. "It's ridiculous to say that girls should only talk to girls. Did I say anything bad to a boy? They're my friends. They're like my brothers. I won't do it, that's all."

I was sent home with a little paper requesting that I transfer to a different school. The charge: **insolence.** My mother, startled to see me home early and on my own, stared out the window when I told her.

 Stop here for **Break Time** on the next page.

Word Power

insolence (in´ sə ləns) *n.* a lack of respect; rudeness

Break Time

The settings are very important in "Thank You in Arabic." Each place in which the narrator lives or visits has an important effect on her feelings and moods. In the column on the left, write the name of a place in which the family has lived or visited. In the column on the right, write descriptions of the place. An example has been provided.

Place	Descriptions
Cairo, Egypt	• Pyramids are on the edge of the city. • The downtown is noisy. • There is a famous hotel near the pyramids.
St. Louis, United States	Possible responses: • There are little shops in neighborhoods; • big shops in downtown hotels; • it has Christian and Hindu schools.
Jerusalem, Israel	Possible responses: • It is a divided city; • has a small airport; • has stone houses; • has a girls' school and a boys' school.

 Turn the page to continue reading.

Old City, Jerusalem

What facts about Jerusalem does this photograph present?

Literary Element

Setting Reread the highlighted sentences. What is the new school like?

Possible responses: It is an old stone building in the Armenian Quarter. It is for Armenian students in grades kindergarten through 12.

Connect to the Text

Reread the boxed sentence. Have you ever felt like your life was changing? How did you react?

Answers will vary.

My father went with me to the St. Tarkmanchatz Armenian School, an ancient stone school tucked deep into the Armenian Quarter. He had already called the school officials on the telephone and tried to enroll me, though they didn't want to. Their school was for Armenian students only, kindergarten through twelfth grade. Classes were taught in three languages: Armenian, Arabic and English, which was why I needed to go there.

The head priest wore a long robe and a tall cone-shaped hat. He said, "Excuse me, please, but your daughter, she is not an Armenian, even a small amount?"

"Not at all," said my father. "But in case you didn't know, in the educational code books of this city, it says no student may be rejected on the basis of ethnic background. If you don't accept her, we will alert the proper authorities."

They took me. But the principal wasn't happy about it. The students, however, seemed glad to have a new face to look at. We wore uniforms, navy blue skirts for the girls, white shirts, and navy sweaters. All the other students knew all three languages with three entirely different alphabets. How could they carry so much in their heads?

I felt I had left my old life entirely.

226

Every afternoon I went down to the basement of the school where the kindergarten class was having an Arabic lesson. More than any of the lessons, I remember the way the teacher hit the backs of the students' hands with his ruler when they made a mistake. Their little faces puffed up with quiet tears. This pained me so much I forgot all my words. The teacher never hit my hand, especially after I wrote a letter to the city newspaper, which my father edited, protesting such harsh treatment of young learners. I wish I had known how to talk to those little ones, but they were just beginning their English studies and didn't speak much yet. They were at the same place in their English that I was in my Arabic.

From the high windows of St. Tarkmanchatz, we saw the barbed wire separating Jordan from Israel. The bleak, **uninhabited** strip of land reminded me how little education saved us after all. People who had differing ideas still imagined fighting could solve things. Staring out over the quiet roofs of afternoon, I thought it so foolish. I asked my friends what they thought about it and they shrugged.

"It doesn't matter what we think about it. It just keeps happening. It happened in Armenia too, you know. Really, really bad in Armenia. And who talks about it in the world news now? It happens everywhere. It happens in *your* country one by one, yes? Murders and guns. What can we do?"

Sometimes after school, my brother and I walked up the road that led past the crowded **refugee** camp of Palestinians who owned even less than our modest relatives did in the village.

Word Power

uninhabited (un´ in hab´ it id) *adj.* not lived in or on
refugee (ref´ ū jē´) *n.* a person who leaves his or her home or country to escape or seek protection

Connect to the Text

Reread the sentences boxed in purple. What would you do if this happened to one of your friends?

Answers will vary.

_____

_____

_____

_____

Comprehension Check

Reread the paragraph boxed in green. What does the grandmother want that makes the narrator nervous? Check the correct response.

☐ to move to the United States

☑ to have the family stay forever

☐ to tell more funny stories about her son

I wanted to go back to the United States. Suddenly I felt like a patriotic citizen. One of my friends, Sylvie Markarian, had just been shipped off to Damascus, Syria, to marry a man who was fifty years old. Sylvie was exactly my age. She had never met her future husband before. I thought this was the most awful thing I had ever heard of. "Tell your parents no thank you," I urged her. "Tell them you _refuse_."

"You don't understand," she told me. "In United States you say no. We don't say no. We have to follow someone's wishes. This is the wish of my father. Me, I am scared. I never slept away from my mother before. But I have no choice. I am going because they tell me to go." She was sobbing, sobbing on my shoulder. And I was stroking her long, soft hair. After that, I carried two fists inside, one for Sylvie and one for me.

Most weekends my family went to the village to sit with the relatives. My father translated the more interesting bits of conversation, the funny stories my grandmother told. She talked about old memories from my father's childhood, before he moved away from her. She wanted to make sure we were going to stick around forever, which made me feel very nervous.

During these long, slow weekends, my crying jags began. I cried without any warning, even in the middle of a meal. My crying was usually noiseless but dramatically wet—streams of tears pouring down my cheeks, onto my collar or the back of my hand.

Someone always asked in Arabic, "What is wrong? Are you sick? Do you wish to lie down?"

My father made brave excuses in the beginning. "She's overtired," he said. "She has a headache. She is missing her friend who moved to Syria. She is homesick just now."

My brother stared at me as if I had just landed from Planet X.

Worst of all was our drive to school every morning, when our car came over the rise in the highway and all Jerusalem lay before us. I cried hardest then. My father pulled over and talked to me. He sighed. He kept his hands on the steering wheel even when the car was stopped and said, "Someday, I promise you, you will look back on this period in your life and have no idea what made you so unhappy here."

"I want to go home." It became my anthem. "This place depresses me. It weighs too much. I hate all these old stones that everybody keeps kissing. I'm sick of **pilgrims.** They act so holy and pure. And I hate the way people stare at me here."

"You could be happy here if you tried just a little harder," my father said. "Don't compare it to the United States all the time. Don't pretend the United States is perfect. And look at your brother—he's not having any problems!"

"My brother is eleven years old."

I had crossed the boundary from simple childhood when happiness was a good ball and lots of candy-coated Jordan almonds.

Didn't I recognize the beautiful oddity of my own life when I sat right in the middle of it? Didn't I feel lucky to be here? Well, yes I did. But sometimes it was hard to be lucky.

When we left Jerusalem, we left quickly. Left in a plane, not sure where we were going. The sounds of fighting with Israel had been growing louder and louder. In the no-man's land visible from the windows of our house, guns shot loudly in the middle of the night. We lived right near the edge. My father heard disturbing rumors at the newspaper that would soon grow into the **infamous** Six Day War of 1967. We were in England by then, drinking tea from thin china cups and scanning the newspapers.

Word Power

pilgrims (pil′ grəmz) *n.* people who travel to a holy place for a religious purpose

infamous (in′ fə məs) *adj.* well-known for being bad

Literary Element

Setting Reread the highlighted paragraph. What about Jerusalem depresses the narrator?

Possible responses: She hates the old stones and is sick of the pilgrims. She hates how people stare at her.

English Coach

The term *no-man's land* means a place that is between groups that are fighting where no one lives. Based on the term, whom do you think the land belongs to?

It belongs to no one.

Comprehension Check

Reread the boxed sentences. Where do the narrator and her family go to live when they return to the United States? Why do they choose this place?

They move to Texas because

it is big and warm.

Reading Skill

Evaluate Reread the highlighted paragraph. In your opinion, was the narrator's year in Jerusalem a good experience for her? Why or why not?

Possible responses: Yes,

it expanded her idea of

"normal" everyday life. She

might be more adventurous

in making new friends and

choosing new experiences.

Bombs were blowing up in Jerusalem. We worried about the village. We worried about my grandmother's dreams, which had been getting worse and worse, she'd told us.

My parents didn't want to go back to Missouri. Texas was big and warm. After a chilly year crowded around the small gas heaters we used in Jerusalem, a warm place sounded appealing. In roomy Texas, my parents bought the first house they looked at.

Back *home* again in my own country, it seemed impossible to forget the place we had just left.

Our father used to tell us that when he was little, the sky over Jerusalem crackled with meteors and shooting stars almost every night. They streaked and flashed in the dark. Our father and his brothers slept on the roof to watch the sky.

During our year in Jerusalem, my brother and I looked upwards whenever we were outside at night, but the stars were different since our father was a boy. Now the sky seemed too orderly, stuck in place. The stars had learned where they belonged. Only people on the ground kept changing.

Respond to Literature

Thank You in Arabic

A Comprehension Check

Answer the following questions in the spaces provided.

1. Why does the narrator's family move to Jerusalem? The family's business is
not doing well, especially after the fire. It is where her father grew up.

2. What does the narrator do to get kicked out of school? The narrator tells
the counselor that she will continue to talk to the boys even though the
counselor orders her not to.

B Reading Skills

Complete the following activities in the spaces provided.

1. **Evaluate** What reason does the narrator give for not following the rules at
the Friends Boys School? Is this a good reason? Possible response: She says
that the boys are her friends and that she should be able to speak to them.
Answers will vary.

2. **Evaluate** Do you think the author gives an interesting and vivid picture of
her experience? Why or why not? Possible response: Yes, her experiences
are interesting because I can relate to having mixed feelings about facing a
new experience.

3. **Paraphrase** Paraphrase this sentence from the selection: "I had crossed the
boundary from simple childhood when happiness was a good ball and lots
of candy-coated Jordan almonds." Possible response: I grew up and cannot
be made happy just by having a ball and some candy.

C Word Power

Complete each sentence below, using one of the words in the box.

underestimated	insolence	uninhabited
refugee	pilgrims	infamous

1. The _____pilgrims_____ from Egypt traveled far to see the religious center.

2. The project took so long because I had _____underestimated_____ how much time it would take to complete.

3. Instead of showing respect, the rude man spoke with great _____insolence_____.

4. Many outlaws in history have become _____infamous_____ for their bad deeds.

5. Because the land had no water source, it was _____uninhabited_____.

6. The _____refugee_____ waited at the center to get papers to enter the country.

D Literary Element: Setting

Read the passages below from "Thank You in Arabic." As you read, think about the importance of the settings in the story. Then answer the questions that follow.

> From the high windows of St. Tarkmanchatz, we saw the barbed wire separating Jordan from Israel.[1] The bleak, uninhabited strip of land reminded me how little education saved us after all.[2] People who had differing ideas still imagined fighting could solve things.[3] Staring out over the quiet roofs of afternoon, I thought it so foolish.[4]
>
> Sometimes after school, my brother and I walked up the road that led past the crowded refugee camp of Palestinians who owned even less than our modest relatives did in the village.[5]

1. What do sentences 1–4 tell you about the place where the narrator lives?

   Possible responses: There is barbed wire between two countries that are

   fighting each other. The empty piece of land and barbed wire are reminders

   that Jerusalem is facing war.

2. What does sentence 5 tell you about some of the people living in
   Jerusalem? Possible responses: Some people have to live together in

   cramped spaces. They do not have much. They are even poorer than the

   narrator's family.

E A Letter

Imagine that you are the narrator. Write a letter to a friend in Missouri. Tell him about your trip to Jerusalem, your new school, and your friends.

Dear _____,

My journey to Jerusalem was interesting. We made many stops. We stopped in New York City, Portugal, Spain, Italy, and Egypt.

_____

The people in Jerusalem are Possible response: different and stare at me

a lot, but I have made some friends.

I've gone to two schools since I've been here. At the first school,

Possible response: they kicked me out because I talked to boys.

At the second school, Possible responses: I took Arabic lessons with

kindergarten students; everyone is Armenian.

My good friend Sylvie had to leave because Possible response: her

parents are forcing her to marry a man more than three times her

age.

I think we will be coming back to the United States because

Possible responses: a war is about to start; the sounds of fighting are

getting louder and louder.

I miss you very much.

Naomi

P.S. I learned a very useful word, shookrun, which means

_____ thank you _____ in Arabic.

Assessment

Fill in the circle next to each correct answer.

1. What does the narrator's brother throw behind the stove?
   - ○ A. a china teacup
   - ○ B. old Christmas lights
   - ● C. his vitamin C tablets
   - ○ D. his oatmeal

2. Which sentence **best** paraphrases this sentence: "But that language had never lived in our mouths"?
   - ○ A. Words died in our mouths.
   - ○ B. We were speechless.
   - ● C. We did not speak that language.
   - ○ D. We could not speak with our mouths full.

3. The narrator's family moves to a place near the border of what two countries?
   - ● A. Israel and Jordan
   - ○ B. Egypt and Israel
   - ○ C. Armenia and Syria
   - ○ D. Spain and Italy

4. How does the narrator protest the harsh treatment of the kindergarten children?
   - ○ A. She leaves the school and goes to another one.
   - ○ B. She talks to the children and reads to them.
   - ○ C. She talks back to the teacher.
   - ● D. She writes a letter to the city newspaper.

5. Which of the following words means "a place that is not lived in"?
   - ○ A. underestimated
   - ● B. uninhabited
   - ○ C. infamous
   - ○ D. insolence

Get Ready to Read!

THE GETTYSBURG ADDRESS

Meet Abraham Lincoln

Abraham Lincoln was born in 1809 in Kentucky. Lincoln was our country's president from 1861 to 1865. He helped end slavery in the United States. Lincoln was known for being honest and well-spoken. He could use few words to explain important truths. This ability has kept Lincoln's words alive even today. Shortly after the Civil War ended in 1865, Lincoln was shot and killed. His speech "The Gettysburg Address" was given on November 19, 1863.

What You Know

What do you know about Abraham Lincoln? Think of words that describe his qualities. Make a list together as a class.

Reason to Read

Read to find out more about the president who helped lead the nation through the Civil War.

Background Info

The Civil War took place in the United States from 1861 to 1865. Northerners and Southerners fought over slavery and states' rights. There were many bloody battles. The Battle of Gettysburg took place in Pennsylvania in July of 1863. In just three days, more than 40,000 soldiers from both sides were killed or wounded. Four months after the battle, a cemetery was built in Gettysburg. President Lincoln gave a now-famous speech at the cemetery to honor the dead.

Word Power *word sums*

conceived (kən sēvd´) *v.* created; imagined; p. 238
The man who *conceived* the high-speed computer was a genius.

con⁺ceive⁺ed

proposition (prop´ ə zish´ ən) *n.* a suggestion; an idea; p. 238
The mayor's *proposition* to start building a new school has been approved.

pro⁺pose⁺ite⁺ion

consecrate (kon´ sə krāt´) *v.* to make, declare, or honor as sacred; p. 240
We will *consecrate* this land in honor of those who made it thrive.

con⁺secr⁺ate

detract (di trakt´) *v.* to take something away; lessen; p. 240
Wearing too much makeup will *detract* from your natural beauty.

de⁺tract

nobly (nō´ bəl ē) *adv.* with honor; in a heroic way; p. 240
The woman *nobly* climbed the tallest mountain in the world.

noble⁺y

**Answer the following questions, using one of the new words above.
Write your answers in the spaces provided.**

1. Which word goes with "doing something bravely"? _____ nobly _____

2. Which word goes with "a plan for something"? _____ proposition _____

3. Which word goes with "thought up"? _____ conceived _____

4. Which word goes with "to take away from something"? _____ detract _____

5. Which word goes with "to declare a place special"? _____ consecrate _____

The Gettysburg Address, 1987. Mort Künstler.
Oil on canvas, 30 x 30 in. Private collection.

THE GETTYSBURG ADDRESS

Abraham Lincoln

Background Info

A "score" is twenty years. Lincoln is referring to the year the United States was founded.

Reading Skill

Evaluate Reread the highlighted sentence. Lincoln believes our country is based on the idea that all people should be free and treated equally. Do you think this is a good idea on which to base a country? Why?

Possible response: Yes, because everyone should be treated fairly and be able to act freely.

Four score and seven years ago our fathers brought forth on this continent a new nation, **conceived** in Liberty, and dedicated to the **proposition** that all men are created equal.

WHAT IT MEANS Eighty-seven years ago, our founding fathers created a new nation. This nation was based on the idea of freedom and equality for everyone.

Word Power

conceived (kən sēvd´) v. created; imagined
proposition (prop´ ə zish´ ən) n. a suggestion; an idea

Now we are engaged in a great civil war, testing whether that nation, or any nation so conceived and so dedicated, can long endure. We are met on a great battlefield of that war. We have come to dedicate a portion of that field, as a final resting place for those who here gave their lives that that nation might live. It is altogether fitting and proper that we should do this.

WHAT IT MEANS Now we are fighting a major civil war to see if this nation, which is based on the idea of equality and freedom, can continue to exist far into the future. We meet on a battlefield of that war. We are here to make part of that field a cemetery for those who died fighting for the survival of this new nation. We are doing the right thing.

The Angle, Gettysburg, Pennsylvania, July 3, 1863, 1988. Mort Künstler. Oil on canvas, 18 x 24 in. Collection of Mr. and Mrs. Robert L. Sharpe.

What lines or ideas in the Gettysburg Address does this painting bring to mind? Explain.

English Coach

The word *great* can mean "very good," but here Lincoln uses it to mean "major" or "important." Use the word in a sentence the way Lincoln meant it.

Possible response: The great

event changed our lives

forever.

Connect to the Text

Reread the boxed sentences. Have you ever been inspired by someone's heroic actions? How did you respond?

Answers will vary.

_____

_____

_____

_____

239

Literary Element

Setting Reread the sentences highlighted in blue. Why is the place where Lincoln is giving his speech important? Check the correct response.

- ☐ It is the building in which the country was founded.
- ☑ It is a battlefield where soldiers fought bravely.
- ☐ It is where the Civil War finally ended.

Reading Skill

Paraphrase Reread the sentences highlighted in green. Lincoln gives his speech to honor the dead. But he also wants his listeners to continue to do something. In your own words, paraphrase what he is saying to the listeners.

Possible response: We need

to continue to fight for

freedom and democracy.

_____

_____

_____

But, in a larger sense, we cannot dedicate—we cannot **consecrate**—we cannot hallow—this ground. The brave men, living and dead, who struggled here, have consecrated it, far above our poor power to add or **detract.** The world will little note, nor long remember what we say here, but it can never forget what they did here. It is for us the living, rather, to be dedicated here to the unfinished work which they who fought here have thus far so **nobly** advanced. It is rather for us to be here dedicated to the great task remaining before us—that from these honored dead we take increased devotion to that cause for which they gave the last full measure of devotion—that we here highly resolve that these dead shall not have died in vain—that this nation, under God, shall have a new birth of freedom—and that government of the people, by the people, for the people, shall not perish from the earth.

November 19, 1863

WHAT IT MEANS However, we cannot make this ground sacred. The men who fought here, those who are still alive and those who are dead, have already made this a sacred place. The world will not remember what we say here, but it will never forget what those who fought here have done. So, it is our job now to make sure we finish the job that they began. We should be inspired by those who have died to become even more devoted to the cause of freedom. If we do not, their deaths are meaningless. We must make sure freedom and democracy survive.

Word Power

consecrate (kon´ sə krāt´) *v.* to make, declare, or honor as sacred
detract (di trakt´) *v.* to take something away; lessen
nobly (nō´ bəl ē) *adv.* with honor; in a heroic way

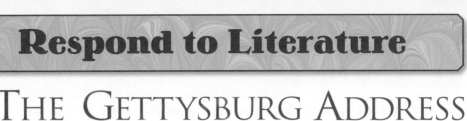

Respond to Literature

THE GETTYSBURG ADDRESS

A Comprehension Check

Answer the following questions in the spaces provided.

1. What ideas does Lincoln say our country is based on? It is based on the ideas of liberty and equality for everyone.

2. What does Lincoln want his listeners to do to make sure that the soldiers did not die without reason? He wants them to continue to fight to keep freedom and democracy alive.

B Reading Skills

Answer the following questions in the spaces provided.

1. **Paraphrase** What is another way of saying "The world will not remember what we say here, but it will never forget what those who fought here have done"? Possible response: The words we say today will be forgotten, but the actions of the soldiers will be remembered.

2. **Evaluate** Lincoln says that no one will remember his words. Yet his speech has become famous. Why do you think that is? Possible response: It has important ideas that are strongly expressed. It is very emotional.

C Word Power

Complete each sentence below, using one of the words in the box.

conceived	proposition	consecrate
detract	nobly	

1. We presented a _____ proposition _____ to our teacher to forbid homework on weekends.

2. Too many weeds _____ detract _____ from the beauty of the lawn.

3. My uncle _____ nobly _____ volunteered to fight in the war overseas.

4. The book was _____ conceived _____ by an author with a wild imagination.

5. The veterans will _____ consecrate _____ this park as a memorial to those who fought in the war.

Circle the word that best completes each sentence.

6. She had to **(nobly, detract)** from his score because he made too many spelling errors.

7. The officials will **(conceived, consecrate)** this cemetery for those who died protecting our freedom.

8. Paul **(consecrate, nobly)** agreed to speak for those who were not allowed to attend.

9. If enough people vote for this **(proposition, detract)**, our town will get a new library.

10. His plan to make computers easier to use was **(proposition, conceived)** in a garage.

D Literary Element: Setting

Read the passages below from "The Gettysburg Address." As you read, think about why Lincoln chose Gettysburg as the place to give his speech.

We meet on a battlefield of that war.[1] We are here to make part of that field a cemetery for those who died fighting for the survival of this new nation.[2]

The men who fought here, those who are still alive and those who are dead, have already made this a sacred place.[3] The world will not remember what we say here, but it will never forget what those who fought here have done.[4]

1. Read sentences 1–2. The place where Lincoln is speaking has had two functions. What are they?

   The place was a battlefield and is now a cemetery.

2. Reread sentences 3–4. According to Lincoln, how has the ground been made sacred? Possible response: The soldiers who fought on the battlefield have made it sacred by fighting to preserve the ideals of the country.

E A Personal Letter

Imagine that you are at Gettysburg and hear Lincoln deliver his speech. Now you are at home thinking about his words. Write a letter to a friend describing what you heard and how you felt about the speech.

Dear _____,

Today I went to the Gettysburg battlefield. There were many people. Some had lost their sons. Some of these people were Possible responses: crying; comforting others in the crowd.

President Lincoln made a speech. He said Possible responses: the Civil War is testing our country; a cemetery is being created to honor dead soldiers and that it is the right thing to do.

He wants us to Possible responses: continue fighting for freedom and democracy; be inspired by those who died.

His words were Possible responses: powerful, moving, inspiring.

They made me feel Possible response: sad, but eager to help our country.

I hope peace will come soon.

Your friend,

_____

Assessment

Fill in the circle next to each correct answer.

1. What is being dedicated at Gettysburg?
   - ● A. a cemetery
   - ○ B. a monument
   - ○ C. a park
   - ○ D. a new nation

2. Why does Lincoln deliver the speech "The Gettysburg Address"?
   - ○ A. He wants to congratulate the soldiers on winning the war.
   - ● B. He is honoring the dead at a battleground.
   - ○ C. He is trying to get votes to become president.
   - ○ D. He is surrendering to the Southern army.

3. Lincoln is dedicating a cemetery at Gettysburg because
   - ○ A. it was the location of the final battle of the Civil War.
   - ○ B. it was where the Southern troops surrendered.
   - ● C. it was a battlefield where many brave soldiers fought.
   - ○ D. it was the meeting place of the country's founding fathers.

4. Choose one of the following statements that **best** paraphrases one of the main ideas of "The Gettysburg Address."
   - ○ A. Everyone should always support the military.
   - ○ B. We should learn from our mistakes and not repeat errors.
   - ● C. We should continue to fight for freedom and democracy.
   - ○ D. To survive, the country needs to constantly change.

5. Which of the following words means "an idea or a suggestion"?
   - ● A. proposition
   - ○ B. nobly
   - ○ C. conceived
   - ○ D. consecrate

This We Know

Meet Chief Seattle

Chief Seattle was born around 1786 near present-day Seattle, Washington. Although he was a warrior for most of his life, Chief Seattle became known for making powerful speeches on behalf of his people. After his fighting days were over, he dedicated himself to helping solve problems among Native American groups and finding ways to get along with white settlers. He died in 1866. The speech "This We Know" is believed to have been given in 1854.

What You Know

Have you ever done something to help protect our environment? Think of ways ordinary citizens can protect the land. As a class, make a list of ideas.

Reason to Read

Read the speech "This We Know" to find out how a Native American leader feels about how we should treat the earth.

Background Info

Native Americans have lived in the Pacific Northwest region of the present-day United States for thousands of years. These groups include the Duwamish and Suquamish Indians, who settled around Puget Sound in what became the state of Washington. In the 1850s, a representative of the federal government met with members of these groups to try to buy the land they lived on. In return, the Native Americans were promised some land and help from the government. "This We Know" is a speech said to have been given by the leader of the Native American groups during the meeting.

Word Power

veins (vāns) *n.* blood vessels that carry blood to the heart from other parts of the body; p. 248
Be careful not to cut the *veins* in your arm.

ancestors (an´ ses´ tərz) *n.* people from whom someone is descended, especially from the distant past; p. 248
My grandmother told me that our *ancestors* lived on a farm in Italy.

contempt (kən tempt´) *n.* a lack of respect; a feeling of hatred toward someone or something; p. 250
The cook treated the lazy boy with *contempt*.

slaughtered (slô´ tərd) *v.* killed in large numbers; p. 250
The sick cows were *slaughtered* so that they would not spread the disease.

preserve (pri zurv´) *v.* to protect from harm or destruction; to maintain; p. 250
We tried to *preserve* the historic houses that were in danger of being torn down.

**Answer the following questions that contain the new words above.
Write your answers in the spaces provided.**

1. If people *slaughtered* a herd of animals, would the animals be alive or dead?

   dead

2. Are *ancestors* people related to you or people who are your friends?

   people related to you

3. If you have *contempt* for someone, would you like or dislike that person?

   dislike that person

4. If a nurse wanted to find *veins*, would she look at your teeth or your arm?

   your arm

5. If you wanted to *preserve* a photo, would you keep it in an album or throw it away?

   keep it in an album

Adapted from

This We Know

Based on a speech by Chief Seattle

English Coach

The suffix -*y* can mean "having or full of." A *sandy* shore has a lot of *sand*. *Rocky* peaks have a lot of *rocks*. What is a word that means "full of mist"?

misty

The President in Washington sends word that he wishes to buy our land. But how can you buy or sell the sky? The land? The idea is strange to us. If we do not own the freshness of the air and the sparkle of the water, how can you buy them?

Every part of this earth is sacred to my people. Every shining pine needle, every sandy shore, every mist in the dark woods, every meadow, every humming insect. All are holy in the memory and experience of my people. We know the sap which runs through the trees as we know the blood that runs through our **veins.** We are part of the earth and it is part of us. The perfumed flowers are our sisters. The bear, the deer, the eagle, these are our brothers. The rocky peaks, the juices in the meadow, the body of the pony, and man, all belong to the same family.

The shining water that moves in the streams and rivers is not just water, but the blood of our **ancestors.** If we sell you our land you must remember that it is sacred. Each ghostly reflection in the clear water of the lakes tells of events and memories in the life of my people. The water's murmur is the voice of my father's father.

Word Power

veins (vāns) *n.* blood vessels that carry blood to the heart from other parts of the body

ancestors (an´ ses´ tərz) *n.* people from whom someone is descended, especially from the distant past

The rivers are our brothers. They quench our thirst. They carry our canoes and feed our children. So you must give to the rivers the kindness you would give any brother.

If we sell you our land, remember that the air is precious to us, that the air shares its spirit with all the life it supports. The wind that gave our grandfather his first breath also receives his last sigh. The wind also gives our children the spirit of life. So if we sell you our land, you must keep it apart and sacred, as a place where man can go to taste the wind that is sweetened by meadow flowers.

Will you teach your children what we have taught our children? That the earth is our mother? What happens to the earth, happens to all the sons of the earth.

This we know: The earth does not belong to man, man belongs to the earth. All things are connected like the blood which unites us all. Man did not weave the web of life, he is merely a strand in it. Whatever he does to the web he does to himself.

What features shown in this picture are mentioned by Chief Seattle in his speech?

Reading Skill

Evaluate Reread the highlighted paragraph. Chief Seattle wants the U.S. government to treat the rivers well. Do you agree with him that rivers should be treated with kindness and respect? Why?

Answers will vary.

_____

_____

_____

_____

Reading Skill

Paraphrase Reread the highlighted sentences. In your own words, paraphrase what Chief Seattle is saying about humans.

Possible response: Humans

did not create the earth;

we are just part of it. What

humans do to the earth, we

do to ourselves.

_____

_____

Background Info

The talking wires are telegraph wires. Before the telephone was invented, telegraphs allowed people to communicate long distances through wires. By 1861, telegraph wires had been placed throughout the United States.

Literary Element

Author's Purpose Reread the highlighted paragraph. This passage explains the purpose of Chief Seattle's speech. What does he want the government to do? Check the correct response.

- [ ] give the land back to the Indians
- [x] love and take care of the land
- [ ] find a place for Indians to live

One thing we know: Our god is also your god. The earth is precious to him and to harm the earth is to heap **contempt** on its creator.

Your future is a mystery to us. What will happen when the buffalo are all **slaughtered**? The wild horses tamed? What will happen when the secret corners of the forest are heavy with the scent of many men and the view of the ripe hills is ruined by talking wires? Where will the thicket be? Gone! Where will the eagle be? Gone! And what is it to say goodbye to the swift pony and the hunt? The end of living and the beginning of survival.

When the last Indian has vanished with his wilderness and his memory is only the shadow of a cloud moving across the prairie, will these shores and forests still be here? Will there be any of the spirit of my people left?

Did You Know?

A *prairie* is a large area of flat or rolling grassland. Few trees grow on prairies.
. . . .

We love this earth as a newborn loves its mother's heartbeat. So, if we sell you our land love it as we have loved it. Care for it as we have cared for it. Hold in your mind the memory of the land as it is when you receive it. **Preserve** the land for all children and love it as God loves us all.

As we are part of the land, you too are part of the land. This earth is precious to us. It is also precious to you. One thing we know: There is only one God. No man, be he Indian or White Man, can be apart. We *are* brothers after all.

Word Power

contempt (kən tempt´) *n.* a lack of respect; a feeling of hatred toward someone or something

slaughtered (slô´ tərd) *v.* killed in large numbers

preserve (pri zurv´) *v.* to protect from harm or destruction; to maintain

Respond to Literature

This We Know

A Comprehension Check

Answer the following questions in the spaces provided.

1. Why does Chief Seattle think that the idea of selling land is strange?

   Possible response: He says that no one can own the land. If no one can own it, no one can sell it.

2. What does Chief Seattle think might happen if the Native Americans sell the land to the U.S. government? Possible response: He thinks that the wildlife may be killed, that the air and the forests might be destroyed, and that too many people might settle on the land.

B Reading Skills

Complete the following activities in the spaces provided.

1. **Evaluate** Do you think this speech is important to people today? Explain your answer. Possible responses: Yes, people still need to respect the land, the air, and the water. It is even more important today because more people are using the land than when Chief Seattle lived. It is up to us to care for our environment.

2. **Paraphrase** In your own words, paraphrase this passage from the speech: "Man did not weave the web of life, he is merely a strand in it. Whatever he does to the web he does to himself." Possible responses: People are just one part of life on earth. Any changes made to one part of life will affect all the other parts of life.

C Word Power

Complete each sentence below, using one of the words in the box.

veins	ancestors	contempt
slaughtered	preserve	

1. While researching her family history, Tamika discovered that she has several famous _____ancestors_____ .

2. When he gets mad, the _____veins_____ in his neck become more visible.

3. One way to _____preserve_____ a work of art is to keep it out of direct sunlight.

4. The protestors had great _____contempt_____ for the company that dumped trash into the river.

5. Because so many blue whales were _____slaughtered_____ , they became an endangered species.

Circle the word that best completes each sentence.

6. They stopped building new houses on the land to **(veins, preserve)** the unique environment.

7. Your **(slaughtered, contempt)** for people who watch television is getting annoying.

8. I learned that my **(contempt, ancestors)** were originally from Spain.

9. Before they were **(slaughtered, preserve)**, wild buffalo roamed the prairie.

10. The blood that flows through your **(veins, ancestors)** looks blue under the skin.

D Literary Element: Author's Purpose

Read the passages below from "This We Know." As you read, think about how the sentences illustrate Chief Seattle's purpose for giving this speech. Then answer the questions that follow.

The rivers are our brothers.[1] They quench our thirst.[2] They carry our canoes and feed our children.[3] So you must give to the rivers the kindness you would give any brother.[4]

As we are part of the land, you too are part of the land.[5] This earth is precious to us.[6] It is also precious to you.[7] One thing we know: There is only one God.[8] No man, be he Indian or White Man, can be apart.[9] We *are* brothers after all.[10]

1. In sentences 1–4, what is Chief Seattle's purpose for speaking these words?

   Possible responses: He wants people to take care of the rivers because they

   provide water to drink, food to eat, and a way to travel. He wants the rivers

   to be treated with respect.

2. In sentences 5–10, who is Chief Seattle addressing? What connections does he want the listeners to make? Possible responses: He is talking to the

   white people who want to buy the land. He wants them to see the

   relationship between the Native Americans and the white people and also

   between nature and all people.

E A Conservation Poster

Create a poster for your community. Your purpose is to persuade people to take care of the earth and not pollute it. Use examples from Chief Seattle's speech to encourage and inspire people to care for the earth.

PROTECT THE EARTH!

Chief Seattle once said, "This earth is precious to us." He also said that

Possible responses: every part of it is sacred and important. We

are part of the earth, and it is part of us. We must preserve the

land and love it.

Do not let our rivers die from pollution. We need our rivers for

Possible response: food, drinking water, and transportation.

We also need to keep our air clean. Chief Seattle said that the air

Possible response: is precious to us and that it shares its spirit

with all the life it supports.

Let's love the earth as Chief Seattle loved it and take his advice to

Possible response: care for it and preserve it for all generations

to come.

Our future depends on how we treat our world today.

Assessment

Fill in the circle next to each correct answer.

1. According to Chief Seattle, who owns the land and the sky?
   - ○ A. white people
   - ○ B. the president
   - ○ C. his people
   - ● D. no one

2. To illustrate how important nature is to his people, Chief Seattle calls the bear, the eagle, and the deer his
   - ○ A. friends.
   - ● B. brothers.
   - ○ C. uncles.
   - ○ D. children.

3. Choose the sentence that **best** paraphrases these words by Chief Seattle: "The rocky peaks, the juices in the meadow, the body of the pony, and man, all belong to the same family."
   - ○ A. The land in Washington belongs only to my people.
   - ○ B. All parts of nature are separate.
   - ● C. All things on the earth are related.
   - ○ D. Nature can be owned only by the government.

4. Why does Chief Seattle make this speech?
   - ● A. He wants to persuade people to maintain the land and keep it beautiful.
   - ○ B. He wants to inform the president that his land is not for sale.
   - ○ C. He wants to persuade his people that selling the land is a good idea.
   - ○ D. He wants to explain that his people are not violent.

5. Which of the following words means "a strong dislike"?
   - ○ A. veins
   - ○ B. ancestors
   - ● C. contempt
   - ○ D. slaughtered

Get Ready to Read!

Nationally Televised Speech
by President John F. Kennedy

Meet
John F. Kennedy

John F. Kennedy was born in 1917. In 1960, after serving as a U.S. senator, he became the thirty-fifth president of the United States. The civil rights movement was in its early stages as he began his term in office. He was a supporter of civil rights laws intended to give equal rights to all Americans. President Kennedy gave this speech to the nation on June 11, 1963. On November 22, 1963, he was shot and killed in Dallas, Texas.

What You Know

What do you know about the civil rights movement in the United States? As a class, make a list of important people and events in the movement.

Reason to Read

Read this speech to learn how President John F. Kennedy asked citizens and the government to help make equal rights a reality for all Americans.

Background Info

In 1954 the U.S. government declared that students could not be put in separate schools based on race. But even by the early 1960s, many schools and other public places still did not provide equal opportunities for African Americans. On June 11, 1963, President John F. Kennedy gave a speech on national television after he sent National Guard troops to the University of Alabama to protect two African American students from acts of violence. President Kennedy gave this speech that night to urge Americans to treat others with respect, regardless of race, and to pass and support new laws that would guarantee every American citizen fair and equal treatment.

Word Power

demonstrate (dem´ ən strāt´) *v.* to take part in a group display of feelings toward a person or an issue; p. 258
The organization's members did not like the governor's idea, so they decided to *demonstrate* on the steps of the state capitol.

segregation (seg´ rə gā´ shən) *n.* the act of separating people by racial or social groups; p. 259
There are still many countries in which *segregation* exists, and children of different races attend different schools.

discrimination (dis krim´ ə nā´ shən) *n.* the act of treating a person or a group of people unfairly or with prejudice; p. 259
The boss told the male workers that *discrimination* against women was not allowed in the company.

injustice (in jus´ tis) *n.* unfair treatment; a wrong; p. 259
It is an *injustice* to be punished without first being able to tell your side of the story.

token (tō´ kən) *adj.* having little value or effect; p. 260
Roberto's *token* apology did not convince his neighbor that he was sorry.

federal (fed´ ər əl) *adj.* of or relating to the central government of the United States; p. 261
My aunt is a *federal* agent who helps people apply for U.S. citizenship.

Answer the following questions, using one of the new words above.
Write your answers in the spaces provided.

1. Which word goes with "national or central government"? _____ federal _____

2. Which word goes with "an act of prejudice toward a group of people"?
_____ discrimination _____

3. Which word goes with "something almost worthless"? _____ token _____

4. Which word goes with "a group displaying their feelings about an issue"?
_____ demonstrate _____

5. Which word goes with "not being treated fairly"? _____ injustice _____

6. Which word goes with "the separation of people according to their race"?
_____ segregation _____

Adapted from
Nationally Televised Speech
by President John F. Kennedy

John F. Kennedy

June 11, 1963

This nation was created by men of many nations and backgrounds. It was based on the idea that all men are created equal; and that the rights of every man are reduced when the rights of one man are threatened.

So, it ought to be possible for American students of any color to attend any public school they select without having to be backed up by troops. It ought to be possible for American customers of any color to receive equal service in public places of business, such as hotels and restaurants, and theaters and stores, without being forced to **demonstrate** in the street.

And it ought to be possible for American citizens of any color to vote in a free election without trouble or fear of punishment.

Word Power

demonstrate (dem´ ən strāt´) v. to take part in a group display of feelings toward a person or an issue

It ought to be possible, in short, for every American to enjoy the rights of being American without regard to his race or his color.

Difficulties over **segregation** and **discrimination** are in every city, in every state. These difficulties cause in many cities a rising tide of unease that threatens the public safety.

In a time of national crisis, good and generous men should be able to come together no matter what their politics are.

This is not even a legal issue alone. It is better to settle these matters in the courts than on the streets. New laws are needed at every level. But law alone cannot make men see right.

We are faced mainly with a moral issue. It is as old as the Scriptures and is as clear as the American Constitution. The heart of the question is whether all Americans are to have equal rights and equal opportunities. Are we going to treat our fellow Americans as we want to be treated?

If an American, because his skin is dark, cannot eat lunch in a restaurant open to the public; if he cannot send his children to the best public schools; if he cannot vote for the public leaders who represent him; if, in short, he cannot enjoy the full and free life which all of us want, then who among us would be happy to have the color of his skin changed and stand in his place?

One hundred years have passed since President Lincoln freed the slaves. But their grandsons are not fully free. They are not yet freed from **injustice.** They are not yet freed from social and economic inequality.

And this nation, for all its hopes and all its pride, will not be fully free until all its citizens are free.

Word Power

segregation (seg′ rə gā′ shən) *n.* the act of separating people by racial or social groups

discrimination (dis krim′ ə nā′ shən) *n.* the act of treating a person or a group of people unfairly or with prejudice

injustice (in jus′ tis) *n.* unfair treatment; a wrong

English Coach

The suffix *-tion* can mean "the act of." The word *segregate* means "to separate people of different races." *Segregation* means "the act of segregating." Write the word that means the "act of graduating."

graduation

Reading Skill

Evaluate Reread the sentences highlighted in green. Kennedy believes that all Americans should have equal rights and that everyone should treat others as he or she wants to be treated. Do you agree with him? Why or why not?

Answers will vary.

Background Info

In the early 1960s, Birmingham, Alabama, was one of the most segregated cities in the country. African Americans faced discrimination and violence. In 1963 protestors of this unfair treament, including children, were beaten by police, attacked by police dogs, and sprayed with fire hoses. These images shocked the country. City officials finally backed down and began to provide some rights to African Americans.

Reading Skill

Paraphrase Reread the highlighted sentence and the rest of the paragraph. Kennedy states that the country is facing a moral problem. In your own words, tell what he says must be done to solve the problem.

Possible response: The

government needs to help

end discrimination, and

people have to treat each

other fairly in everyday life.

Have you seen any demonstrations or marches in person or on television? What issues were the people supporting?

Now the time has come for this nation to fulfill its promise. The events in Birmingham and elsewhere have so increased the cries for equality that no city or state or lawmakers can wisely choose to ignore them.

The fires of anger and disagreement are burning in every city, North and South. Where legal solutions are not at hand, correction is looked for in the streets in demonstrations, parades and protests. These actions create tensions and threaten violence—and threaten lives.

We face a moral crisis as a country and a people. It cannot be met by police action. It cannot be left to increased demonstrations in the streets. It cannot be quieted by **token** moves or talk. It is time to act in the Congress, in your state and local government, and, above all, in all of our daily lives.

I am, therefore, asking the Congress to create laws giving all Americans the right to be served in places which are open to the public—hotels, restaurants and theaters, stores and similar places of business. This seems to me to be a basic right.

Word Power
token (tō′ kən) *adj.* having little value or effect

I'm also asking Congress to let the **Federal** Government more fully be a part of lawsuits designed to end segregation in public education. We have succeeded in persuading many districts to desegregate. Dozens have accepted Negroes without violence.

Other features will also be asked for, including greater protection for the right to vote.

But laws, I repeat, cannot solve this problem alone. It must be solved in the homes of every American in every community across our country.

> In this respect, I want to honor those citizens, North and South, who've been working in their communities to make life better for all.
>
> They are acting not out of a sense of legal duty but out of a sense of human goodness. Like our soldiers and sailors in all parts of the world they are meeting freedom's challenge on the battlefield. I salute them for their honor—their bravery.

How are the students in this picture similar to the students at your school? How are they different?

_____

Word Power

federal (fed′ ər əl) *adj.* of or relating to the central government of the United States

Literary Element

Author's Purpose Reread the highlighted paragraph. One purpose of Kennedy's speech is to persuade the national government to take action. What does Kennedy want the outcome of this action to be? Underline the answer in the paragraph.

Comprehension Check

Reread the boxed text. Whom does Kennedy want to thank and honor? To what group does he compare them?

He honors people who

are working to end

discrimination. He compares

them to soldiers and sailors

on the battlefield.

_____

Respond to Literature

Nationally Televised Speech
by President John F. Kennedy

A Comprehension Check

Answer the following questions in the spaces provided.

1. What idea does Kennedy say our country is based on?

   Kennedy says our country is based on the idea that all men are created

   equal.

2. What two main things does Kennedy want Congress to help achieve?

   Kennedy wants Congress to create laws protecting the right of all

   Americans to be served in public places and to end public-school

   segregation.

B Reading Skills

Complete the following activities in the spaces provided.

1. **Evaluate** In your opinion, do you think President Kennedy is convincing? Why or why not? Use parts of his speech to support your answers.

   Answers will vary.

2. **Paraphrase** In your own words, tell what President Kennedy means when he says, "And this nation, for all its hopes and all its pride, will not be fully free until all its citizens are free."

   Possible response: Until all citizens, regardless of race, have equal rights,

   the United States will not be a free country.

C Word Power

Complete each sentence below, using one of the words in the box.

> demonstrate   segregation   discrimination
>
> injustice   token   federal

1. Jeff knew that arguing would not change my mind, so he offered only a ___token___ resistance to my plan.

2. The nurses decided to ___demonstrate___ in front of the hospital to protest unfair wages.

3. When you get a job, you must pay taxes to the ___federal___ government.

4. My grandfather told me that when he first came to the United States, he faced prejudice and ___discrimination___ because he could not speak English.

5. When ___segregation___ was legal, African Americans were not permitted to drink from the same water fountains as white Americans.

6. Willie suffered a serious ___injustice___ when he was wrongly accused of stealing the bike.

D Literary Element: Author's Purpose

Read the passages below from President John F. Kennedy's speech. As you read, think about how the passages illustrate Kennedy's purpose for giving this speech. Then answer the questions that follow.

> If an American, because his skin is dark, cannot eat lunch in a restaurant open to the public; if he cannot send his children to the best public schools; if he cannot vote for the public leaders who represent him; if, in short, he cannot enjoy the full and free life which all of us want, then who among us would be happy to have the color of his skin changed and stand in his place?[1]
>
> Like our soldiers and sailors in all parts of the world they are meeting freedom's challenge on the battlefield.[2] I salute them for their honor—their bravery.[3]

1. In sentence 1, how does Kennedy try to make the listener understand the injustices that African Americans have endured?

   Possible responses: He asks if non-African American listeners would want

   to trade places with an African American. He asks listeners if they would be

   happy being denied a full and free life.

2. In sentences 2–3, why does Kennedy compare the people fighting against discrimination with U.S. soldiers and sailors?

   Possible response: He compares them with soldiers and sailors to show

   how brave and noble they are and to show that they are also fighting for

   freedom.

E Equality in Our Country

Think about the points that President Kennedy makes in his speech. Then fill in the diagram. The rights that Kennedy says all Americans should have are stated in the top three circles of the diagram. Write specific examples of each right using Kennedy's words. A sample answer has been provided for you. Then tell how these rights can best be achieved in the fourth circle of the diagram.

The right to equal education

All students should be able to attend public schools of their choice.

Possible responses: African Americans and whites should be free to go to school together. All students should get the same opportunity for an education.

The right to equal service

Possible responses: All Americans should be treated equally in public places. No one should be denied the right to be in these places because of their race.

The right to vote

Possible responses: All Americans who are citizens have the right to vote. They should be allowed to vote for public leaders without interference.

How we can achieve equality

Possible responses: We need to have laws that guarantee the same rights for all citizens. We must all stop discriminating against people because of their race in all parts of our daily lives.

Assessment

Fill in the circle next to each correct answer.

1. Choose the sentence that **best** paraphrases these words by President Kennedy: "This nation . . . was based on the idea that all men are created equal; and that the rights of every man are reduced when the rights of one man are threatened."

   ○ A. All people lose their rights if we treat everyone equally.

   ○ B. The idea of equality is difficult to achieve.

   ○ C. One threatening person can ruin the rights of everyone.

   ● D. If just one person is denied his or her rights, everyone suffers.

2. What is one right that President Kennedy says all American citizens should have?

   ● A. the right to vote in a free election

   ○ B. the right to deny service in public places

   ○ C. the right to treat others any way we want

   ○ D. the right to be wealthy

3. Whom does Kennedy salute for their bravery?

   ○ A. Congress and the Federal Government

   ○ B. the grandchildren of freed slaves

   ● C. citizens working to better their communities

   ○ D. owners of public places of business

4. What is one reason President Kennedy gives this speech?

   ○ A. to end a war between the North and South

   ● B. to ask the government to create laws against discrimination

   ○ C. to organize protests throughout the country against discrimination

   ○ D. to send National Guard troops to Birmingham, Alabama

5. Which of the following words means "not having much value"?

   ○ A. segregation

   ○ B. discrimination

   ● C. token

   ○ D. injustice

Wrap-up

UNIT 5

. . . .

Compare and Contrast

Author's purpose is an important literary element in the speech "This We Know" by Chief Seattle and the "Nationally Televised Speech by President John F. Kennedy." Although the speeches were given almost one hundred years apart and are on different topics, their purposes are central to both speeches. Think about what each speaker is saying in each speech. Think about what each speaker is trying to persuade his audience to do.

Complete the chart below. In the left column, explain how the authors' purposes are alike. In the right column, explain the differences between the authors' purposes in each speech. Examples have been provided.

Alike	Different
• Both are written to persuade their listeners to do the right thing. • Both describe problems that are happening or will happen without changes in attitude. • Both ask the government to take responsibility.	• Chief Seattle's speech is directed at people from the government trying to buy land; Kennedy's speech is directed at all U.S. citizens. • Chief Seattle's speech focuses on preserving nature; Kennedy's speech focuses on ending segregation. • Kennedy warns about things happening in the present; Chief Seattle warns about things that might happen in the future.

Glossary

A

afterthought (af´ tər thôt´) *n.* an idea that occurs or comes to mind later; p. 21

ancestors (an´ ses´ tərz) *n.* people from whom someone is descended, especially from the distant past; p. 248

arrogant (ar´ə gənt) *adj.* full of undeserved pride; p. 162

astonishment (əs ton´ ish mənt) *n.* surprise; amazement; p. 52

B

banished (ban´ishd) *v.* forced to leave a country or a community; p. 162

baptism (bap´ tiz´ əm) *n.* a ceremony in which a person becomes a member of the Christian religion; p. 34

bawling (bôl´ ing) *v.* crying loudly; p. 205

C

captive (kap´ tiv) *adj.* imprisoned; kept within bounds; p. 194

clan (klan) *n.* a group of families that have a common ancestor; p. 177

commended (kə men´did) *v.* gave approval of; gave praise; p. 167

commotion (kə mō´shən) *n.* noise and confusion; a noisy uproar; p. 164

compassionate (kəm pash´ ə nit) *adj.* kindhearted; concerned; p. 136

conceal (kən sēl´) *v.* to hide something; p. 8

conceived (kən sēvd´) *v.* created; imagined; p. 238

conquer (kong´kər) *v.* to take over, usually by force; p. 164

consecrate (kon´ sə krāt´) *v.* to make, declare, or honor as sacred; p. 240

conspicuous (kən spik´ ū əs) *adj.* easily seen; obvious; p. 139

contempt (kən tempt´) *n.* a lack of respect; a feeling of hatred toward someone or something; p. 250

croon (kro͞on) *v.* to gently sing or hum; p. 205

crouch (krouch) *v.* to stoop low with bent knees; p. 69

cunning (kun´ ing) *adj.* skillful and clever; sly; p. 194

D

demonstrate (dem´ ən strāt´) *v.* to take part in a group display of feelings toward a person or an issue; p. 258

descendants (di sen´dənts) *n.* people related to a person who lived in the past; p. 116

detract (di trakt´) *v.* to take something away; lessen; p. 240

discomfort (dis kum´fərt) *n.* the state of being uncomfortable; a bother; p. 117

discrimination (dis krim´ ə nā´ shən) *n.* the act of treating a person or a group of people unfairly or with prejudice; p. 259

E

eerie (ēr´ ē) *adj.* weird, especially in a frightening way; p. 103

embraced (em brāsd´) *v.* hugged or held in the arms; p. 186

emigrated (em´ ə grāt´ id) *v.* left one's country to move to another; moved to another place; p. 137

exhaled (eks hāld´) *v.* breathed out; p. 103

Glossary

F

fantasy (fan´ tə sē) *n.* expression of the imaginary; ideas about things that are not real; p. 65

fatigue (fə tēg´) *n.* weakness or tiredness; p. 115

federal (fed´ ər əl) *adj.* of or relating to the central government of the United States; p. 261

G

glimpse (glimps) *n.* a very quick look; a peek; p. 195

gloated (glōt´ id) *v.* felt or expressed a greedy pleasure or satisfaction in one's own success or achievement, especially in a slightly nasty way; p. 81

grogginess (grog´ ē nis) *n.* a state of being sleepy or not fully alert; p. 81

H

hideous (hid´ē əs) *adj.* horrible, ugly, or nasty; p. 10

I

incident (in´sə dənt) *n.* an event that happens; an experience; p. 51

infamous (in´ fə məs) *adj.* well-known for being bad; p. 229

injustice (in jus´ tis) *n.* unfair treatment; a wrong; p. 259

insolence (in´ sə ləns) *n.* a lack of respect; rudeness; p. 224

interval (in´ tər vəl) *n.* a length of time between events; p. 143

involuntary (in vol´ ən ter´ ē) *adj.* not done willingly or by choice; p. 98

involvement (in volv´ mənt) *n.* the act of being a part of or taking part in something; p. 19

K

keen (kēn) *adj.* highly sensitive; sharp; p. 179

L

liable (lī´ə bəl) *adj.* likely; p. 65

linoleum (li nō´ lē əm) *n.* a type of material used for covering floors; p. 35

loathe (lōth) *v.* to consider with extreme disgust; hate; p. 152

lurched (lurchd) *v.* moved suddenly in a jerky and uneven way; p. 88

M

meager (mē´ gər) *adj.* not enough in amount or quality; p. 83

meaningless (mē´ ning lis) *adj.* pointless; without importance; p. 53

mercurial (mər kyoor´ ē əl) *adj.* moody; quick to change; p. 140

mock (mok) *v.* to tease or make fun of someone; p. 10

N

nobly (nō´ bəl ē) *adv.* with honor; in a heroic way; p. 240

O

offering (ô´ fər ing) *n.* a gift, often given for a religious purpose; p. 196

ominous (om´ ə nəs) *adj.* threatening harm or evil; p. 103

Glossary

P

persisted (pər sist´ id) *v.* refused to give up; continued in a stubborn way; p. 19

pilgrims (pil´ grəmz) *n.* people who travel to a holy place for a religious purpose; p. 229

plungers (plun´ jərz) *n.* large rubber cups attached to long handles that are used to unclog drains; p. 35

precious (presh´ əs) *adj.* valuable; highly cherished; p. 34

prejudiced (prej´ə disd) *adj.* having a bad opinion without enough knowledge or good reasons; p. 45

preserve (pri zurv´) *v.* to protect from harm or destruction; to maintain; p. 250

procession (prə sesh´ ən) *n.* a march; people moving forward in an orderly way; p. 115

proposition (prop´ ə zish´ ən) *n.* a suggestion; an idea; p. 238

psychiatrists (sī kī´ ə trists) *n.* doctors who specialize in helping people with mental problems; p. 23

psyching (sī´ king) *v.* making someone fearful or uneasy; p. 69

pursue (pər soo´) *v.* to chase; to seek; p. 182

Q

quench (kwench) *v.* to satisfy; to put an end to a need or desire; p. 196

R

reassuringly (rē´ ə shoor´ ing lē) *adv.* in a manner that restores confidence; p. 145

refugee (ref´ ū jē´) *n.* a person who leaves his or her home or country to escape or seek protection; p. 227

rejected (ri jekt´ id) *adj.* unwanted; unaccepted; p. 49

reluctantly (ri luk´tənt lē) *adv.* with hesitation; unwillingly; p. 116

rouses (rou´zez) *v.* stirs up emotion or excites; p. 7

S

sacred (sā´krid) *adj.* holy; worthy of great respect; p. 121

scorned (skôrnd) *v.* treated with dislike or disrespect; p. 205

scrunched (skrunchd) *v.* crouched; squatted; p. 205

scuffed (skufd) *adj.* scraped or scratched through use; p. 35

segregation (seg´ rə gā´ shən) *n.* the act of separating people by racial or social groups; p. 259

seize (sēz) *v.* to grab and take hold of someone or something, possibly by force; p. 207

sheepishly (shē´pish lē) *adv.* in an embarrassed way; shyly; p. 116

sinewy (sin´ ū ē) *adj.* physically tough or powerful; p. 184

slaughtered (slô´ tərd) *v.* killed in large numbers; p. 250

sophisticated (sə fis´ tə kā´ tid) *adj.* having or showing knowledge or experience of the world; p. 83

spare (spār) *v.* to treat with mercy; to hold back from harming or injuring; p. 184

sparsely (spärs´ lē) *adv.* in an uncrowded or thinly spread way; p. 135

stalking (stô´king) *v.* following someone in a secretive manner; p. 6

suspicion (sə spish´ən) *n.* a feeling that something is wrong; p. 8

Glossary

T

taunt (tônt) *v.* to make fun of in an insulting way; p. 83

tentatively (ten′ tə tiv lē) *adv.* in an uncertain way; hesitantly; p. 97

tirade (tī′ rād) *n.* a long, angry or scolding speech; p. 86

token (tō′ kən) *adj.* having little value or effect; p. 260

tradition (trə dish′ ən) *n.* a custom; a long-accepted practice; p. 72

U

underestimated (un′ dər es′ tə māt′ id) *v.* placed too low a value on; guessed too low; p. 220

uninhabited (un′ in hab′ it id) *adj.* not lived in or on; p. 227

V

veins (vāns) *n.* blood vessels that carry blood to the heart from other parts of the body; p. 248

veterans (vet′ ər ənz) *n.* people who served in the armed forces, such as the navy, air force, marines, or army; p. 18

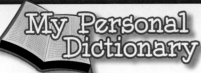

My Personal Dictionary

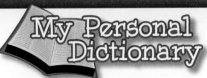

My Personal Dictionary

My Personal
Dictionary

My Personal Dictionary

My Personal Dictionary

280

My Personal Dictionary

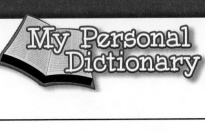

My Personal Dictionary

ACKNOWLEDGMENTS

LITERATURE
UNIT 1

Adapted from "Stop the Sun" Copyright © 1986 by Gary Paulsen, from *Boy's Life,* January 1986. Reprinted by permission of Flannery Literary on behalf of the author.

"Chanclas" from *The House On Mango Street.* Copyright © 1984 by Sandra Cisneros. Published by Vintage Books, a division of Random House, Inc. and in hardcover by Alfred A. Knopf in 1994. Reprinted by permission of Susan Bergholz Literary Services, New York. All rights reserved.

Adaptation of "Everybody Knows Tobie" by Daniel Garza, from *Descant,* the literary Journal of Texas Christian University, Vol. VII, No. 3, 1963. Reprinted by permission of the author and Texas Christian University.

UNIT 2

"Raymond's Run," copyright © 1971 by Toni Cade Bambara, from *Gorilla, My Love* by Toni Cade Bambara. Adapted and reprinted by permission of Random House, Inc.

"Mother and Daughter" from *Baseball in April and Other Stories,* copyright © 1990 by Gary Soto, reprinted by permission of Harcourt, Inc.

Adapted from "The Treasure of Lemon Brown" by Walter Dean Myers. Adapted and reprinted by permission of Miriam Altshuler Agency, on behalf of the author.

Adapted from "The Medicine Bag" by Virginia Driving Hawk Sneve. Adapted and reprinted by permission of the author.

UNIT 3

From *The Diary of Anne Frank (Play)* by Frances Goodrich and Albert Hackett, copyright © 1956 by Albert Hackett, Frances Goodrich Hackett and Otto Frank. Used by permission of Random House, Inc.

UNIT 4

Adapted from "The Wise Old Woman" by Yoshiko Uchida, courtesy of the Bancroft Library, University of California, Berkeley.

"Racing the Great Bear," by Joseph Bruchac. Reprinted by permission of Barbara S. Kouts.

"The People Could Fly" from *The People Could Fly: American Black Folktales* by Virginia Hamilton, illustrated by Leo and Diane Dillon, copyright © 1985 by Virginia Hamilton. Illustrations copyright © 1985 by Leo and Diane Dillon. Used by permission of Alfred A. Knopf, an imprint of Random House Children's Books, a division of Random House, Inc.

UNIT 5

Adapted from "Thank You in Arabic" by Naomi Shihab Nye. Adapted and reprinted by permission of the author.